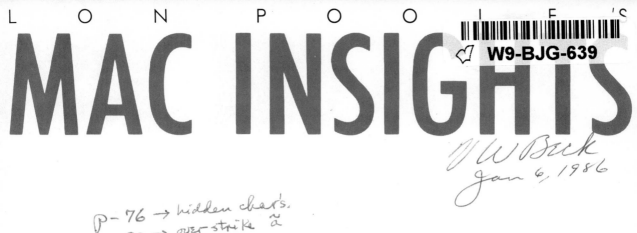

LON POOLE'S
MAC INSIGHTS

J W Beck
Jan 6, 1986

P- 76 → hidden char's.
-80 → over-strike ã
142 → separation lines
147 — TABS & Margins
159 — Wider documents (pages)

L O N   P O O L E ' S
MAC INSIGHTS

Secrets,
shortcuts,
and solutions
for the
Apple®
Macintosh™

MICROSOFT.
P R E S S

PUBLISHED BY

Microsoft Press
A Division of Microsoft Corporation
16011 N.E. 36th Way, Box 97017, Redmond, Washington 98073-9717

Library of Congress Cataloging in Publication Data
Poole, Lon
Mac insights.
Includes index.
1. Macintosh (Computer)
I. Title.
QA76.8.M3P659   1986   004.165   86-8495

ISBN 0-914845-73-X

Printed and bound in the United States of America.

1 2 3 4 5 6 7 8 9   FGFG   8 9 0 9 8 7 6

Distributed to the book trade in the
United States by Harper & Row.

Distributed to the book trade in Canada
by General Publishing Company, Ltd.

Distributed to the book trade outside the
United States and Canada by Penguin Books Ltd.

Penguin Books Ltd., Harmondsworth, Middlesex, England
Penguin Books Australia Ltd., Ringwood, Victoria, Australia
Penguin Books N.Z. Ltd., 182-190 Wairau Road, Auckland 10, New Zealand

British Cataloging in Publication Data available

TABLE OF CONTENTS

ACKNOWLEDGMENTS

The tips in this book are not all my original ideas. Many were suggested by the thousands of questions sent to my "Get Info" column in *Macworld* magazine. I'd like to thank everyone who has taken the time to write; your letters inspired this book.

Other tip ideas came from reading many Mac-related periodicals, including *Macworld, Mac User,* and *MacInTouch.* I particularly want to thank the following groups and the editors of their publications:

Ann Arbor Macintosh Users Group, *MacTechnics News*

Apple University Consortium, *Wheels for the Mind*

Berkeley Macintosh Users Group (BMUG), *Spring '85 Journal* and *Fall '85 Journal*

Brigham Young University Apple Users Group, *Apple Chatter*

Carnegie-Mellon Macintosh Users Group (CMU-MUG), *MacNuggets*

Drexel University computer center and Lucy Anne Wozny, *Macintosh Information*

Macintosh Users Group for Writers and Users of Mac Programs (MUGWUMP) and the Distributed Computing Services of Cornell University, *Muggers' Monthly*

Notre Dame MadMacs Users' Group, *ROM Warrior*

San Diego Macintosh Users Group, *Resources*

University of Rochester user services, *FindUR*

University of Utah Macintosh Users Group (UUMUG), *MacFUG News*

Yale Macintosh Users Group (YMUG), *The Desktop Journal*

Thanks to the following individuals for their help: Harvey Alcaves, Marein Cremer, Chris Espinosa, John Fenwick, Scott Holmes, Prasad Kaipa, Barbara Knaster, Scott Knaster, Mike Koss, John R. Love, Lonna McDowell, Johnathan Price, Bryan Stearns, and Martha Steffen.

I'd like to thank my wife, Karin, for her steady support, especially for listening to my circumlocutions and for filling in elsewhere while I spent too much time with the Mac.

INTRODUCTION

The chief strength of the Apple Macintosh, its ease of use, is paradoxically a major weakness. Mac users learn so much by doing that they don't bother reading manuals and introductory texts. That's too bad, because the Mac has another level of performance that is hard to discover by unguided experimentation but is easy to master with brief explanation. That's what this book is all about: tips to help you learn new ways to perform everyday Mac tasks and in the process gain insights into more efficient and productive ways to use your Mac.

Mac Insights can help you start and quit applications faster, find disk space you didn't know was there, troubleshoot when your Mac doesn't work right, rescue lost and damaged files, and transfer information to and from other types of computers, including mainframes and IBM PCs. It gives you advice on organizing applications and documents on disks, printing envelopes on an ImageWriter or LaserWriter, and formatting for a LaserWriter even if you don't have one.

With this book, you can find out how to best eject disks, select options in dialog boxes, draw dotted and dashed lines, mix text attributes on the same line in MacPaint and MacDraw, and select words, lines, sentences, phrases, paragraphs, and other large areas of text. You also get tips on creating custom MacPaint brush shapes, using several MiniFinders, adding Command-key shortcuts to menus, personalizing icons and pointers, printing pin-feed labels, and adding characters of your own design to any font.

Tip sources

For well over two years I have been reading and answering letters that Macintosh users write to my "Get Info" column in *Macworld* magazine. Much of what has appeared there appears in *Mac Insights*. I've selected the best information from "Get Info" and included it here to save you from hunting through back issues.

But material from "Get Info" only accounts for about a third of the tips in this book. The rest of the tips come from research I've done both for my column and specifically for this book. I have scoured countless newsletters, magazines, books, information-service databases, electronic bulletin boards, and so on (see the acknowledgments for a complete list of my sources).

Using this book

To get the most out of *Mac Insights,* you should already be familiar with the Macintosh. Do you know what I mean by menu, menu bar, pointer, insertion point, desktop, window, title bar, scroll bar, folder, application, document, icon, highlight, dialog box, and button? Can you select, choose, open, close, click, double click, drag, and scroll? If not, please spend a couple of hours with your Macintosh owner's manual before reading this book.

Where a tip applies to just one application program, you need a fundamental knowledge of the application's features and operation to be able to make use of the tip. For example, don't bother with the word-processing tips unless you know how to use MacWrite or another word processor to write, edit, print, and save a letter.

You can use *Mac Insights* in several ways. Read the entire book—or a complete section—from beginning to end, if you like. But if you're like most Mac users, you'll probably pick up the book and browse through it, looking for suggestions that intrigue you and ideas you want to try. Or perhaps you'll go directly to the subjects that interest you—advice on using modem commands, help with formatting text documents, a cure for worn-out mouse feet, and so on. Are you having trouble printing a document? Turn immediately to the troubleshooting chapter's concise list of common ImageWriter and LaserWriter problems and their cures. Perhaps scan the printing chapter for more help. Or check the index and discover other tips that mention printing problems. Because I think you'll use the *Mac Insights* index often, I've prepared as complete and helpful an index as possible.

I've tried every one of the tips in this book on several variations of the Mac. The tips all work on the standard Mac 512K, the Mac 512K Enhanced, and the Mac Plus. Most tips also work on Macs with the original 64K ROMs and on the Mac XL, but I did not test the tips extensively on those machines. When testing, I used the latest program versions available as of April 1986. Naturally, if (perhaps I should say when) a software publisher distributes a new version of a particular application program, you may have to experiment a bit to make some tips work properly.

Where appropriate, I name the specific products, especially software, that you'll need for the tips. In case your local Apple dealer or software store does not stock all these programs, I've listed sources at the end of the book.

I think you'll find *Mac Insights* informative, fun, and easy to use. I hope it will stimulate your curiosity and sense of adventure, and encourage you to experiment and explore. If you have any suggestions for tips you'd like to see included in the next edition, please send them to me at Microsoft Press, 16011 N.E. 36th, Box 97017, Redmond, WA 98073-9717.

Shortcuts

The Macintosh user interface makes learning applications easy, but may get in the way once you master basic skills. Fortunately, there are shortcuts for bypassing many easy-but-lengthy procedures. Some shortcuts are fairly obvious, such as the Command-key shortcuts listed in the menus. For example, everyone soon discovers that pressing Command-X, Command-C, or Command-V is quicker than choosing Cut, Copy, or Paste from the Edit menu. This chapter describes some equally useful shortcuts that Mac users don't always find on their own.

USING THE MOUSE

Dragging a window without activating it

When several windows are displayed on the screen, dragging one window by its title bar normally puts it on top of all others and makes it the active window. If you want to move a window aside to see what's underneath it, but don't want to activate it, press the Command key when you start to drag. You can release the Command key after you begin dragging.

This trick will not work with the Alarm Clock desk accessory's window. Like all windows without title bars, the Alarm Clock window always comes to the top and becomes active when you drag it.

Opening a compatible document from the Finder

It's usually easy to open a document directly from the Finder's desktop. You either select the document's icon and choose Open from the Finder's File menu, or double click on the icon. However, if the application that created the document is not on any of the disks whose icons appear on the desktop, the Finder complains *An application can't be found for this document.*

Suppose that your goal is to open the document, not with the application that created it, but with a compatible application; for example, you might want to open a MacTerminal document with MacWrite. To open the document:

1. Select the document and application icons.
2. Choose Open from the Finder's File menu.

The document and application must be in the same folder, since the Finder won't let you select items from different folders at the same time.

This shortcut works with some applications, but not all. For example, MacWrite can open any plain-text document, but not a formatted Jazz or Microsoft Word document. MacPaint and MacDraw cannot open any documents but their own.

Opening several documents from the Finder

Applications such as MacDraw and Microsoft Excel can open more than one document from the Finder at a time. To open several documents at once:

1. Select all the documents.
2. Choose Open from the Finder's File menu.

The Finder can't simultaneously select documents from different folders, so all the documents must be in the same folder.

This shortcut doesn't work for all applications capable of opening several documents at once. For example, Microsoft Word opens only one document from the group you select. If you want to work with more than one Word document at a time, you have to start Word and open each document individually.

Removing disk icons

Early versions of the Finder did not allow you to drag a disk icon to the Trash unless you ejected the disk first. Beginning with Finder version 4.1, however, you can drag any disk icon—except the icon of the startup disk—into the Trash. The Finder removes the disk icon from the desktop and, if the disk is inserted, ejects it. Version 5.1 or above also lets you drag the startup-disk icon into the Trash; the startup disk is ejected, but its dimmed icon remains on the desktop.

USING THE KEYBOARD

Using the Edit-menu command equivalents

Get in the habit of using Command-Z, Command-X, Command-C, and Command-V instead of choosing the Undo, Cut, Copy, and Paste commands from the Edit menu. You have two hands: Use them both to save time and effort!

Ejecting disks

You can usually eject the disk in the internal drive by pressing Command-Shift-1, or the disk in the external drive by pressing Command-Shift-2. One notable occasion when these keyboard shortcuts do not work is when the disk-swapping alert box commands *Please insert the disk...*

Avoid any temptation to shut down or restart your Mac after you have pressed Command-Shift-1 or Command-Shift-2 to eject a disk, especially if any documents are open at the time. At the very least, you'll probably disrupt the Finder's desktop, and you may corrupt the open documents, too.

Saving screen snapshots

You can record the current screen image as a MacPaint document, called a screen snapshot or screen dump, by pressing Command-Shift-3. Screen snapshots are saved on the disk that contains the application program you're using, and each snapshot requires anywhere from 2 to 56K of disk space. The Mac beeps if you press Command-Shift-3 when there's not enough disk space available to save a screen snapshot.

You can record up to ten snapshots, which will automatically be named Screen 0 through Screen 9, at a time. If you try to record an eleventh snapshot without first removing or renaming some of the Screen 0 through Screen 9 documents, the Mac will beep at you.

Printing screen snapshots

To print a screen image, turn on the ImageWriter and press Command-Shift-4. If the Shift Lock key is depressed, you get a snapshot of the whole screen. If not, only the active window is printed.

Disposing of applications, system files, and locked items

Errare humanum est, the Romans said, and the Finder got wind of it. As a result, it asks you *Are you sure you want to remove...?* every time you drag an application or system file to the Trash. You have to click OK to confirm that you know what you are doing. The Finder takes an even harder stance if you try to discard a locked item. *That item is locked or in use, and can't be removed,* it chides, and makes you use the Get Info command to unlock the item before trying again.

If you never make mistakes, you can circumvent the Finder's warnings about removing applications, system files, and locked items by pressing the Option key as you drag icons to the Trash.

Fast finding of file names

When you choose the Open command from within an application that uses the hierarchical file system (HFS), you are presented with a scrollable list of file names from which to select the one you want to open. Searching a long list can be tedious. To narrow the search, type the first part of the name you want. When you stop typing, the first name that matches your entry is automatically found and selected. The keyboard touch setting in the Control Panel desk accessory determines how long you can pause while typing without starting a new request.

Tabbing to change drives

On systems with more than one drive, the dialog boxes for disk commands such as Open and Save As contain a Drive button. Clicking the Drive button changes drives. On a Mac Plus or other Mac that uses the hierarchical file system (HFS), pressing the Tab key has the same effect.

Arrow-key navigation in Open and Save dialog boxes

The mouse is the standard tool for scrolling through the file and folder names listed in the Open, Save, and Save As dialog boxes, and for opening folders and selecting a file by name. On a Mac Plus, you can use the arrow keys to navigate the list of file and folder names. Pressing the Up or Down Arrow key selects the file or folder name listed above or below the currently selected name, scrolling the list if necessary. To open a selected folder, press Command-Down Arrow. To back up to the previous folder, press Command-Up Arrow.

The same keyboard navigation is available on any Mac that uses the hierarchical file system (HFS) and has either a Mac Plus keyboard or a numeric keypad.

Tabbing in dialog boxes

In dialog boxes where you must type several items, you can usually advance from one item to the next by pressing the Tab key. The whole of the next item is usually selected, so you can change it simply by typing its replacement. Pressing Tab when you reach the last item in the box takes you back to the first item.

Pressing Return or Enter in dialog boxes

Pressing the Return or Enter key when you're in a dialog box usually has the same effect as clicking the OK button. However, if a button other than the OK button is surrounded by a thick border, pressing Return or Enter effectively clicks the thickly bordered button.

In dialog boxes that have no OK button, pressing Return or Enter usually confirms the dialog box. Here again, a thickly bordered button takes precedence.

Scrolling through MacPaint's fonts and font sizes

MacPaint, like most applications, provides no shortcuts for choosing a specific font name or font size. However, you can use the keyboard to step consecutively up or down through the list of fonts or the list of sizes.

- ☐ Press Command-Shift-Period to advance to the next font.
- ☐ Press Command-Shift-Comma to back up to the previous font.
- ☐ Press Command-Period to advance to the next larger font size.
- ☐ Press Command-Comma to back up to the next smaller font size.

Notice that the symbols < and >, which are the uppercase symbols on the Comma and Period keys, suggest direction.

Grabbing the page in MacPaint and Microsoft Excel

When working with the pencil in MacPaint, you may want to bring another part of your picture into view. You simply press the Option key to temporarily turn the pencil into a grabber, then slide the page in the desired direction.

When previewing printed pages on the screen in Microsoft Excel, you normally see a reduction of the entire page, but you may want to see part of the page image in its full size. You can click on the area you want to check and then press the Option key, temporarily changing the pointer into a grabber that you can use to bring any part of the full-size page image into view.

Undoing in MacPaint

The Undo feature is particularly valuable in MacPaint. If at first you don't draw a line or shape correctly, undo and try again. For a super-quick undo, just hit the

Tilde key. Except when you are typing, pressing Tilde has the same effect as pressing Command-Z or choosing Undo from the Edit menu.

Selecting or deleting the previous word in Microsoft Word

If the insertion point is between words in a Microsoft Word document, pressing Shift-Backspace selects the word to the left of the insertion point. Pressing Option-Backspace deletes the word to the left of the insertion point. If the insertion point is not between words, the word containing the cursor is selected or deleted.

Microsoft dialog boxes

Most Microsoft products, including Excel, Word, Multiplan, File, Chart, and BASIC, have a number of keyboard shortcuts that operate in dialog boxes. You can usually operate the displayed buttons by pressing the Command key as you type the first letter of the button name. For example, in the Open dialog box, you can eject a disk by pressing Command-E. Pressing Command-Period cancels the dialog box, as if you had clicked the Cancel button.

In Microsoft Excel, and to a lesser extent in other Microsoft products, the same keyboard technique works for other options listed in dialog boxes. In a dialog box where there is no place to enter text, you can omit pressing the Command key, and simply type the first letter of the button name. In some cases, you can also use the mouse to effectively select a dialog-box option and click the OK button, by just double clicking on the option. You can also select an option and at the same time OK the dialog box by combining the double-clicking technique with the keyboard shortcut; simply double type the first letter of the option while pressing the Command key.

Opening MacProject's Task Info window

Each task in a MacProject schedule chart lasts a specific duration and uses specific resources. You enter and edit duration and resource information for a task in its Task Info window. While working on the schedule chart, you can bring up the Task Info window by pressing the Tab key. Once the Task Info window is active, you can move from entry to entry by pressing the Tab key.

You can also open the Task Info window by pressing Command-T; you close it by pressing Command-T again.

Selecting the next MacProject task

When working on a schedule chart in MacProject, you can select the next task or milestone box to the right by pressing the Return key. However, if you are editing the text inside a task or milestone box, pressing Return breaks the line of text at the insertion point. To advance to the next task or milestone, you must select the task or milestone box before pressing Return.

Pressing Return while working in the Task Info window also moves you to the next task or milestone.

Saving time online

Here are several keyboard shortcuts that can save you time and money when you're connected with many online information services, including CompuServe and Delphi:

- ☐ Command-O cancels output so that you can type another command right away. It saves you the time and expense of reading menus you know or messages and information you don't care about.
- ☐ Command-C cancels the command you last typed and returns you to the previous menu.
- ☐ Command-S temporarily suspends the display of information on the screen. (Careful—the meter is still running!)
- ☐ Command-Q resumes screen display of information that was suspended when you pressed Command-S.

Troubleshooting

Having trouble with your Macintosh system? The troubleshooting table in this section summarizes common problems and ways to cure or prevent them. First, find the problem area in the first column of the table. (Sometimes you'll have to scan more than one problem area; for example, trouble you consider part of starting or restarting may be listed not under "Can't start," but under "Mac," "Error alerts," "Keyboard," or "Disks.") Then scan the second column for symptoms like those you're experiencing. The last two columns explain what's probably wrong and what you can do to fix the trouble or work around it.

COMMON PROBLEMS

Problem area	Symptoms	Likely causes	Cures
Mac	Dark screen	Brightness turned down	Turn brightness control clockwise
		Screen-saver desk accessory installed	Tap any key, or move mouse to deactivate desk accessory
		Mac broken	Have Mac repaired
	Bright screen but no picture	Mac broken	Have Mac repaired
	Flashing apple in menu bar	Alarm clock "ringing"	Turn off alarm clock using Alarm Clock desk accessory
	Pointer gone or doesn't move	Mouse cable loose	Plug mouse cable firmly into Mac
		Program crashed	In Switcher, press Command-Option-Shift-Period; otherwise, restart Mac
		Mouse broken	Repair or replace mouse
		Mac broken	Have Mac repaired
	Pointer moves erratically	Dirt on mouse roller	Remove roller, then clean and reassemble mouse
		Rolling mouse on uneven surface	Provide smooth surface
		Mouse feet worn off	Install Magnum's Mouse Mover / Replace mouse
	Broken lines and static	Program crashed	In Switcher, press Command-Option-Shift-Period; otherwise, restart Mac
		Too much picture-tube coating	Turn Mac off and back on for temporary fix; have excess coating removed

(cont.)

COMMON PROBLEMS

Problem area	Symptoms	Likely causes	Cures
Error alerts	System error	Program crashed	In Switcher, press Command-Option-Shift-Period; otherwise, restart Mac
			After restarting crashed program, check for damage to document you were using (gnash teeth, if necessary); see "System error ID table" for possible enlightenment. If problem persists, try to discern sequence of events that causes problem and avoid repeating sequence; yell at software publisher
		Bad disk	Use another disk
		Dirty disk drive	Clean drive with disk-cleaning kit
		Disk drive broken	Use another drive; have broken drive repaired
		Missing Hard Disk 20 file	Start up with single-sided disk whose System Folder contains these files: Hard Disk 20, System (version 3.1.1 or above), and Finder (version 5.2 or above); drag copy of these files to double-sided disk
		Too much picture-tube coating	Turn Mac off and back on for temporary fix; have excess coating removed
	Too little memory	Too many windows open	Close desk accessories; if application allows multiple documents to be open at once, close some
		Document too large or complex	With programs that keep entire document you're working on in memory, such as MacDraw, MacProject, ThinkTank, and most spreadsheet programs, split document in two by cutting and pasting several pages of document to new documents (via Scrapbook if necessary), and then save smaller documents
		Large Clipboard	Select one letter or similar small object, choose Copy from Edit menu, then choose Copy again
		Memory cluttered	Save document you're working on
			Quit, restart application program, and reopen document you were working on

(cont.)

COMMON PROBLEMS

Problem area	Symptoms	Likely causes	Cures
Error alerts (cont'd.)	Other alert with error code	Program surprised	Something you did created error situation that program author did not anticipate (perhaps you used another program, with Switcher, or a desk accessory to delete or rename a file the program was using); see "Miscellaneous error ID table" for more possibilities
Can't start up	Dark screen	No power	Check power switches, cords, and circuit breakers or fuses
			SCSI devices attached to Mac Plus must be on
	Disk drive doesn't operate	Bad cable connection	Turn off power and check cable for tightness
		Disk drive broken	If you can start up from another drive, have broken drive repaired
		Mac broken	If you can't start up from another drive, have Mac repaired
	Flashing X on disk icon	Disk not startup disk	Use disk that contains System file and Finder
			Try cures listed under "Disk drive doesn't operate"
	Disk ejects prematurely	Disk not startup disk	Use disk with System file and Finder in same folder
			Try cures listed under "Disk drive doesn't operate"
	Sad Mac icon	System file missing	Start up with disk that contains System file, then copy System file from startup disk
		Missing Hard Disk 20 file	Start up with single-sided disk whose System Folder contains these files: Hard Disk 20, System (version 3.1.1 or above), and Finder (version 5.2 or above); drag copy of these files to double-sided disk
			Try cures listed under "Flashing X on disk icon"
		Memory tests failed	If code beneath sad Mac icon doesn't begin with 0F, some of Mac's memory may be bad; have Mac repaired

(cont.)

COMMON PROBLEMS

Problem area	Symptoms	Likely causes	Cures
Can't start up (cont'd.)	System error		Restart while holding down Option and Command keys
			Try cures listed under "Sad Mac icon"
	Can't load Finder	Finder damaged or missing	Start up with disk that contains good Finder, then copy Finder to problem disk
	Can't start from hard disk	Normal with some hard disks	Use special diskette for startup with hard disk
		System file missing or damaged	Start up with diskette and then copy diskette's System file to hard disk's System Folder; with some hard disks, you must also run a special disk-installation program provided by the hard-disk manufacturer (consult your hard disk owner's manual)
		Hard disk not ready	Turn on hard disk, wait minute or so, and try restarting Mac
		Hard-disk cable loose	Turn off all power switches, check cable tightness, turn on power, and try again; with internal hard disk, have internal connections checked
		Hard disk broken	If you can start up with diskette, have hard disk repaired
		Hard disk needs reformatting	Start up with diskette and reformat according to instructions in hard-disk manual
		Mac broken	If you can't start up at all, have Mac repaired
	Mac clicks or chirps	Mac broken	Have Mac repaired
Keyboard	Keyboard dead	Sometimes no typing is expected	Use mouse
		Program crashed	In Switcher, press Command-Option-Shift-Period; otherwise, restart Mac
		Cable loose	Ensure cable securely inserted in Mac and keyboard
		Keyboard or cable broken	Repair or replace keyboard or cable
		Mac broken	Have Mac repaired

(cont.)

COMMON PROBLEMS

Problem area	Symptoms	Likely causes	Cures
Keyboard (cont'd.)	Keyboard erratic	Debris inside keyboard	Repeatedly tap faulty keys to dislodge debris
			Open keyboard case, vacuum or blow out dust and debris, and reassemble keyboard
		You switched to startup disk that doesn't include HFS	Update that disk or remove its System Folder
	Equal-sign key generates comma	Startup disk has old System file	Update startup disk with latest System file (dated after January 4, 1986)
		You switched to startup disk with old System file	Update that disk or remove its System Folder
Clock	Clock inaccurate	Battery low or dead	Replace clock battery with EverReady No. 523 or equivalent
Disks	Can't open from disk	Disk askew in drive	Eject disk and reinsert it
		Dirty drive	Clean drive with disk-cleaning kit
		Bad disk	Use backup copy of document or application
		External drive cable loose	Use internal drive; then quit, shut down, turn off power, and check cable for tightness
		Drive broken	Try opening from other drive (if you have two); have broken drive repaired
	Can't save on disk	File locked	Save under different name
		Disk locked	Slide disk-locking tab so no hole shows in corner of disk
		Disk full or nearly full	Save on another disk; later, reorganize documents
		Disk, drive, or cable not functioning	Try cures listed under "Can't open from disk"

(cont.)

COMMON PROBLEMS

Problem area	Symptoms	Likely causes	Cures
Disks (cont'd.)	Folders or files missing	Startup disk doesn't include HFS	Update startup disk with latest Finder and System files (dated after January 4, 1986)
			Macs without 128K ROM also require Hard Disk 20 file to use HFS
		You switched to startup disk that doesn't include HFS	Update that disk or remove its System folder
	Can't eject disk	Mac drives have no eject lever	In Finder, select disk's icon and choose Eject from File menu, or drag disk's icon to Trash
			In most applications, choose Open or Save As and then click Eject button in dialog box that appears
			Press Command-Shift-1 for internal drive, or Command-Shift-2 for external drive
		Program crashed	In Switcher, press Command-Option-Shift-Period; otherwise, hold down mouse button as you restart Mac
			As last resort, push straightened paper clip into hole near disk insertion slot
	Drive doesn't spin	Mac confused	Press Command-Shift-1 or Command-Shift-2 to eject disk and then reinsert disk
		Disk, drive, or cable not functioning	Print document, type it using typewriter, or read it aloud to tape recorder, in case you have to recreate it
			Send document to another Mac via serial port, using modem and phone lines if other Mac is not nearby
			Try cures listed under "Can't open from disk"

(cont.)

COMMON PROBLEMS

Problem area	Symptoms	Likely causes	Cures
Disks (cont'd.)	Good disk unreadable	Double-sided (800K) disk in single-sided (400K) drive	Use 800K disks only in 800K drives
		400K HFS disk in old Mac	Use disks initialized with HFS only in 800K drive or in 400K drive with HFS
		Disk, drive, or cable not functioning	Try cures listed under "Can't open from disk"
	Can't initialize disk	Defective disk	Use another disk
		Missing Hard Disk 20 file	Start up with single-sided disk whose System Folder contains these files: Hard Disk 20, System (version 3.1.1 or above), and Finder (version 5.2 or above); drag copy of these files to double-sided disk
	All disks unreadable	Mac confused	Quit, turn off Mac, remove clock battery, wait five minutes, install clock battery, restart Mac, and try inserting disks again
	Can't fully insert disk	Disk held upside down	Insert disk with locking tab on left
		Drive broken	Have drive repaired
	Disk drive spins nonstop	Defective disk	Use another disk
		Disk, drive, or cable not functioning	Try cures listed under "Can't open from disk"
ImageWriter	Doesn't print anything	Power switch off	Turn on
		Select lamp unlit	Press Select switch once
		Cable loose	Plug cable securely into ImageWriter and Mac

(cont.)

COMMON PROBLEMS

Problem area	Symptoms	Likely causes	Cures
ImageWriter (cont'd.)		Cover off or loose	Place cover securely on ImageWriter
		Out of paper	Put more paper in printer and make sure Select lamp is lit
		Disk full	Copy document, application, or both to blank disk; remove from original disk after copying
			Print one page at a time, indicating page to print in page-range fields in Print dialog box
		Mac confused	Verify printer and port choices with Chooser desk accessory
			Use Apple's Installer program to install Chooser desk accessory and new ImageWriter printing resource (version 2.2 or above)
			Quit, turn off Mac, remove clock battery, wait five minutes, install clock battery, restart program, and try printing again
		Bad disk	Quit, copy document to another disk, restart program, and try printing again
		Program malfunction	Quit, restart program, and try printing again
		ImageWriter broken	Check ImageWriter by turning it off and holding down Form Feed button while turning it back on; it should repeatedly print line of letters, numbers, and symbols; if it doesn't, have it repaired
	No standard or high quality	Disk locked	Slide disk-locking tab so that no hole shows in corner of disk
	Prints gibberish	ImageWriter switches set wrong	See tip in Printing chapter for correct switch settings
		Wrong cable	Try new cable
		Printer buffer/ spooler malfunction	Disconnect printer buffer or turn off spooler, and try again

(cont.)

COMMON PROBLEMS

Problem area	Symptoms	Likely causes	Cures
ImageWriter (cont'd.)	Prints only *U*'s	Mac confused	Quit, turn off Mac, remove clock battery, wait five minutes, install clock battery, restart program, and try printing again
			See tip in Printing chapter for explanation
	Compressed line near top of page	Normal with some pin-feed paper	Try different weight of paper
			Use single-sheet paper
			Apply even, gentle tension to paper coming out of printer
		Paper-feed lever set wrong	Set lever for pin-feed or pressure-feed paper
		Slack in gears	Turn printer off and on just before printing
	Line height uneven	Normal condition	No cure for variations in line height with small font sizes on original ImageWriter; use larger font size or get ImageWriter II
	Picture lighter than text	Normal on original ImageWriter	Get ImageWriter II or use FixPic desk accessory
	Macpaint pictures distorted	Wrong orientation selected	Select Tall Adjusted or Wide in Page Setup dialog box
	Thin lines across patterns	Normal condition	ImageWriter has trouble with some patterns; try heavy paper with different combinations of paper feed settings
	Print quality poor	Paper-thickness lever set wrong	Set thickness lever (under printer cover) all the way up for one-part paper, or down one notch for each additional copy

(cont.)

COMMON PROBLEMS

Problem area	Symptoms	Likely causes	Cures
ImageWriter (cont'd.)	Top or bottom margin off	Wrong measurements in Page Setup dialog box	Choose Page Setup from File menu, change margin measurements, and print again
		On ImageWriter II, switch SW1-5 set wrong	Remove front cover and set switch SW1-5 to Open
	Muddy colors on ImageWriter II	Pigment transfer on ribbon	Replace ribbon and use color sparingly (white background and sparse patterns)
	Paper wrinkles or tears	Paper supply obstructed	Clear paper path
		Paper-feed lever set wrong	Set lever for pin-feed or pressure-feed paper
LaserWriter	System error	Unprintable character in document	Print small sections of document until you find section that causes error; retype that section to eliminate bad character
	Doesn't print anything	Still preparing page image	Wait as long as middle light on LaserWriter blinks; complex page may take 20 minutes or more to prepare
		Out of paper	Add paper
		Paper jam	Remove printed pages from output tray
			Clear paper path
		Mac confused	Verify printer and port choices with Chooser desk accessory
			Use Apple's Installer program to install Chooser desk accessory and new LaserWriter printing resource (version 3.0 or above)
		LaserWriter not selected	Verify printer and port choices with Chooser desk accessory
		AppleTalk not connected	Use Control Panel desk accessory to connect AppleTalk
	Excess space between words	Font Substitution option selected	Cancel Font Substitution option in Page Setup dialog box; select all text and manually change to LaserWriter font

(cont.)

19

COMMON PROBLEMS

Problem area	Symptoms	Likely causes	Cures
LaserWriter (cont'd.)	Slow to print	Normal under some conditions	Avoid large, heavy screen fonts such as Athens, London, and Venice
			Avoid frequent switching from one screen font to another
			In MacDraw, avoid patterns other than black, white, and shades of gray
			Avoid bitmap graphics, such as MacPaint images
Switcher	Out of memory	RAM cache on	Turn RAM cache off or reduce memory allotted to it; then quit Switcher and restart it
	Can't load set	Applications in different folders	Move all applications in set to same folder as Switcher document, or to System Folder

SYSTEM-ERROR IDS AND THEIR MEANINGS

	ID	Meaning
System errors	1	Bus error: Memory-reference problem occurred on Mac XL, or on modified Mac or Mac Plus
	2	Address error: Program referred to odd memory address
	3	Illegal instruction: MC68000 microprocessor encountered machine-language instruction it did not recognize
	4	Zero divide: Signed Divide (DIVS) or Unsigned Divide (DIVU) machine-language instruction had divisor of 0
	5	Check exception: Check Register Against Bounds (CHK) machine-language instruction failed; perhaps Pascal value-out-of-range error occurred
	6	TrapV exception: Trap On Overflow (TRAPV) machine-language instruction failed
	7	Privilege violation: Mac always runs in privilege (supervisor) mode; perhaps erroneous Return From Execution (RTE) machine-language instruction encountered
	8	Trace exception: Trace bit on microprocessor's status register set
	9	Line 1010 exception: 1010 trap dispatcher failed, making it impossible to use ROM
	10	Line 1111 exception: Unimplemented machine-language instruction encountered; perhaps leftover breakpoint from program debugging
	11	Miscellaneous exception: Nonspecific error condition caught by microprocessor
	12	Unimplemented core routine: Microprocessor encountered nonexistent trap number, perhaps fictitious ROM routine
	13	Spurious interrupt: Interrupt vector table entry for particular level of interrupt is NIL; usually occurs with level 4, 5, 6, or 7 interrupts
	14	I/O system error: Mac's File Manager found bad type field in entry on I/O request queue, or dCtlQHead field was NIL during Fetch or Stash call in custom driver routine, or needed device-control entry has been purged
	15	Segment Loader error: GetResource procedure unable to read segment into memory
	16	Floating-point error: Halt bit in floating-point environment word set
	17-24	Can't read PACK resource into memory
	25	Memory full or fragmented: Memory Manager unable to fill program's request for more memory
	26	Segment Loader error: GetResource procedure encountered nonexecutable resource or unable to read 'CODE' segment 0 into memory for some other reason
	27	File map destroyed: Volume contains block with block number higher than last block or lower than first block on volume
	28	Stack overflow error: Memory problem occurred because stack expanded into heap

(cont.)

NONSYSTEM-ERROR IDS AND THEIR MEANINGS

	ID	Meaning
Input/output device errors	−17	Can't perform requested control procedure
	−18	Can't perform requested status procedure
	−19	Can't read
	−20	Can't write
	−21	Device or driver unknown (reference number doesn't match unit table)
	−22	Device or driver unknown (reference number specifies NIL handle in unit table)
	−23	Driver not opened for requested read or write; attempt to open RAM serial driver failed
	−25	Attempt to remove open driver
	−26	Driver resource missing
	−27	Input or output request aborted, or error while aborting print operation
	−28	Driver not open
File errors	−33	Directory full
	−34	Disk full (all allocation blocks on volume full)
	−35	No such volume
	−36	I/O error
	−37	Bad name (perhaps zero length)
	−38	File not open
	−39	End of file reached while reading
	−40	Attempt to position before start of file
	−42	Too many files open
	−43	File not found
	−44	Volume physically locked
	−45	File locked
	−46	Volume locked by software flag
	−47	File busy; attempt to delete open file(s)
	−48	Duplicate file name
	−49	File already open for writing; multiple paths for writing not allowed
	−50	Error in file specification; parameters don't specify existing volume, and there's no default volume; bad disk-drive positioning information; bad drive number
	−51	Attempt to use nonexistent access path
	−52	Error getting file position
	−53	Disk ejected or volume off-line
	−54	Attempt to open locked file for writing
	−55	Volume already mounted and on-line

(cont.)

NONSYSTEM-ERROR IDS AND THEIR MEANINGS

	ID	Meaning
File errors	−56	No such drive
(cont.)	−57	Not Macintosh disk; volume lacks directory in Macintosh format
	−58	External file system; file-system identifier is nonzero, or path reference number is greater than 1024
	−59	Problem during rename
	−60	Bad block on master directory; must reinitialize volume
	−61	Writing not allowed
Disk errors	−64	Drive disconnected
	−65	No disk inserted
	−66	Disk seems blank
	−67	Can't find address mark
	−68	Verification of read failed
	−69	Bad address mark
	−70	Bad address mark
	−71	Missing data mark
	−72	Bad data mark
	−73	Bad data mark
	−74	Write underrun occurred
	−75	Drive error
	−76	Can't find track 0
	−77	Can't initialize disk controller chip
	−78	Tried to read side 2 of disk in single-sided drive
	−79	Can't correctly adjust disk speed
	−80	Drive error
	−81	Can't find sector
Clock-chip	−85	Can't read clock
errors	−86	Verification of time change failed
	−87	Verification of parameter RAM failed
	−88	Validity status not $A8
AppleTalk	−91	Socket already active; socket not known; no room for more sockets
errors	−92	Data-size error
	−93	Bridge between two AppleTalk networks missing
	−94	Protocol error
	−95	Can't get clear signal to send
	−97	Can't open driver because port already in use
	−98	Can't open driver because port not configured for this connection

(cont.)

NONSYSTEM-ERROR IDS AND THEIR MEANINGS

	ID	Meaning
Scrap errors	− 100	Desk scrap (Clipboard) not initialized
	− 102	Scrap doesn't contain data of type requested
Memory errors	− 108	Not enough room in heap zone
	− 109	NIL master pointer
	− 111	Attempt to use free block
	− 112	Attempt to purge locked block
	− 117	Block is locked
Resource errors	− 192	Resource not found
	− 193	Resource file not found
	− 194	Unable to add resource
	− 195	Unable to remove resource
More AppleTalk errors	− 1024	Buffer overflow (Name-Binding Protocol—NBP)
	− 1025	Name not confirmed (NBP)
	− 1026	Name confirmed for different socket (NBP)
	− 1027	Duplicate name (NBP)
	− 1028	Name not found (NBP)
	− 1029	Names information socket error (NBP)
	− 1096	Send request failed (AppleTalk-Transaction Protocol—ATP)
	− 1097	Too many concurrent requests (ATP)
	− 1098	Too many responding sockets (ATP)
	− 1099	Bad responding socket (ATP)
	− 1100	Bad sequence number (ATP)
	− 1101	No release received (ATP)
	− 1102	Control block not found (ATP)
	− 1103	Additional response packet sent before first response packet (ATP)
	− 1104	Too many outstanding calls (ATP)
	− 1105	Request aborted
	− 3101	Too much data for buffer
	− 3102	MPP driver not installed
	− 3103	Bad checksum (Datagram-Delivery Protocol—DDP)
	− 3104	Can't find name-address pair in buffer (NBP)
	− 3105	Socket or protocol type invalid or not in table
	− 3106	Response message too large (ATP)
	− 3107	Bad response from ATPRequest function
	− 3108	AB Record not found
	− 3109	Asynchronous call aborted because socket closed before call completed

Hardware hints

The Mac is a simple machine, as computers go. It's easy to set up and requires little maintenance. This chapter offers ideas for installing the Mac in unusual situations, for prolonging trouble-free operation, and for fixing common minor problems yourself.

DISKS AND DISK DRIVES

Disk life

The specification for 3½-inch disks calls for them to operate without dropouts (that is, with less than 10 percent loss of signal amplitude) for 10 million passes, with the drive head positioned over one track. What does that mean to you and me? Disk manufacturers—including Sony, BASF, and others—are reluctant to state a theoretical disk life in terms of hours of operation, because so many factors can affect it. High or low temperatures, high humidity, dusty or smoky air, magnetic fields, vibration, and dirty drive heads can all reduce the useful life of a disk.

Statistics on 3½-inch disk longevity are incomplete, but for comparison, 5¼-inch disks tend to last one to two years before reaching retirement age. History has shown that 5¼-inch disks generally fail because of physical abuse—bending, denting, folding, and so forth—before they wear out.

By the way, disks have an indefinite shelf life as long as they're kept in pleasant surroundings. To a disk, "pleasant" means clean, dry (between 8 and 90 percent relative humidity, with no water forming on the disk surface), between 39 and 127 degrees F, and away from magnetic fields. As long as you meet these conditions, you don't have to worry about your disk archives fading or developing worm holes.

External drive placement

There are two things to consider when deciding where to put your external disk drive: safety and convenience. Magnetic disturbance from the Mac's power supply can permanently destroy information on the disk in the external drive. Since the power supply is located against the left side of the Mac's case, its magnetic influence may affect an external drive placed on the top or to the left of the machine.

Placing the external drive on top of the Mac is also risky for another reason: If the disk drive is allowed to soak up the heat steaming out of the top of the machine for a long time, the drive's head may expand enough out of alignment that it cannot read relatively cold disks. The drive will usually work again if you take it off the Mac and allow it to cool down.

The only place left for the external drive is on the right side of the Mac. You can reduce the desk space the external drive occupies by setting it on its side, with its feet facing the right side of the Mac. The drive should work reliably in this position, though inserting disks sideways does take some getting used to.

THE MOUSE

Avoiding worn-out mouse feet

The two "feet" that support the front of the mouse can wear off after several months' continuous use on a hard surface. Without its front feet, the mouse wobbles and doesn't glide smoothly. To keep your mouse's feet from wearing out, you can buy or make a mouse pad.

To make a pad, you'll need a piece of the nylon-covered neoprene used for wet suits. Use the type called Nylon I, which has nylon on one side only. A 4- by 6-inch piece is adequate; 8 by 10 inches is ample. Place the fabric nylon side up, rubber side down.

If this advice comes too late and your mouse's feet are already worn out, try applying self-adhesive Velcro strips to the bottom of the mouse, adjacent to the worn feet. Use the soft, fuzzy half of the Velcro, not the half with stiff plastic hooks. Or buy Magnum Software's Mouse Mover. It is a sort of three-wheeled, ball-bearing roller skate that clips to the base of your mouse, eliminating the worn-feet syndrome and making the mouse somewhat easier to move precisely. Its 99 ball bearings are a bit noisy, especially on hard surfaces—it makes your mouse sound like it's trying out for a roller derby.

Replacing the mouse-button switch

Lots of clicking and double clicking may wear out the switch on your mouse button. You can have the switch replaced, or you can replace it yourself if you are mechanically inclined. If you're doing it yourself, you'll need the following:

- [ ] A pair of needle-nose pliers.
- [ ] A small soldering iron (15 to 30 watts) and some $^{60}/_{40}$ rosin-core solder.
- [ ] Radio Shack part number 275-017 or 275-016, or an equivalent subminiature single-pole, double-throw (SPDT) switch that measures ¾ by ¼ by ⅜ inch and is rated 0.1 amp 250 volt or better.

Once you've assembled these items, proceed as follows:

1. There is a metal lever attached to the Radio Shack switch. Remove the lever with the needle-nose pliers.
2. Remove the two screws that hold the mouse case together and put them aside where they won't get lost.

3. Holding the mouse upside down, separate the two halves of its case. They don't pull straight apart; you must slide the bottom half forward slightly. When the case comes apart, take care not to lose the plastic mouse button and its spring.

4. Remove the entire switch and cable assembly from the mouse as a unit. The switch is held in place by a small knob that sticks into the side of the switch. Carefully pry the support bracket arm that contains the knob back just far enough to release the switch.

5. One at a time, desolder the two wires attached to the old switch, and then solder them in the corresponding places on the new switch.

6. Reinstall the cable assembly and new switch in the mouse.

7. Reassemble the mouse. Before screwing the case together, click the mouse button to make sure it feels right. If it doesn't, its spring may be crooked; open up the mouse again and check.

THE SCREEN

Etching

A stationary image, such as the Mac's menu bar, displayed continuously for weeks or months, may etch the screen's phosphor, leaving a shadow. The Macintosh owner's manual suggests dimming the screen with the brightness control whenever you leave the machine on and unattended for a long time. The brightness control is located at the front of the Mac on the overhang under the Apple logo.

The Fade to Black desk accessory, by Brian L. Matthews, eliminates this problem. It automatically paints the entire screen black after a period of no keyboard or mouse-button activity, leaving only a wandering icon visible to remind you that the Mac is still switched on. A click of the mouse brings the screen back to life. You choose the length of the inactive period in seconds or minutes. You should be aware that Fade to Black does not always restore the screen properly with some programs, notably MacPaint, and that it may cause problems while you are printing or telecommunicating.

Mac XL distortion

Compared with the 9-inch screen of the Mac 512 and Mac Plus, the 12-inch screen of the Macintosh XL has room for larger windows, more icons, wider word-processing lines, more spreadsheet columns, and so on. However, the images are taller and thinner, making squares look like rectangles and circles look like ovals. The problem is the different dot shapes on the two screens: Dots on the Mac XL are rectangular instead of square.

The dot shape of the Mac XL can be made square by installing an accessory inside the machine. Apple offers a Mac XL screen-modification kit that irrevocably alters the dots. Two other products, BitFixer from All Star Computer Services and LisaVision from the company of the same name, give you a choice: You can have rectangular dots for programs written for the Lisa computer, such as Lisa 7/7, the Pascal Workshop, or UNIX; or, with just the flip of a switch, you can have square dots for Mac programs.

THE SPEAKER

Amplified sound

The audio-output jack lets you pipe the Mac's sound output to an external speaker, an audio amplifier, or even a tape recorder. The jack accepts a standard 1/8-inch phone plug.

Electronics stores carry adapter cables that send the monaural sound from the Mac to both channels of a stereo amplifier; Radio Shack part number 42-2153 is one such cable. Connect the cable to high-level input jacks on the amplifier or tape recorder. The Mac's sound output signal will overload low-level input jacks, such as those intended for a magnetic phono cartridge or microphone, resulting in loud but distorted sound.

Speaker placement

If you attach an external speaker to your Mac, don't place the speaker on or near an external disk drive or disk storage cabinets. The speaker contains a magnet that could destroy the information on your disks.

COOLING

Don't block vents

If you place your hand over the vents at the top of the Mac, you'll feel hot air escaping, particularly on the side where the power switch is located. As the hot air escapes, it draws cooler air into the machine through vents near the bottom of the case. The cooler air gets hot as it passes over the electronic components inside the Mac and rises out the top, drawing in more cool air.

If you block the vents, you stop the flow of air, and the Mac may overheat and die. Hence, do not leave papers, books, cats, or other objects on top of the Mac, or stack anything against its sides.

Avoiding sunstroke

Heat builds up rapidly inside a car parked in the sun. The same thing happens inside a Mac if you leave it in the sun, and you can't cool the Mac off by rolling down the windows! The electronic components inside your Mac are at least as sensitive to heat as you are, so find it a cool place in the shade.

Adding a fan

If you want to make sure your Mac stays cool, you can add a fan. One model, the Fanny Mac from Beck-Tech, fits into the handle recess at the top of the machine and increases the volume of air flowing through it. The fan includes an electrical surge suppressor and a power switch, which you use instead of the Mac's power switch.

Another model, the MacBreeze from Levco, clips inside the Mac. Instead of boosting the general airflow through the machine, the MacBreeze blows air directly at the power-supply components, which run much hotter and tend to fail earlier than the Mac's other components.

ELECTRICITY

Ungrounded fears

Many older buildings have no electrical grounding available. You may be able to get around ungrounded outlets with adapter plugs, but they only provide a true ground if used properly. In some cases, connecting the small wire of the adapter to the screw on the outlet's cover plate is adequate. But often that cover-plate screw is not grounded.

You can ground the cover-plate screw by running a 14-gauge insulated wire from the screw to the nearest cold-water pipe. Use a cold-water pipe, not a hot-water pipe or radiator, because the hot-water boiler may interrupt the ground. A hardware store or electrical supply store should have a bracket that clamps to the pipe and has a terminal to which you can attach the wire.

To be really secure, you should also ground the cold-water pipes by connecting them to a grounding rod ahead of the water meter. Typically, the rod is 8 feet long, but to be sure it will function properly, it ought to reach down into the water table.

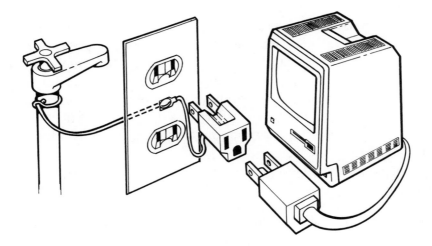

To reliably ground your Mac in an older building, you may need to run a wire from the plug adapter at the electrical outlet to the nearest cold-water pipe.

12-volt battery power

Although the Macintosh is designed to use the 120-volt alternating current (AC) that comes out of power outlets in residences or business offices, it can also be powered by 12-volt direct current (DC) from car batteries. You'll need a device called an inverter, which transforms direct current to alternating current.

There are two types of inverters: sine-wave and square-wave. Sine-wave inverters produce a smooth alternating current and are expensive. Square-wave inverters are inexpensive, but alternate abruptly between the negative and positive flow of electrical current. If these transitions occur too quickly, the filter capacitors in the Mac's power supply could heat up. However, this situation is unlikely to cause a problem because the inverter would probably fail before the capacitors did. Most inexpensive square-wave inverters contain transformers that produce comparatively slow voltage transitions.

The inverter must produce AC power between 95 and 120 volts under load; that is, when the Mac is plugged into it and turned on. Inexpensive inverters may produce peak voltages outside that range under no load, but the peaks usually smooth out when a load is applied. The frequency of the inverter's AC output is unimportant, because the Mac controls the frequency internally as needed.

The inverter must also produce enough power for whatever you plug into it. The Mac draws between 40 and 60 watts. Inverter output is usually given in amps, but you can convert the amps to watts by multiplying them by the number of volts. Thus, the Mac requires 0.33 to 0.5 amp at 120 volts. Attaching an external disk drive does not increase the power requirement significantly, but plugging in a printer or hard disk does. For example, an Apple HD 20 hard disk draws 30 watts (0.25 amp at 120 volts), and an ImageWriter draws 20 watts on standby and 180 watts while printing (0.13 to 1.5 amps at 120 volts).

How long will a battery last? That depends on how much you plug into the inverter and on the capacity of the battery. Battery capacity is measured in amp-hours. If you divide the battery's amp-hour rating by the total amps drawn by the devices attached to it, you come up with the number of hours the battery will last. For example, the Mac itself draws between 3.5 and 5 amps at 12 volts DC (40 to 60 watts divided by 12 volts), so a 55-amp-hour battery will last between 11 and 16½ hours.

Foreign power

The US models of Macintosh and ImageWriter are designed to operate at 107 to 132 volts AC, at a frequency of 50 to 60 hertz. In countries with 220- or 240-volt power, you can operate a US-type Mac and ImageWriter with a 220- to 110-volt (a "two-to-one") step-down transformer. For the Mac alone, the transformer must be rated at 60 watts (60 VA) or higher. For the Mac and ImageWriter together, the rating must be 240 watts (240 VA) or higher. Get a good-quality, grounded (three-prong plug) isolation transformer. Do not use a cheap transformer; it may ruin your computer equipment.

By the way, you may encounter some difficulty should your "foreign" computer need repairs, since Apple dealers generally stock parts only for equipment designed for their country. They should be able to order parts for any model, but that involves waiting for the parts to arrive. Also, your Apple warranty or AppleCare service contract is valid only in the country of purchase. For warranty repairs or AppleCare service, you must return the malfunctioning equipment to the country where you bought it. So if you're thinking about sending your equipment abroad, take the time to put it through its paces first, so that any problems covered under the warranty can be corrected before you export it.

MAINTENANCE

ImageWriter head breakdown

If you print large pictures containing many solid black areas, the print head of an original-model ImageWriter may overheat and fail, requiring a new head. To avoid this expense, design your pages so that they are no more than 25 to 30 percent solid black. Allowing the head to cool off between pages also helps prevent overheating. The ImageWriter II comes with built-in protection against head overheating.

Squeaky ImageWriter

The ImageWriter user's manual suggests lubricating the shaft on which the head mechanism travels with a light machine oil once a year. However, it cautions that you should not use electric-motor oil or any lubricant that contains rust inhibitors. The problem is that it's almost impossible to find a machine oil without rust inhibitors. Apple recommends sewing-machine oil—even if it contains a rust inhibitor—for lubricating the ImageWriter.

Removing fingerprints from disks

A single fingerprint can render a disk unreadable. Fingers don't often find their way past the metal shutter on a 3½-inch disk, but it does happen: Young fingers, especially, have a way of circumventing the protective shutter. Should one of your disks suddenly turn up unreadable, you can check it for fingerprints by sliding open the shutter and looking at the disk surface under a strong light.

Remove any fingerprints you find with a cotton swab moistened with alcohol. Twirl the swab to pick up any loose strands of cotton, and blow gently on the disk to dry the alcohol.

If you spill coffee on the keyboard...

If you spill liquid on your keyboard and it stops working, unplug the keyboard, turn it upside down to drain out the liquid, and let it dry for a day. If that doesn't do the trick, you'll have to take it in for repair.

Opening the case

You may have seen ads for do-it-yourself memory upgrades, cooling-fan kits, and replacement disk drives, and wondered how difficult they would be to install. To see whether you want to tackle making internal modifications yourself, start by trying to open the Mac's case. (A word of warning: Opening the case does not void the warranty, but any damage you cause in the process is not covered under warranty.) The five screws you must remove, including the one hidden behind the clock-battery cover, require a special screwdriver with a Torx T-15 tip and an 8-inch shaft. After you remove the screws, a friction coating makes it very difficult to remove the back cover; use a ruler edgewise as a wedge to pry the case apart.

As you open the case, a piece of foil may fall off the sockets at the back of Mac. Don't be alarmed. Save the foil so you can slip it back over the sockets when you reassemble your Mac.

Inside the case, you will see the following:

☐ A large vertical circuit board called the analog or power-supply board.
☐ A large horizontal circuit board called the digital or logic board.
☐ The picture tube.
☐ Beneath the picture tube, the disk drive.

Caution: Look, but don't touch unless you know what you're doing. The power-supply board and picture tube may contain dangerous residual high voltages.

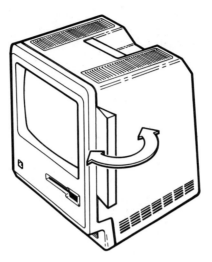

To open a Macintosh case, you must first remove five screws, one from behind the battery cover, with a Torx T-15 screwdriver. Then use the edge of a ruler to pry the case apart.

Peak performance

Originally, the Mac suffered the fate of all generalists: It did many things adequately, but nothing exceptionally well. That situation changed markedly as more memory and other hardware improvements became available, and with the introduction of software that takes advantage of the additional hardware power. This chapter introduces some of what you can do to soup up your Mac.

SPEED

Faster application startups

From the Macintosh desktop, you can designate one application on each disk to be the "startup application." Then whenever you start the Mac with that disk, the startup application is automatically opened, bypassing the Finder's desktop. Assuming you are using a floppy disk, this gets the application going 5 to 20 seconds faster.

To designate the startup application:

1. Select the icon of the application you want started automatically.
2. Choose Set Startup from the Finder's Special menu.

Undoing the Set Startup command

To change a disk so that it once again starts up the Finder's desktop, instead of an application such as MacWrite, make the Finder the startup application. If you have removed the Finder from the disk to free up space, you will have to copy it from another disk, such as the System or System Tools disk that came with your Mac, before you can make it the startup application. Then proceed as follows:

1. Display the Finder's desktop by quitting the startup application.
2. Open the System Folder and select the Finder icon.
3. Choose Set Startup from the Special menu.

Adding more memory

Most application programs run noticeably faster on a Mac with 512K or more of memory than they do on a Mac with 128K. The extra memory stores more fonts and other resources, more program segments, and more of the document you're working on. As a result, the Mac makes fewer trips to the disk when you change fonts, choose from menus, or bring different parts of a document into view. Fewer trips to the disk mean better performance.

MacPaint (versions 1.5 and above), for example, keeps an entire drawing in memory on a 512K Mac. Thus when you move the drawing with the grabber, the formerly unseen parts of the drawing appear immediately. On a 128K Mac, you must wait as MacPaint retrieves the formerly unseen parts of the drawing from the disk.

Upgrading with 128K ROM and 800K disk drive

Upgrading a 512K Mac that still has the original 64K ROM and single-sided (400K) disk drive by installing the Mac Plus 128K ROM and double-sided (800K) disk drive improves its performance significantly. The QuickDraw procedures in the 128K ROM display text 50 percent faster and draw graphics an average of twice as fast as the QuickDraw procedures in 64K ROM. The larger ROM includes many of the most commonly used resources that formerly had to be transferred from disk, such as the 12-point Chicago font. The 800K disk drives are two to three times faster than 400K disk drives, not counting the speed improvements that result when you activate the disk caching included with the upgrade.

RAM disks

Few programs require or can take advantage of 512K of memory. Only the most powerful or complex programs, such as Jazz, Microsoft Excel, and Helix, will use every bit of memory available, and they use it only when working on extremely large files. You can exploit fallow memory by turning it into an electronic disk drive, called a RAM disk.

You can create a RAM disk with programs such as Mac Memory Disk from Assimilation, Quick Disk from Symmetry, MacMate! from SMB Development, or the public-domain RamStart by George A. Nelson. With these programs, you specify how much memory to allot to the RAM disk, and most have a method for designating which files are to be copied onto the RAM disk once it has been created. If you have a Mac Plus or Mac 512K Enhanced, make sure the RAM disk program works with the 128K ROM before using it.

Transferring information from an electronic RAM disk is much faster than from a mechanical disk. However, there are some drawbacks. When the Mac's power goes off, the RAM disk vanishes and all the information on it is instantly erased. As a result, you must recreate the RAM disk every time you restart the Mac. Recreating it and transferring information onto it adds about 30 seconds to startup time. And keep in mind that because the RAM disk is so volatile, it's a bad place to save documents you are working on.

A RAM disk sounds like a great place to put the System file and the Finder, and perhaps a few application programs—that is, until you think about how much space all those files require. On a 512K Mac, RAM-disk size is limited to about 350K, room enough for only the System file, the Finder, and a small application program. Such a small RAM disk probably won't have room to support printing, which requires the ImageWriter file and may require an extra 50K of workspace on the RAM disk. Unless your Mac has a megabyte of memory or more, you'll find a RAM disk most useful in cases like the following:

☐ If you like to switch back and forth between applications, put the Finder and the System file on the RAM disk for all applications to use. Add an ImageWriter file if you want to try printing with the RAM disk. But remove the System file from each application-program disk you plan to use, or drag it out of the System folder on a double-sided disk or other disk that uses the hierarchical file system (HFS), so that one of those System files doesn't take over when you start the application.

☐ If you plan to use just one application, put it on the RAM disk along with the System file, the Finder, and the ImageWriter or LaserWriter file.

Disk caching

Unused memory can be put to work as a disk cache for frequently used information. The Mac Plus and Mac 512K Enhanced have a built-in disk-caching feature, as does every 512K Mac that has been upgraded with a new 128K ROM since January 1986. You can also buy special disk-caching programs, such as Nevins' TurboCharger and Mainstay's MacBooster, to use with other Macs.

Here's how disk caching works: As information is transferred from disk, a copy of it is kept in the area of memory set aside as the disk cache. When that information is needed again, it can be copied quickly from the disk cache instead of slowly from disk. If the cache becomes full, the oldest or least used information in it is discarded. Thus, if you switch applications, parts of the first application program in the cache are eventually replaced by parts of the second application.

A disk cache trades the raw speed of a RAM disk for versatility and safety. Because it is constantly copying and recopying information from the disk, it is not as fast as a RAM disk. In addition, documents are normally saved on disk, not in the disk cache. However, the disk cache is especially useful for the following:

☐ Searching and sorting database files.

☐ Scrolling back and forth in long documents.

☐ Frequent switching among two or three applications that are collectively too large for a RAM disk.

☐ Long sessions with a single application that, together with the System file, is too large for a RAM disk.

THE SWITCHER

Including the Finder

When you use the Switcher, try to find room for the Finder as the first application in the set. The amount of memory that the Finder requires depends on the number of windows it has open and on the number of disk icons on its desktop. You'll need a minimum of 106K for one disk icon and 128K or more for several.

Normally you quit an application to remove it from the Finder, but the Finder's File menu has no Quit command. However, when using the Finder version 5.1 and above from the Switcher, the Shut Down command in the Special menu changes to Quit. If you use an earlier version of the Finder with the Switcher, you must start another application from the Finder, and then quit that application to return to the Switcher with the Finder's former slot vacant.

To quit the Switcher itself when the Finder is among the active applications, first quit all active applications except the Finder. Then quit the Switcher. The Switcher hands the Mac over to the Finder, since it is the only remaining active application.

Conserving memory

The Switcher's Save Screen feature uses 22K per application. By turning it off, you can reduce the amount of memory the Switcher itself uses and free up more memory for applications. To turn off Save Screen before installing an application, use the Configure Then Install command in the Switcher menu. After installing an application, you can turn the Save Screen feature on and off by clicking the screen in the Mac icon to the right of the application name in the Switcher's list of installed applications. If you attempt to turn on Save Screen when there's insufficient memory, the Switcher beeps. In that case, use the Show Info Window command in the Switcher's File menu to see how memory is being used.

Speeding up switching

Turning off the Switcher's Save Screen feature may save memory, but it slows down switching between applications. If fast switching is more important to you than conserving memory, turn on the Save Screen feature for every application by clicking the screen of every Mac icon in the Switcher's main window.

Turning off other optional Switcher features also speeds up switching between applications. Choose the Options command from the Switcher menu and make sure the Always Convert Clipboard and Switching Animation options are not checked. With the Always Convert Clipboard option off, you must hold down the Option key in order to convert the Clipboard when you switch applications.

Why convert the Clipboard?

Why is Clipboard conversion necessary when switching applications? Many applications maintain a private clipboard for cutting, copying, and pasting within the application. Most applications convert their private clipboard to the universal Mac Clipboard document when you quit the application or choose a desk accessory from the Apple menu.

When you request Clipboard conversion from the Switcher by turning on the Always Convert Clipboard option or by pressing the Option key when you switch, the Switcher fools the application you're switching from into thinking you've just chosen a desk accessory from the Apple menu, forcing the conversion of the private clipboard to the Clipboard document. It also fools the application you're switching to into thinking you've just closed a desk accessory, forcing conversion of the Clipboard document to that application's private clipboard. Without the conversions, what you cut or copy in the first application remains on its private clipboard, unknown to the second application.

Application sets and attached documents

Once you have configured a set of applications with the Switcher, you can use the Save Set command from the Switcher's File menu to save the configuration as a Switcher document. The Load Set command then installs the set of applications.

You can also attach a document to each application in the set and have the Switcher open the attached documents when it installs the set. You attach a document to an application as follows:

1. Install or configure the application.
2. Select the application by clicking its name in the Switcher's main window.
3. Choose Attach Document from the Switcher's File menu and, in the Open dialog box that appears, select the name of the document you want to attach to the application.

All the applications in a set must be present on one of the disks inserted when you load the set. With Switcher 4.4, if any application in a set is on a disk that uses the hierarchical file system (HFS), all applications in the set must be in the same folder on that disk. Later versions of the Switcher do not have this restriction. If the Switcher can't find an application called for in the set, it stops installing the set and displays an explanatory message. If an attached document is missing, the Switcher ignores it and installs the application with a new document.

Automatically installing an application set

If you want one set of applications and their attached documents automatically installed when you start Switcher, name the set *Switcher.startup* when you use the Save Set command to save it. To have that set automatically installed when you start the Mac, use the Set Startup command from the Finder's Special menu to make the Switcher the startup application.

Using the Switcher with a disk cache or RAM disk

Both the Switcher and the applications you start through the Switcher can use the memory you set aside for a disk cache or RAM disk. Practically speaking, you'll need a megabyte or more of memory to use the Switcher together with a disk cache or RAM disk.

Set up the cache or RAM disk first, and be sure to leave enough room for all the applications you want to install with the Switcher. Once they are installed, you must not change the size of the cache or RAM disk.

How much memory does an application need?

When you install some applications, they tell the Switcher how much memory they prefer and the minimum amount they must have. For applications that don't specify preferred and minimum memory sizes, the Switcher allocates 128K.

You can set memory-allocation sizes yourself using the Configure Then Install command in the Switcher's Switcher menu. But why bother with changing memory-allocation size? On the one hand, many programs perform better or accommodate larger documents when more memory is available. For example, MacPaint works fine with 128K, but works faster with 179K; Microsoft Excel requires at least 256K, but works better with 304K and can take advantage of even more memory to open a larger document or more documents. On the other hand, you may need to reduce an application's memory size in order to install another application as part of the same Switcher set.

If an application doesn't specify its preferred and minimum memory sizes, and they're not listed in the application's manual, you will have to determine what they should be by trial and error. Here's how you determine the preferred memory size:

1. With no RAM disk installed and the disk cache off, start the Switcher.

2. Click a vacant slot in the Switcher menu, and choose Configure Then Install from the Switcher menu. The standard Open dialog box appears.

3. Open the application you want to configure. A configuration dialog box opens, showing the preferred and minimum memory sizes for the application.

4. Enter the Preferred Memory Size. Try a large number initially, but not more than 420 on a Mac 512K or 935 on a Mac Plus. Click the Temporary button to put the dialog box away and reveal the main Switcher window.

5. Start the application by double clicking on its icon in the main Switcher window. Open a document and use the application heavily for several minutes. Try as many commands as you can, especially those that make the disk operate.

6. When the disk quiets down, or after five to ten minutes' use, return to the Switcher by clicking between the two-headed arrow in the menu bar or by choosing Switcher from the Apple menu.

7. Choose Show Information Window from the Switcher's File menu. The Switcher Information window appears, showing memory usage with a bar chart. The dark gray area of the bar chart shows how much of the allocated memory the application is actually using. If less than 90 percent of the bar is dark gray, you can probably get away with allocating less memory for the application. To do that, quit the application and repeat the process beginning with step 2, but use a slightly smaller memory size in step 4.

8. When you decide on an optimum size, make a note of it and reconfigure the application with the Configure Then Install command, but this time click the Permanent button.

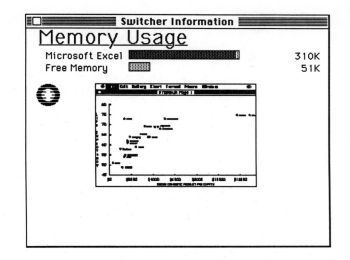

Use the memory-usage bar chart in the Switcher Information window to see whether an application is actually using all the memory allocated for it. Here, Microsoft Excel is using almost all of the 310K it has available.

For the minimum memory size, try 128K. Very few applications work reliably with less. If an alert message appears when you try to start the application, advising you the program failed or couldn't be run, try a larger size.

Emergency exit

If the pointer freezes, the keyboard goes dead, or you get a system error message while using an application with the Switcher, don't restart the Mac. Instead, press Command-Option-Shift-Period; you may have to press these keys several times to get a response. This emergency exit usually returns you to the Switcher with the other installed applications intact. A message appears advising you that the application was terminated by the emergency exit. Although you can't resume the particular application that failed, you can switch to the other installed applications. After using the emergency exit, it's a good idea to quit the other applications in an orderly manner and restart the Mac.

Disks and files

*You shouldn't have to think about which disk is
the startup disk, but you do. You don't have
to think about icon names, but you should.
No one wants to think about copying files and folders
from disk to disk, but everyone does,
and you soon forget which disk contains what.
Thinking about speeding up the switch from one
application to another, or about finding more
disk space? The tips in this chapter help
you deal with these bothersome disk, file, and
folder details—and more.*

STARTUP DISKS

What makes a disk a startup disk?

Starting up a Mac requires a startup disk, which is any disk that contains a System file and, in most cases, a Finder. Furthermore, on a double-sided disk, a hard disk, or any other disk that uses the hierarchical file system (HFS), both of these files must be in the same folder. By convention, the System file and Finder are usually kept in the System Folder. A single-sided startup disk, which normally does not use HFS, need not contain the Finder, provided it contains either a MiniFinder or an application that has been designated a startup application with the Finder's Set Startup command.

In addition, a startup disk usually contains the following:

☐ The Scrapbook File, Note Pad File, and Clipboard File.

☐ One or more application-program and document files.

Most applications also expect to find printing resource files, such as the ImageWriter, AppleTalk ImageWriter, or LaserWriter file, on the startup disk, whether or not the application itself is on the startup disk.

The System file on the startup disk determines which fonts and desk accessories are available. You can use the Font/DA Mover program to add and remove fonts or desk accessories in any System file, so that different startup disks have different sets of fonts and desk accessories.

The startup disk may be a 3½-inch disk in the internal drive, a 3½-inch disk in the external drive, an internal hard disk, a hard disk attached to the external drive port, or, on a Mac Plus, a disk drive attached to the SCSI (small computer system interface) port. At startup time, the Mac looks in those places in that order and uses the System file, Finder, and other files from the first startup disk it finds.

Switching startup disks and System files

The System file on the startup disk affects the settings in the Chooser (or Choose Printer) and Control Panel desk accessories and the contents of the Scrapbook and Note Pad desk accessories, as well as which fonts are available and which desk accessories are listed in the Apple menu. The Mac switches startup disks, and concomitantly switches System files, when you do any of the following:

☐ Start an application located on another startup disk. To switch from some hard disks, notably Apple's Hard Disk 20, you must hold down the Option key while you start an application on another drive.

☐ Open a document that is not itself located on another startup disk, but whose application is. To switch from a hard disk, you may have to hold down the Option key while you open the document.

☐ Restart the Mac with a different 3½-inch startup disk.

☐ Hold down the Option and Command keys while you double click the Finder icon on the startup disk you want to switch to.

Preventing System-file switching

You can prevent the switching of System files and thereby avoid the chance of attendant changes to Chooser and Control Panel settings, Scrapbook and Note Pad contents, font and desk-accessory availability, and so on—all of which may occur when you start an application or open a document from the Finder or MiniFinder. Here's how:

☐ If you are starting an application on a disk that contains Finder version 5.1 or above, simply drag the Finder—and MiniFinder, if one is present—out of the folder it shares with the System file on that disk.

☐ If you are opening a document whose application is on a disk that contains Finder version 5.1 or above, separate the System file from the Finder and any MiniFinder on the application disk.

☐ If you are starting an application on a single-sided disk or other disk that does not use the hierarchical file system (HFS), you must either rename the Finder icon or make the icon invisible on that disk.

Finder versions 5.2 and above won't let you rename their icons, but you can make any icon invisible with a disk-editing program such as Fedit, or with Apple's resource-editor program, ResEdit. Follow the steps on the next page to make the Finder invisible using ResEdit.

1. For safety, make a copy of the disk whose Finder you want to make invisible. If possible, copy ResEdit version 1.0D7 or above onto that disk.

2. Start ResEdit. A small window appears for each disk currently inserted. The title at the top of each window identifies which disk it is for; a list of names inside the window shows which application, document, and other files are on the disk. For double-sided disks, hard disks, and other disks that use HFS, folders are also listed.

3. On an HFS disk, open the folder that contains the Finder; usually it is in the System Folder.

4. Locate the Finder in the disk or folder window and select it by clicking its name (make sure you select the Finder on the correct disk!).

5. Choose Get Info from ResEdit's File menu. An information window appears.

6. Find the check box labeled *Invisible* and click it so that an *X* appears in it.

7. Close the information window. ResEdit asks if you want to save the change you made; click the Yes button.

8. Quit ResEdit.

9. If there is a MiniFinder installed on the disk whose Finder you made invisible, return to the Finder and remove the MiniFinder.

The MiniFinder will always switch to the System file on a single-sided disk or other disk that doesn't use HFS, even if the Finder on that disk is invisible. Therefore, you must remove all MiniFinders in order to prevent switching System files when you start an application on a non-HFS disk. If you want to use MiniFinders but you want to avoid switching System files, stick to opening applications from HFS disks.

Using desktop patterns as System-file ID

The current desktop pattern is kept in the System file, so if you assign a different pattern to each System file, you'll be able to tell when the Mac has changed System files. Whenever you switch to a new version of the System file for the first time, use the Control Panel desk accessory to change the desktop pattern.

A couple of applications, notably MacPaint and the MiniFinder, always use the standard gray desktop pattern regardless of the Control Panel setting, so there's no use trying to change them.

THE FINDER

Optimal use of windows

Optimize the use of windows in the Finder by placing seldom-used icons at the bottom of the window and then shrinking the window so that the icons are no longer visible. Keeping windows small makes it easier to work with more of them at a time. But don't make them so small that you spend more time hunting for icons in them with the scroll bars than you would spend moving windows around.

If you usually use only one or two of the items in a window, consider moving them onto the desktop. Then you'll rarely need to open the window they came from. For example, if you are a Microsoft Excel user, you could move the Resume Excel icon to the desktop and leave the Excel disk window closed.

Sorting icons

Have you ever wished the By Name, By Date, By Size, and By Kind commands in the View menu would rearrange the icons in a window, rather than displaying sorted text information about the icons? It turns out that, indirectly, you can make them do this. Here's what you do:

1. Open the window whose icons you want to organize, and choose By Icon or By Small Icon from the View menu. If you chose By Small Icon, press the Option key and choose Clean Up from the Special menu, thereby compacting the small icons in the window.

2. Choose By Name, By Date, By Size, or By Kind from the View menu. Information about the icons is displayed in text format in the order you requested.

3. Choose Select All from the Edit menu, highlighting everything in the window.

4. Drag all the selected items out of the window, onto the desktop. When you release the mouse button, the items appear as a pile of icons on the desktop.

5. Immediately drag the still-selected icons back into their original window, where they are again displayed in text format in the order you requested in step 1.

6. Choose By Icon or By Small Icon from the Special menu the same as in step 1, and the icons are displayed left to right and top to bottom in the same order as the text information they have replaced.

Aligning dragged icon

Want some help straightening up icons? With Finder versions 5.1 and above, press the Command key as you start to drag an icon or group of icons. When you release the mouse button to end the drag, all highlighted icons automatically line up along an invisible grid. This feature works in the small icon view as well as the standard icon view.

Realigning all icons

Pressing the Option key while you choose Clean Up from the Special menu forces the Finder (versions 5.1 and above) to move all icons in the active window to the upper left corner of that window while aligning them with an invisible grid.

Don't open any windows

When you start up, insert a disk, or quit an application, the Finder normally opens the same disk and folder windows that were open when you last shut down, started the application, or ejected the disk. To eliminate the time-consuming automatic window opening, hold down the Option key until you see the Finder's menu bar or the icon of the disk you inserted. This feature is only present in Finder versions 5.1 and above.

Forget opening this window

The Finder normally remembers when you open windows, and automatically re-opens the same windows the next time it encounters the corresponding disk. If you hold down the Option key while opening a window, the Finder (versions 5.1 and above) will not remember the event. When you next start up the Mac or quit an application with the same disk inserted, or when you insert that disk, the window will not reopen automatically.

Closing all windows at once

With versions 5.1 and above of the Finder, you can close all windows by pressing the Option key while choosing Close from the File menu or while clicking the close box of any window.

Generic and name-brand icons

What are those blank, featureless icons that sometimes haunt the desktop? Where do they come from? Where do they go? The Finder has the answers.

The Finder is responsible for drawing icons on the desktop, but it contains images for only the folder icon, the trash icon, the System-file icon, a generic application icon, and a generic document icon. The Finder does not contain images for the unique icons that most application programs and documents use. Instead, applications such as MacWrite and MacPaint contain within their programs icons for themselves and for the documents they create.

To understand how the Finder assigns icons, you need to know how a document and an application program are linked. Each document and application has two hidden attributes—four-letter codes called Creator and Type—that tell the Finder which icon to use. An application's Creator attribute is a unique monogram, such as MPNT, and its Type is always APPL. A document's Creator attribute specifies which application contains its icon and its Type attribute specifies which of the Creator application's set of icons to use. Hence the application that creates a particular type of document, not the document itself, knows what the document icon should look like.

For all the applications and documents on a disk, the Finder initially fetches icon images from the appropriate applications. Rather than repeat this process every time you insert the disk, the Finder copies the icon images it fetches into an invisible document called the Desktop file. Whenever the Finder encounters a document for which it cannot find a matching Creator application, it searches the Desktop file for another document of the same Creator and Type and uses that document's icon. If the Finder cannot find a matching application or document, it substitutes its generic document icon, which looks like a blank page with the right corner folded over. Pressing Command-Shift-3, for example, creates a snapshot of the screen as a MacPaint-type document. But if none of the disks inserted at the time contains MacPaint or MacPaint documents, the new document gets a generic icon.

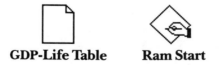

GDP-Life Table   **Ram Start**

*Generic document icons (left) usually appear when a document is saved on a disk
that does not contain similar documents or the application that created the document.
Generic application icons (right), though, appear when no one has yet created unique
icons for the applications.*

If a document you have created shows up on the desktop as a generic icon, you can replace it with a "name-brand" icon, as follows:

1. Drag the generic document icon to a disk that contains a name-brand icon for another document of the same type. The Finder then converts the generic icon to a name-brand icon.

2. Copy the newly converted name-brand icon back to its original disk.

When an application has a generic icon, it usually means no one has ever created a unique icon for the application. You can create an application icon using an icon-editing program or resource editor, as described in the Resources chapter.

Finding a hidden window

To bring the open window of a folder or disk icon to the front, double click on the hollow folder or disk icon.

Wrong Finder font?

The Finder determines which font to use for the names of icons by looking at the parameter RAM area of memory, which contains standard settings for the printer selection, speaker volume, keyboard repeat rate, and so on. If a program changes the parameter RAM settings, the Finder may use the wrong font, resulting in distorted icon names. To clear the parameter RAM so that is will be reset to standard settings during the next startup, you must remove the clock battery, as follows:

1. Shut down, turn off the Mac, and remove the clock battery for approximately five minutes.

2. Replace the battery, turn on the Mac, and start up with the formerly corrupted disk.

3. After startup, use the Control Panel desk accessory to reset the time, date, and other settings.

GET INFO

Unreliable file locking

The Finder's Get Info command includes an option for locking a document, application, or folder in order to prevent erasing it or replacing it. Most applications respect this lock, but not all do. Microsoft Word and MacWrite, for example, both save over a locked file without warning. Before entrusting the safety of an important document to the Get Info lock, test the lock's efficacy on an unimportant document.

When you need long comments...

You can describe the purpose or contents of a disk, application, document, or folder in the comments box at the bottom of a Get Info window. The box can hold 50 words, but only three lines of the comment are visible at once. On a Mac Plus or a Mac 512K equivalently upgraded, the text scrolls automatically as you enter it. You can see text that has scrolled out of view by placing the pointer near the middle of the box, pressing the mouse button, and dragging the pointer out of the box. On an earlier model Mac, you can bring the last two lines of a five-line comment into view by temporarily cutting the first two lines out; be sure to paste them back before closing the Get Info window.

NAMES

Keep icon names brief

Keep icon names brief if you prefer the By Icon view to the others available in the View menu. Icon names longer than about 12 characters tend to overlap when you arrange icons with the Clean Up command.

Accommodating long icon names

If you must use long icon names, you can arrange the icons so that their names do not overlap. The following method staggers alternate columns quickly and neatly:

1. Arrange the icons into rows and columns by pressing the Option key while choosing Clean Up from the Finder's Special menu, or by sorting the icons as described in "Sorting icons."
2. Select every other column of icons by pressing the Shift key as you click on each icon in the column, or as you drag selection rectangles around the icons.
3. Drag the selected group of icons down a half-inch or so.

Including dates in names

You may want the date in the names of some documents, such as correspondence. The Finder can list documents by date, but the Open dialog box cannot.

Compacting long names

Use lowercase letters, which are narrower than uppercase, to squeeze longer file names into less space.

Rules for names

A disk name can contain up to 27 characters. A document, application, or folder name can contain up to 31 characters. On a single-sided disk or any other disk that does not use the hierarchical file system (HFS), a document, application, or folder name can contain up to 63 characters. Do not use colons in names, and avoid putting a period at the beginning of a name.

COPYING

Flagging new documents for moving

When you first save a document that you know you'll later have to move to another disk, prefix the document name with a special character, such as @. Back in the Finder, you'll see the prefix and remember to make the move.

Moving by dragging

Save time when moving an icon to another folder or copying it to another disk by dragging it directly to the destination folder or disk icon—don't bother hunting for the folder or disk window. If the destination folder or disk icon is open, drag the file's icon to its hollow folder or disk icon. And if the destination folder or disk icon is closed, don't bother opening it. The Finder will still copy the icon you're dragging into the next available spot in the destination folder or disk.

Excluding files or folders when copying disks

The Finder completely replaces the contents of one disk with the contents of another disk when you drag the source disk's icon over the destination disk's icon—provided both disks are the same type and have the same storage capacity. However, the Finder does not copy any documents, applications, and folders whose icons you have previously dragged onto the desktop. After copying the disk, you can return the icons on the desktop to their former locations in the source disk window by selecting the icons and choosing Put Away from the Finder's File menu.

Think twice when copying folders

When the Finder asks, *Replace items with same names with the selected items?*, take a mental inventory of the destination disk before clicking OK. If you are copying a folder to a disk that contains a folder by the same name, the new folder will replace the old—and every last thing in it. Unfortunately, the Finder doesn't warn you that it is about to replace the "entire contents" of one folder with those of another, as it does with disks. Until Apple makes this change (if ever), be alert when copying folders.

CATALOGS

Printing catalogs of MacPaint documents

MacPaint's Print Catalog command prints a catalog of the MacPaint documents in the folder that contains the currently open MacPaint document. If the currently open document is on a single-sided disk or other disk that doesn't use the hierarchical file system (HFS), the catalog includes all documents on the disk, regardless of folders. MacPaint itself does not need to be in the same folder or even on the same disk as the currently open document.

Obtaining disk catalogs

In order to print a complete directory of every file in every folder on a disk, you'll have to use something other than the Finder's Print Catalog command or the screen-snapshot feature (which you activate by pressing Command-Shift-4).

The MDC II program from New Canaan Microcode constructs and prints a complete directory of one disk or a catalog of a disk collection. It displays two catalog windows. One window lists the disks in the catalog and the other lists the files. For each file on every disk, it shows the name, date created, date modified, size, creator, type, and disk (volume). Folders on disks that don't use the hierarchical file system (HFS) are completely ignored. MDC II handles about 5000 files and has a search feature to help you find a file in the catalog. With special icons, it also identifies which of 32 categories you have put the file in. Files can be listed in alphabetical order by name, by either date created or date modified, by creator, by type, or by volume. All this information can be printed on paper, 3-by-5 cards, or special pin-feed labels.

MINIFINDERS

Using a MiniFinder for faster startups and quits

If you have lots of documents and applications on a hard disk or even on a double-sided disk, the time spent waiting for the Finder to construct its desktop can be annoying. One way to speed up disk operation is to use the MiniFinder rather than the Finder to open applications. For example, starting up the Mac with two double-sided disks takes 10 seconds less with a MiniFinder than with the Finder.

The MiniFinder allows you to install up to 12 document or application icons on its own abbreviated version of the desktop. If you need to open other applications, clicking the MiniFinder's Open Other button causes a standard Open dialog box to appear, from which you can open any application (but no documents) on any disk.

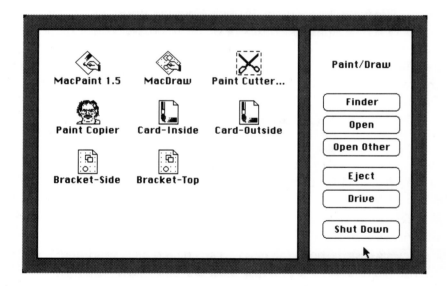

The speedy MiniFinder allows you to open 12 selected documents and application icons, open other applications from a standard Open dialog box, eject disks, shut down, and switch to the standard Finder.

To install a MiniFinder:

1. Select the icons of up to 12 applications and documents you want imme-
    diately available from the MiniFinder. All icons, including the icons of the
    applications required to open the selected documents, must be in the
    same window.

2. Choose Use MiniFinder from the Special menu. In the dialog box that ap-
    pears, click the Install button. A MiniFinder icon is created on the current
    startup disk. If the current startup disk uses the hierarchical file system
    (HFS), the MiniFinder icon will be in the same folder on the startup disk
    as the Finder.

You can double click the MiniFinder icon to start the MiniFinder. Whenever you
start up the Mac, the MiniFinder, rather than the Finder, takes control.

Arranging icons in a Minifinder

Once you install icons in a MiniFinder, they are fixed in place; you can't drag
them around as you can in the standard Finder. However, you can decide what their
positions will be before installing them in the MiniFinder. Before choosing Use
MiniFinder from the Finder's Special menu, arrange the icons in four rows of three,
starting with the left icon in the top row and working left to right and top to bottom.
If you have fewer than 12 icons, the unused slots must be in the bottom rows.

Using several MiniFinders

The MiniFinder is limited to 12 icons, but you can set up multiple levels of
MiniFinders that accommodate many application and document icons. For example, using two levels, you can install 132 documents and applications. The first-level
MiniFinder contains up to 12 renamed MiniFinder icons. Double clicking one of
these icons opens a second-level MiniFinder. Each second-level MiniFinder contains
the icon of the first-level MiniFinder and up to 11 application and document icons.

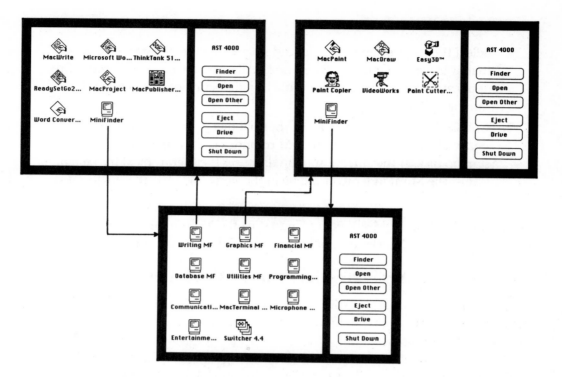

You can install two levels of MiniFinders that let you quickly access up to 132 applications and documents. From the first-level MiniFinder, double click on a renamed MiniFinder icon to move to the second level. To return to the first level, double click on the icon labeled MiniFinder.

When creating two levels of MiniFinder, you create and rename the MiniFinder icons in the second level before you create the first. (There's a trick to renaming MiniFinder icons for the second level: The Finder won't let you rename a MiniFinder icon directly, but you can rename a duplicate of the icon.) Create the second level as follows:

1. Arrange the application and document icons in folders so that all the icons for any one MiniFinder are in the same folder. Once you install a set of icons in a MiniFinder, you must not move the icons to different folders.

2. If you want to be able to move from a second-level MiniFinder back to the first level, the folder must also contain a MiniFinder icon named *MiniFinder*. This icon acts as a placeholder for the final first-level

MiniFinder, which you'll create later. To create the placeholder, select any application icon and choose Use MiniFinder from the Special menu. In a few seconds, an icon named *MiniFinder* appears (it will probably be in the System Folder).

3. Drag the placeholder MiniFinder into the folder in which you're collecting applications and documents.

4. Select the 11 application and document icons, plus the placeholder Mini-Finder icon, choose Use MiniFinder from the Special Menu, and click Install in the dialog box that appears.

5. On a double-sided disk, hard disk, or other disk that uses the hierarchical file system (HFS), the new MiniFinder icon appears in the System Folder. You no longer need the placeholder MiniFinder icon you used in step 4, so drag it to the Trash. However, on a single-sided disk or other disk that doesn't use HFS, the new MiniFinder icon replaces the placeholder you used in step 4, so do not remove it.

6. Select the new MiniFinder icon (remember to use the one in the System Folder on an HFS disk), and choose Duplicate from the File menu. A duplicate MiniFinder icon appears, labeled *Copy of MiniFinder.*

7. Rename the duplicate MiniFinder icon. If it's not already in the System Folder, drag it there. If you're going to create another second-level Mini-Finder, use the existing MiniFinder icon as the placeholder in step 3.

Repeat steps 3 through 7 for each second-level MiniFinder. Then you're ready to create the first-level MiniFinder, as follows:

1. Open the System Folder and select all the renamed second-level MiniFinder icons you have created.

2. Choose Use MiniFinder from the Special Menu. A few seconds after you click Install, an icon named *MiniFinder* appears in the System Folder.

Bypassing the MiniFinder when quitting

To bypass the MiniFinder and go directly to the Finder when you quit an application, press the Option key while choosing Quit from the application's File menu.

FREEING DISK SPACE

Removing the Finder

Removing the Finder from a disk frees up about 56K of disk space. The Finder is not required on single-sided disks, which normally do not use the hierarchical file system (HFS). Provided you first designate a startup application with the Finder's Set Startup command, you can remove the Finder and still use the single-sided disk as a startup disk.

Warning: Quitting most applications when there is no Finder or MiniFinder present usually results in a serious system error.

The Mac will not let you remove the Finder from the current startup disk by dragging the Finder icon to the Trash. First you must switch startup disks as described in "Switching startup disks and system files."

If you remove the Finder from an HFS disk, the disk is no longer a startup disk, in which case you may as well remove the System file, Scrapbook File, Note Pad File, and Clipboard File.

Removing unused printing resources

You can save space on your startup disks by removing printing resources you don't need from the System Folder. To remove unused printing resources, drag them to the Trash.

What kinds of resources might you discard? Well, you almost certainly do not need both the ImageWriter and AppleTalk ImageWriter resources. To print on an ImageWriter II with an AppleTalk card, the AppleTalk ImageWriter resource must be present. To print on an ImageWriter or ImageWriter II without AppleTalk, most applications need the ImageWriter resource. Microsoft Excel, Word, and Multiplan need the ImageWriter resource to print in standard or high quality, but not in draft quality. For draft-quality printing in these applications, use the Printer Setup command from their File menus to pick a printing resource such as Typewriter or TTY.

Other candidates for the Trash are the LaserWriter and Laser Prep resources, which you need only if you have a LaserWriter or if you prepare documents on your Mac for later printing on a LaserWriter attached to a different Mac. You can remove the LaserWriter and Laser Prep resources from any disk that you never use for LaserWriter printing or preparation.

Omitting needless fonts

One way to free up space on a startup disk is to remove fonts you never use. Each size of every font is a separate entity that you can add or remove from a System file using the Font/DA Mover program. Removing all sizes of the New York font, for example, frees almost 27K.

Small font sizes tend to require the least space, usually on the order of 1.5K to 2.5K each. Large sizes may take more than 13K apiece. Before you remove large sizes, make sure you don't need them for best-quality printing on an ImageWriter. The Mac obtains best-quality print by condensing a font size that is double the size to be printed. For example, you need Geneva 24 to get best-quality Geneva 12.

Fonts you remove need not be lost forever. The Font/DA Mover lets you save them in font files before removing them; later you can copy them back to a System file from the font files.

Removing desk accessories

Desk accessories are part of the System file and, as with fonts, you can remove disused ones with the Font/DA Mover program. The amount of space required by an individual desk accessory may be anywhere from less than 1K to more than 40K, though few are larger than 10K.

In addition to removing desk accessories you never use, you may want to consider removing ones you seldom use from most of your startup disks. For example, if you use only one printer, you don't really need the Chooser on every disk. The Control Panel and Alarm Clock are two other desk accessories you might need on only one disk. When you need to change settings with one of those desk accessories, it's no great inconvenience to have to switch to the disk they're on.

Purging the Scrapbook

Old clippings in the Scrapbook waste disk space. Ideally, you should purge your Scrapbook file regularly, but if you can't bear to throw old stuff away, you can keep a copy of the Scrapbook file under a different name, perhaps on another disk. Here's how:

1. Select the Scrapbook-file icon, which is usually in the System Folder, and choose Duplicate from the File menu.
2. Change the name of the copy of the Scrapbook file, if you want, and drag its icon to another disk.

3. Choose Scrapbook from the Apple menu and remove all the deadwood from the Scrapbook window.

Later, if you want to retrieve a clipping from an old Scrapbook, temporarily re-name the Scrapbook file on the startup disk, change the name of the old Scrapbook icon back to *Scrapbook File,* and drag it to the current startup disk. Now when you choose Scrapbook from the Apple menu, the Scrapbook window displays the contents of the old Scrapbook.

Saving unformatted documents to save space

An unformatted, text-only document usually takes up less disk space than the same document with character- and paragraph-formatting information. So if you can live without font, style, size, margin, tab, paragraph indent, and other formatting, you can consume as much as 30 percent less space by clicking the Text Only option in those Save and Save As dialog boxes that offer it.

Deleting from a desk accessory

How many times have you wished you could delete a file while using an application instead of having to go back to the Finder? There are several desk accessories that allow you to delete files from almost any application. One such desk accessory, DiskInfo from Maitreya Designs, displays a scrollable list of file names—in name or date order—similar to the one you see in the Finder when you choose By Name or By Date from the View menu. You select one file at a time from the list for deletion, verify your selection in a separate dialog box, and verify again if the file is locked.

Warning: Delete files with caution, or you may cause the application program hosting the desk accessory to fail spectacularly. Don't delete files that are still open, or temporary files with names like Paint1, MW0001, Print File, and UndoFile. When you're using the Switcher, be especially careful that you don't delete a file from one partition that's in use in another partition.

When you don't need help...

Applications that provide built-in help information usually keep that information in a separate disk file. In most cases, you can remove the help file and free up a substantial amount of disk space. So if you are beyond help, look for an icon with the word *help* in its name, copy that icon to a backup disk, and then drag it from the working disk into the Trash.

Lean MacPaint

MacPaint has two screens of built-in help information, which you access with the Introduction and Shortcuts commands on its Goodies menu. Both help screens are MacPaint resources that you can remove using a resource-editor program, thereby making MacPaint about 13K lighter. Use Apple's general-purpose resource editor, ResEdit version 1.0D7 or above, as follows:

1. For safety's sake, make a copy of your MacPaint disk. Copy ResEdit onto that disk.
2. Start ResEdit. A small window appears for each disk currently inserted. The title at the top of each window identifies which disk it is for, and a list of names inside the window shows which application, document, and other files are on the disk. For double-sided disks, hard disks, and other disks that use the hierarchical file system (HFS), folders are also listed.
3. Locate MacPaint in its disk window and double click it. Another small window opens, listing all the resources in MacPaint by their four-letter names.
4. Find the resource named PICT in the MacPaint window and click it to select it.
5. Choose Clear from ResEdit's Edit menu.
6. Close the MacPaint window. ResEdit asks if you want to save the change you made; click the Yes button.
7. Quit ResEdit.

After removing the PICT resource from MacPaint, choosing Introduction or Short Cuts from the Goodies menu does nothing.

WHERE TO PUT IT?

Squeezing more files onto single-sided disks

Apple's hierarchical file system (HFS), which is used automatically on hard disks and double-sided disks, does not limit the number of files you can store on a disk. However, the flat file system normally used on single-sided disks does limit the number of files on a disk. As a result, a single-sided disk that contains only small documents (for example, 2K correspondence documents) may have as much as 200K of disk space still available when the number-of-files limit occurs.

The number of files allowed on a disk depends on the length of the file names, and the dependency is not linear. You can have at most 84 files on a single-sided disk where the average file name length is between 14 and 22 characters. If the file name length averages 6 to 13 characters, you can put 96 files on the same disk. There's no point making all names shorter than five characters, since you won't get more than 108 files on any single-sided disk by doing so.

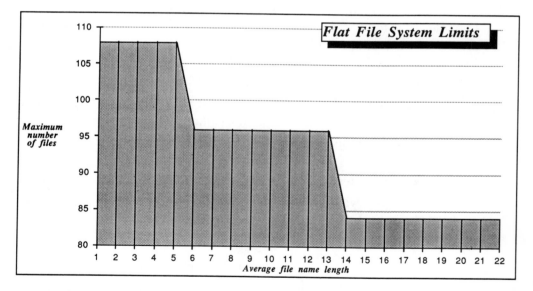

The number of files that can be stored on a single-sided disk, which normally uses the flat file system, depends on the length of the file names.

On a Mac Plus or other Mac that uses HFS, you can set up a single-sided disk to use HFS and thereby get around the number-of-files limit. The method differs for new and old disks:

☐ Set up a new single-sided disk for HFS when you first initialize it. When you finish typing the disk name at the end of the initialization process, hold down the Option key as you press Return.

☐ To convert an old single-sided disk to HFS, you must erase it. Choose Erase from the Finder's Special menu and hold down the Option key as you click the One-Sided button in the dialog box that appears. For best results, hold down the Option key until the box goes away.

Working efficiently with one drive

If your Mac has only one built-in 3½-inch disk drive—no external drive and no hard disk—you must organize the contents of your disks carefully to avoid excessive disk swapping. First, put every application program on its own startup disk. In whatever space remains on each application's disk, put the documents you are still working on with that application. Most applications need some disk space for temporary work files, so be sure to leave 50K or more free on each disk. If all the documents-in-progress for a particular application won't fit on one disk, put the overflow on another startup disk along with another copy of the application program. When you finish working on a document, copy it onto a disk that contains only documents and remove it from the application disk to make room for the next document you create. (Avoid keeping multiple copies of the same document on different disks; you can waste lots of time figuring out which has the most recent changes.)

Disks multiply rapidly on one-drive Mac systems, so try to develop some compulsive habits with regard to labeling and storing your disks. Otherwise, finding a particular document may take 10 minutes or more. When your collection grows to more than 30 disks, seriously consider cataloging it with a program such as MDC II from New Canaan Microcode.

If your one-drive Mac has a megabyte or more of memory, you can use half the memory as if it were a disk drive (see "RAM disks" on page 39 in the "Peak performance" chapter). Programs such as the public-domain RamStart can automatically create a RAM disk, copy the System Folder to it, and make it the startup disk. Your Mac essentially becomes a two-drive system and your 3½-inch disks no longer need to carry the 200K burden of a System file and Finder, leaving more room on them for documents. There may even be room on the RAM disk for an application, freeing up even more actual disk space.

Working efficiently with two drives

On a Mac with two or more disk drives, you'll probably want to reserve one drive for applications on startup disks and the other drive for documents on non-startup disks. If an application is particularly large and there is not enough room for it on a startup disk, you can keep it, along with its documents, on a non-startup disk in the other drive. If the applications you want to work with are small, you may be able to fit more than one on the same startup disk, making switching between them faster. But be sure to leave 50K or so free on the startup disk. Most applications need work space on that disk even if the document you're working on is on another disk.

With some applications, the ImageWriter file or other printing resource, the Clipboard file, and the Scrapbook file must be on the application disk, which may or may not be the startup disk. You'll know an application requires this arrangement if you can't print a document or you can't find a clipping in the Scrapbook.

You don't need as many startup disks with two drives as you do with one drive. This means you'll use fewer disks overall, because they won't be filled with duplicates of the System Folder and the application programs.

TO THE RESCUE

Rebuilding the Finder's desktop

If a *Serious system error...* message appears when you insert a disk, it's possible the Finder's invisible Desktop file has become corrupted. The Desktop file keeps track of which documents, applications, and folders are present on a disk, what their icons look like, where the icons are located on the desktop, and so on.

Usually the Finder recognizes a corrupt Desktop file and rebuilds it automatically; occasionally, however, the Finder falls down on the job. To force the Finder to rebuild the Desktop file for a disk, follow these steps:

1. Start up with another disk.
2. Hold down the Option and Command keys while you insert the troublesome disk. The Finder asks if you're sure you want to rebuild the desktop; click Yes.

Rebuilding the Desktop file erases any comments you might have entered in Get Info windows and, on single-sided disks, erases the names of folders.

You can forestall about 90 percent of the problems you're likely to encounter with the Desktop file if you always eject your disks before switching off the Mac.

Repairing damaged startup disks

It's sometimes possible to restore a damaged startup disk by starting with another disk and copying the System file from the good disk to the damaged disk.

Retrieving documents from bad disks

If you're unable to start up with a disk that contains valuable documents, you may be able to retrieve the documents by treating the bad disk as a non-startup disk. This technique works—sometimes—because the Finder is more finicky than most applications with regard to damaged disks. Here are the steps to follow:

1. Start the Mac with a good startup disk, preferably one that contains the application that created the documents you want to retrieve.
2. Start the application.
3. Open a document from the bad disk with the application's Open command and save the document on a good disk with the Save As command.

Repeat step 3 for each document on the bad disk.

Salvaging a damaged file or disk

When all else fails, you may be able to recover a lost file or rescue a damaged file or disk with a disk-editor program. For example, John Mitchell's Fedit allows you to easily recover lost files, such as ones you've deleted, and to repair such esoteric items as the disk directory and volume map. By following directions in the program's documentation, you may also be able to rescue portions of a damaged text file.

If you're unable to salvage the contents of a disk, you may still be able to re-initialize and reuse it. Follow these steps:

1. Start up with another disk, one that contains the Finder version 5.1 or above.
2. Hold down the Option, Command, and Tab keys while you insert the troublesome disk. The Finder asks if you're sure you want to completely erase the disk; click Yes.

Resources

In the '50s and '60s they painted flames on cars.

*In the '70s they sewed patches on bluejeans
and they tie-dyed T-shirts.*

In the '80s, they're customizing computers.

*You can get in on the latest trend by changing fonts,
icons, pointers, menus, and dialog boxes in your Mac
applications. Read all about it in this chapter.*

ABOUT RESOURCES

Although the System file seems to hog disk space, it actually conserves it. The System file serves as a public library of information useful for many programs. Among other things, it contains descriptions of fonts, menus, windows, pointers, icons, buttons, and scroll bars. These pieces of information are called resources. Unlike a real library, the System file hands out an unlimited number of copies of its resources to application programs and never expects the resources to be returned.

Application programs can also have their own private collection of resources. Even documents can have resources. Usually, the private application and document resources do not duplicate the System-file resources. It is by cutting down on the duplication of resources that the System file actually saves disk space.

Resources are classified by type and each type has a four-character name; any that appear to have shorter names contain a mandatory blank space. The table on the facing page lists some standard resource types, many of which are found in a typical System file, and explains what each contains. Every individual resource has an ID number that uniquely identifies it among all other resources of the same type.

Although application resources generally do not duplicate System-file resources for space-economy reasons, this doesn't mean that they can't duplicate them. If an application resource has the same type and ID number as a System-file resource, the application resource is used. For example, applications that need to modify the standard Open or Save As dialog boxes might have their own resources for these functions. Similarly, resources in document files can override duplicate resources in application files (though many application programs disable this feature).

STANDARD RESOURCES

Type	Contents
ALRT	Alert box templates
BNDL	Correlator of local ID numbers for icon lists and file references to their actual ICN# and FREF ID numbers
CDEF	Program code that constructs and handles operation of controls such as scroll bars and buttons
CNTL	Control templates
CURS	Pointer shapes
DITL	Items (text, controls, and graphics) used in dialog and alert boxes
DLOG	Dialog-box templates
DRVR	Program code for desk accessories and device drivers
DSAT	Definition of system startup alert box and its contents, and program code that displays it
FKEY	Program code for Command-Shift-*number* key sequences (for example, Command-Shift-3)
FOND	Font family description
FONT	Font definitions
FREF	Correlation of file types with local icon ID numbers
FRSV	Identity of fonts reserved for system use
ICN#	Icon lists; typically icons with shadow-like masks, which permit icons to look active, inactive, or hollow, and to be highlighted or not highlighted in any of those three states, like disk and document icons that can appear against the background of the desktop
ICON	Icons, without masks, that can only look plain, like the icons for the printer and modem ports, and alert boxes
INIT	Information used at startup time, including definition of system-error alert box and its contents, and program code that displays and handles it; also contains standard keyboard configuration
INTL	Formats and rules for specific countries, including number punctuation, currency symbol, time and date formats, metric system or not, and alphabetization rules
MBAR	Number of menus and their resource ID numbers
MDEF	Program code for drawing menus
MENU	Menu contents
PACK	Packages of program code that serve as extensions to ROM and perform less common functions, such as disk initialization
PAT	Single patterns, such as scroll bar "elevator" and current desktop pattern
PAT#	Lists of patterns, such as standard desktop and MacPaint pattern palettes
PDEF	Program code to drive printer
PICT	MacPaint-style pictures, such as those used in Control Panel and Alarm Clock desk accessories
PREC	Printer driver's private data storage
SICN	Small icons, such as those used in hierarchical file system's Open dialog box
STR	Assorted bits and pieces of text
STR#	Lists of text strings
WDEF	Program code for drawing windows
WIND	Window templates

The fact that resources are tucked away in the System file does not mean that they are inaccessible. If you are adventurous, you can use a program called a resource editor to change the resources, and therefore the look of the application, without changing the program's code. There are two basic kinds of resource-editor programs: General-purpose resource editors, such as Apple's ResEdit, work with all types of resources; other resource editors, such as FONTastic from Altsys and Icon Switcher from PBI Software, are specialized for working on one particular resource type.

The ResEdit program

Apple's ResEdit program is a general-purpose resource editor. With it, you can edit, copy, and paste all types of resources. It includes several specialized editors for specific types of resources, such as fonts, icons, and dialog boxes. Apple informally distributed unfinished versions of ResEdit throughout 1985 and 1986. All the tips in this book have been tested with version 1.0D7, created in January 1986. Many of the tips do not work with earlier versions, so be sure you have ResEdit 1.0D7 or above.

Since resources are vital to the functioning of a program, editing them may cause the program to fail. For safety's sake, always make a copy of the disk that contains the resources you plan to change. Experiment only on the copy, never on the original disk.

For best performance on a Mac that has only one disk drive, copy the ResEdit program onto the experimental disk. This expedient may not always be possible, since ResEdit is a large program, but it saves much disk swapping if you can manage it.

When you start ResEdit, a small window appears for each disk currently inserted. The title at the top of each window identifies its disk, and a list of names inside the window shows which application, document, and other files are on that particular disk. For double-sided disks and other disks that use the hierarchical file system (HFS), folders are also listed, with small folder icons alongside the folder names. You can open a folder, revealing its contents, by double clicking on its name.

Although you can edit any file listed, you should avoid editing the ResEdit and System files currently in use. Instead, edit a copy of those files from another disk. You don't have to quit ResEdit to switch disks: First eject the disk you want to change by closing its disk window, then insert the desired disk in its place. A window appears for the new disk, listing its files.

To locate the particular resource you want to edit:

1. Double click on the name of the file in the appropriate disk or folder window. For example, if you want to edit a resource in the System file, double click on its name in the disk window. (On an HFS disk, the System file is usually inside the System Folder, so you must first double click on the System Folder's name to open up its folder window, where the System file will be listed.) When you double click on the file name, another window opens up, listing all the resource types in the file by their four-letter names. You may also type the first part of a file or folder name to select it, and then press Return to open it.

2. Double click on the name of the resource type you want to edit; you may also type the first part of the name and press Return. A window displaying a list of the individual resources of that type opens up. This window's title always starts with the name of the resource type, but its format depends on the resource type. For example, the ICON and ICN# windows display pictures of icons. For many resource types, individual resources are listed in a general format: by type, name, and ID number. You can force ResEdit to display the resources in the general format by pressing the Option key while you double click on the name of the resource type.

3. Double click on the name of the individual resource in the resource window. A window in which you can actually edit the resource opens up. Since most individual resources are identified only by ID number, you may have to double click several, one after the other, until you find the right one.

Changes you make to a resource with ResEdit are not saved to disk until you close the file window, close the disk window, or quit ResEdit. At that time, ResEdit asks whether you want to save the changes before closing; you click a Yes or No button to answer. Until you click Yes, you can revert to the last saved version of the resource by choosing Revert from the File menu.

The rest of this chapter explains how to edit individual resources of several types once they are displayed in their windows.

FONT RESOURCES

Changing the default application font

MacWrite and most other application programs use the Geneva font by default because the System file designates it as the standard application font. It has not always been so; longtime Mac users will remember that New York was the standard application font for the first five months of 1984.

You could designate a different font as the standard application font by changing the System file with a resource editor such as ResEdit or a disk editor such as Fedit, but there are easier alternatives. The desk accessory variously called ApplFont1.03 and Change Font D.A. (which doesn't yet work on the Mac Plus), written by Lofty Becker, lets you change the standard application font to any available font by clicking buttons. It's available from users' groups, as is an application-program form of the desk accessory.

✳Secret characters

Most fonts contain a hidden character that you can type by pressing Option-Shift-Tilde. Different sizes of the same font may contain a different character.

〰〰〰〰	New York 9	⌒⌒⌒⌒	Geneva 9	•••••••••••	Toronto 9
～～～～～	New York 10	▣▣▣▣	Geneva 10	‹‹‹‹‹‹‹	Toronto 12
✝✝✝✝✝✝	New York 12	⚘⚘⚘⚘	Geneva 12	🍎🍎🍎🍎	Toronto 14
♫♫♫♫♫	New York 14	＿＿＿＿	Geneva 14	⊗⊗⊗⊗⊗	Toronto 18
♥♥♥♥	New York 18	☁☁☁☁	Geneva 18	‹‹‹‹	Toronto 24
👾👾👾	New York 24	𝄞 𝄞	Geneva 24	☘☘☘☘☘	London 18
▬▬▬▬	Monaco 9	⚘ ⚘ ⚘	Athens 18	••••••••••	Venice 14
‖‖‖‖‖‖‖	Monaco 12	▲▲▲	San Francisco 18		

Many fonts have a hidden character you can type by pressing Option-Shift-Tilde.

Changing a font

Most fonts displayed on the Mac are resources contained in the System file. Using a special program, such as FONTastic from Altsys, you can easily edit fonts to change the look of the letters, to change the symbols, and so forth. With more work, you can also edit fonts using the ResEdit program. Prepare a font for editing with ResEdit as follows:

1. Start ResEdit, insert a copy of the disk containing the font you want to change, and find and open the System file; the file may be inside a folder on a hierarchical file system (HFS) disk. Then open the resource window for the FONT resources, all as described in "The ResEdit program" earlier in this chapter.

2. Each size of every font is a separate resource, so look for the name and size of the font you want to edit and double click on it. A large font-editing window opens; you may have to move it in order to see all of it.

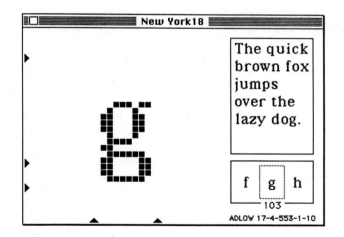

Fonts displayed on the screen are FONT resources that you can edit in a ResEdit font-editing window.

A sample piece of text written in the font appears boxed in the upper right part of the font-editing window. If you want to see characters not currently displayed, you can include them in the sample text using normal text-editing methods.

An enlargement of the character currently selected for editing appears near the middle of the font-editing window. The three black triangles along the left edge of this font-editing window define the vertical dimensions of the entire font, in the selected point size. The middle triangle marks the baseline, where most letters end. The bottom triangle shows how far lowercase letters with descenders, such as *y* and *g*, descend below the baseline. The top triangle shows how far the tallest letters ascend above the baseline. Independent of the ascender and descender markers, every FONT resource specifies one to three dots of space, called leading, for separation between lines of text. You cannot change the amount of leading from the font-editing window.

The two black triangles along the bottom edge of the editing window define the horizontal dimensions of the currently selected character. The left triangle marks the character's offset, which determines how close the selected character is to the character on its left. The right triangle marks the character's width, which determines how close the selected character is to the character on its right.

The code that begins *ADLOW* in the bottom right corner of the font-editing window numerically reports the Ascent, Descent, Location, Offset, and Width of the character selected for editing. The ascent, descent, offset, and width are all measured in dots from the character's origin, which is the point on the baseline used as a reference for drawing the character. The location specifies where the character image starts in the FONT resource.

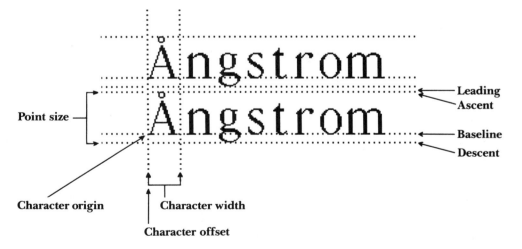

The vertical size of a font (its point size) is measured above and below a baseline. The horizontal dimensions of a character are measured left and right of its origin point.

The selected character appears in its actual size inside a selection rectangle near the bottom right corner of the window. Beneath the selected character is the ASCII code number assigned to the character. Characters with adjacent code numbers flank the selected character. (Character code numbers range between 0 and 255. Normally, code 65 is assigned to an uppercase A, which is produced by pressing the Shift-A key combination, 66 is assigned to uppercase B, and so on.)

For each character you want to edit, follow these steps:

1. Select the character you want to change simply by typing it. Alternatively, scroll rapidly through the characters by dragging the selection rectangle right or left or scroll one character at a time by clicking beside the selection rectangle.

2. Edit the enlargement of the character as if it were in MacPaint's FatBits. Click on a black dot to make it white and click on a white space to make a black dot.

3. If you want to change the horizontal dimensions of the character, drag the black triangles at the bottom of the editing window. Watch in the sample text at the right side of the window to see the results.

4. To adjust the vertical dimensions of the font as a whole, drag the top and bottom black triangles along the edge of the character-editing window. (The baseline marker cannot be moved.) Watch the effects of your changes in the sample text in the right side of the font-editing window.

When you have finished making changes to the font, close the file window. ResEdit asks if you want to save the changes you just made; click either Yes or No. Quit ResEdit when you have finished editing resources.

On a Macintosh Plus, Mac 512K Enhanced, or other Mac equivalently upgraded, the Chicago 12 font is included in the 128K ROM. The FONT resource in the ROM overrides the same resource on a disk, so editing the font on disk has no effect on what is displayed or printed.

There is also no point in changing FONT resources for LaserWriter fonts, such as Times, Helvetica, and Courier. The FONT resources for LaserWriter fonts are used only to display the fonts and printing on an ImageWriter. The LaserWriter has its own built-in font definitions and they override any like-named FONT resources when printing on the LaserWriter.

Creating overstrike characters

Do you sometimes wish the Mac had a non-erasing backspace key, like a type-writer, so you could combine two or more characters to put accents over any letter or create otherwise unavailable mathematical symbols? <u>You can put an accent, circum-flex, umlaut, or tilde over some letters by typing</u> Option-Apostrophe, Option-E, Option-I, Option-U, or Option-N followed by another letter. You can get the same results with any combination of characters by manipulating the two triangles that determine character width in the ResEdit font-editing window. Here's how:

1. While editing any character as described in "Changing a font" earlier in this chapter, drag the right horizontal black triangle to the left, so that it is directly under the character's origin. The last two numbers in the bottom right corner of the character-editing window, the offset and the width, will now match.

2. Try typing the character you have just edited before and after some other characters in the sample text area in the upper right corner of the font-editing window. When you type a character whose width and offset match, the insertion point does not move, so the next character you type overstrikes the first.

For best results, all the characters that overstrike one another must be the same number of dots wide.

The method described here for adjusting character widths doesn't work on all fonts. If moving the black triangles in the FONT resource-editing window has no effect on displayed characters, chances are the font in question has a corresponding FOND resource that contains a character width table. That table overrides the width settings in the FONT resource. Changes to the FONT resources for LaserWriter fonts don't affect printing on a LaserWriter, because the LaserWriter has its own definitions for Times, Helvetica, and Courier. Also, the 128K ROM present in every Mac Plus and many other Macs contains a FONT resource for Chicago 12 that overrides the System-file Chicago 12 resource.

Adding characters to a font

There are more than 30 key combinations involving the Option key for which no particular character has been defined. (With most fonts, typing an unused key combination produces a rectangle.) The exact set of undefined combinations varies from font to font. For example, the character generated by pressing Option-Shift-Tilde is defined in some fonts but not others. LaserWriter fonts generally have no undefined combinations.

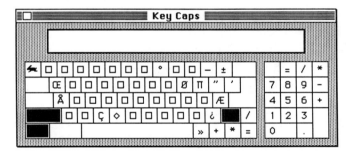

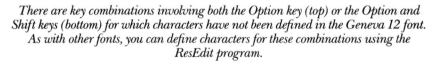

There are key combinations involving both the Option key (top) or the Option and Shift keys (bottom) for which characters have not been defined in the Geneva 12 font. As with other fonts, you can define characters for these combinations using the ResEdit program.

You can use the ResEdit program to assign your own characters to undefined combinations. Once you have the font-editing window on the screen, type a key combination that selects one of the undefined ASCII code numbers. (Code numbers between 217 and 251 are usually undefined.) Then just follow the instructions for editing a character in "Changing a font" to add the newly defined character to the font.

Creating a unique customized font

If you want to have both modified and unmodified versions of a font available, they must have different names. Otherwise, you won't be able to tell them apart in a Font menu. But renaming one of them is not enough, because Mac application programs do not use the font name to identify a font. They use the FONT resource ID number. For example, neither you, the program, nor MacWrite can tell the difference between a customized Geneva 10 and a standard Geneva 10 unless you change the name and resource ID numbers of one. Specialized font-editor programs, such as FONTastic, take care of this for you. You can also change font names and resource ID numbers using the ResEdit program.

In order to change resource ID numbers, you must understand how they are derived. A resource ID number is computed from two other numbers: the font number and the font size. The font number is a number between 0 and 511 that uniquely identifies the font among all fonts that are either in the System file now or might be there at some point in the future. Font numbers 0 through 127 identify fonts that are created by Apple, numbers 128 through 383 are assigned by Apple to certain fonts that are created by others, and numbers 384 through 511 are open for general use. You should therefore give your customized font a number between 384 and 511 in order to avoid conflict with "official" fonts.

To compute the resource ID number, you multiply the font number you have selected by 128 and add the point size. The table on the facing page lists font and resource ID numbers for several sizes of some common fonts and for font numbers 508 through 511.

Having chosen a font number and computed the resource ID number for your customized font, assign the resource ID number to the font using ResEdit, as follows:

1. Start ResEdit, insert a copy of the disk you want to change, and find and open the System file. On a hierarchical file system (HFS) disk, it may be inside a folder. Then open the resource window for the FONT resources, all as described earlier in "The ResEdit program."

2. Select your customized font by clicking its name in the resource window, and then choose Get Info from ResEdit's File menu. An information window opens, with the resource ID number selected.

3. Edit the resource ID number you computed and close the information window.

Repeat steps 2 and 3 for each size of your customized font.

RESOURCE ID NUMBER FOR POINT SIZE

Font Name	Font Number	Point Size 0*	9	10	12	14	18	24
Chicago	0	0	9	10	12	14	18	24
New York	2	256	265	266	268	270	274	280
Geneva	3	384	393	394	396	398	402	408
Monaco	4	512	521	522	524	526	530	536
Venice	5	640	649	650	652	654	658	664
London	6	768	777	778	780	782	786	792
Athens	7	896	905	906	908	910	914	920
San Francisco	8	1024	1033	1034	1036	1038	1042	1048
Toronto	9	1152	1161	1162	1164	1166	1170	1176
Seattle	10	1280	1289	1290	1292	1294	1298	1304
Cairo	11	1408	1417	1418	1420	1422	1426	1432
Los Angeles	12	1536	1545	1546	1548	1550	1554	1560
Times†	20	2560	2569	2570	2572	2574	2578	2584
Helvetica†	21	2688	2697	2698	2700	2702	2706	2712
Courier†	22	2816	2825	2826	2828	2830	2834	2840
Taliesin	24	3072	3081	3082	3084	3086	3090	3096
Your Font	508	65024	65033	65034	65036	65038	65042	65048
Your Font	509	65152	65161	65162	65164	65166	65170	65176
Your Font	510	65280	65289	65290	65292	65294	65298	65304
Your Font	511	65408	65417	65418	65420	65422	65426	65432

* The point size 0 font contains the font name.
† FONT resources do not affect the look of text printed on a LaserWriter.

You probably noticed that the information window for each font resource had a space for a name, but that the space was blank. That space is for the name of the resource, not the name of the font. The name for the entire font is kept in the information window for that font's 0-point resource, which contains no character definitions. You get at the 0-point resource by reopening the FONT resource window in the following special manner:

1. Close the FONT resource window, if it is open.
2. Reopen the window by double clicking the resource named FONT in the file window while pressing the Option key. A resource window opens, listing font resources in the general format, with their types, resource names, and resource ID numbers. Every resource listed has an ID number but only a few have names.

3. Click the 0-point resource for the font you want to rename; usually it's the only resource for that font with a name. Choose Get Info from the File menu. An information window opens.

4. Edit the font name and resource ID number in the information window using normal text-editing methods. (Remember, this is the 0-point size, so the ID number equals 128 times the font number.) When you have finished editing, close the information and FONT windows.

Many fonts have a FOND resource in addition to FONT resources. The FOND resource contains the name, FONT resource ID numbers, and other information about an entire font family, such as Geneva or Times. If your custom font has a FOND resource, you must change the name and FONT resource ID numbers in it to match the changes you just made to the FONT resources. Use ResEdit as follows:

1. Look for the FOND resource right above the FONT resource in the file window. If none is listed, skip to step 7. Otherwise open the FOND resource by double clicking its name. A resource-editing window opens.

2. Change the number in the second box, labeled *Family ID,* to the new font number (not one of the computed resource ID numbers).

3. Scroll down past the boxes labeled *Ascent, Descent, Offset* ..., and *Extra....* Stop scrolling when you find the phrase *# of Font entries.* Below it are one or more sets of three boxes labeled *Font Size, Font Style,* and *Res ID.* There is one set for each font size in the FONT resource, and the sets are separated by lines of five asterisks.

4. In each set, change the box labeled *Res ID* to the new resource ID you calculated for the accompanying font size.

5. When you have finished entering the resource ID numbers, choose Get Info from the File menu. An information window appears.

6. Enter the name of the custom font in the box labeled *Name:,* and then close the information and FOND windows.

7. When you have finished changing the FONT and FOND resources for your customized font, close the file window. Answer Yes when ResEdit asks if you want to save changes.

Fonts in application files

Fonts customarily reside in the System file, where they are available from any application for use in any document. But fonts can also reside in application program files. Fonts from the application file appear on the font menu along with fonts from the System file. Transferring the burden of specialty fonts from the System file to an application file helps to reduce the size of the System file, and may make the difference between a common System file fitting in a small RAM disk on a Mac 512K or not.

You can copy a font to an application program file using Apple's Font/DA Mover program. Normally, it only lets you open the System file and font files; they are the only files listed in the Open dialog box. But if you press the Option key while clicking the Open button, the Open dialog box lists all the files on the disk. You'll even see the names of invisible files such as DeskTop. After opening an application file, you'll be able to copy fonts to it as if it were a System file. You may discover some applications already secretly contain a font or two. MacPaint, for example, has a font named 12 that contains all the icons for the drawing tool palette and the various brush shapes for the paintbrush tool. Don't forget to remove fonts from the System file after copying them to application files.

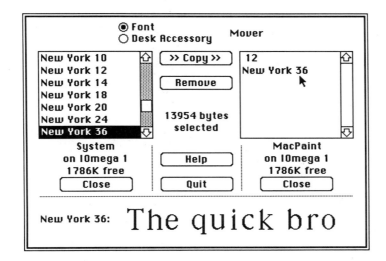

Pressing the Option key while clicking the Open button in the Font/DA Mover program lets you open any copy fonts to and from any file, not just the System file and fonts files.

ICON AND POINTER RESOURCES

Personalizing icons

Tired of the same old icons? They're easy enough to change with a special program, such as Icon Switcher from PBI Software. And, since most icon resources are stored in the System file or an application file, you can also edit them with a general-purpose resource editor, such as Apple's ResEdit, though it takes some work.

An application's icon and the icons of its documents are ICN# resources that are stored in the application file. The application may use other icons too, such as the drawing of Bill Atkinson in MacPaint's About MacPaint window. Those icons are ICON resources; they are also stored in the application file.

Customize your Mac applications with icons that express your personality.

Using ResEdit, locate the icon you want to edit as follows:

1. Start ResEdit, insert a copy of the disk containing the icon you want to change, and open the application program file where the icon resides. The file may be inside a folder on a hierarchical file system (HFS) disk.

2. Double click on the ICON and ICN# resource types. Two resource windows open, showing pictures of the icons comprising each type of icon resource. Move the windows so they don't overlap.

3. Find the icon you want to edit and double click it. A large icon-editing window opens; you may have to move it in order to see it all.

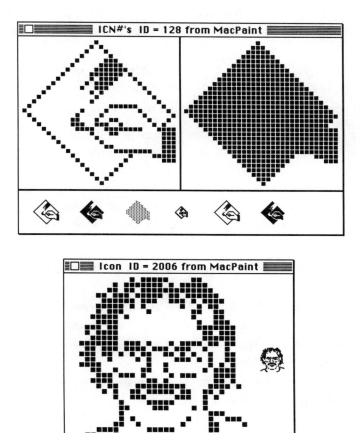

Most icons are resources that you can edit in a ResEdit icon-editing window. There are two types of editing windows: one for ICN# resources (top) and the other for ICON resources (bottom).

ResEdit has two styles of icon-editing windows, one for each type of icon re-source. The editing window for ICON resources shows the icon both magnified and in its actual size. The editing window for ICN# resources shows the icon magnified, a shadow-like mask of the magnified icon, five variations of the icon in its actual size, and a miniature version of the icon. To edit an icon:

1. Edit the enlargement of the icon as if it were in MacPaint's FatBits. Click on a black dot to make it white and click on a white space to make a black dot.

2. Make the mask of an ICN#-type icon conform to your edited icon by choosing Data − >Mask from the Icn# menu.

3. When you have finished editing, close the editing window.

Repeat these steps for each icon you want to change in the file.

If you have edited only ICON resources, there's nothing more to do but close the file window, answer Yes when ResEdit asks if you want to save your changes, quit ResEdit, and enjoy using your personalized icon. However, if you have edited ICN# resources, you must first take additional steps to let the Finder know about the changes. This involves copying all the changed ICN# resources to the DeskTop file on the same disk, as follows:

1. If you have closed the ICN# resource window for the application pro-gram file, reopen it.

2. Look in the disk window for the DeskTop and double click its name. Every disk has a DeskTop file, so make sure you open the one from the disk on which you edited the icons. A window opens, listing the resource types in the DeskTop file.

3. Double click the ICN# resource type. A resource window opens, showing which icons are in the DeskTop file.

4. There should now be two windows showing ICN# resources: one window for the DeskTop file, showing the *original* versions of the icons you have edited, and the other for the application file, showing the *edited* versions of the same icons. Move the ICN# windows so they are side by side.

5. In the DeskTop's ICN# window, find an original icon that needs replacing with its edited version; use the scroll bar if necessary. Double click the icon and, when the icon-editing window opens, note the resource ID number in its title bar. Then close the editing window.

6. Click the application's ICN# window to activate it, click the corresponding edited icon to select it, and then choose Copy from the Edit menu.

7. Activate the DeskTop's ICN# window again and choose Paste from the Edit menu. The edited icon is pasted into the DeskTop's ICN# window (you may have to scroll to see it).

8. Select the original icon in the DeskTop's ICN# window and choose Clear from the Edit menu. The original icon vanishes.

9. Select the replacement icon in the DeskTop's ICN# window and choose Get Info from the File menu. An information window appears, showing the unedited icon's resource ID number.

10. Change the resource ID number to match the one you noted in step 5 and close the information window.

11. Repeat steps 5 through 10 for each icon in the DeskTop file that needs replacing. When you have finished replacing the icons, close the ICN# windows.

12. Close the DeskTop file window and answer Yes when ResEdit asks if you want to save your changes.

13. Close the application file window and answer Yes when ResEdit asks if you want to save your changes.

14. Finally, you can quit ResEdit.

Personalizing pointers

All pointers but one—the standard arrow—are CURS resources stored in the System file or in an application file, so you can edit the pointer shapes with a general-purpose resource editor such as ResEdit. (ResEdit calls each CURS resource a cursor.) You can also change each pointer's "hot spot," which aligns the pointer with the mouse location. Here's how you locate a pointer shape that is defined in the System file:

1. Start ResEdit, insert a copy of the disk containing the pointer shapes you want to change, and find and open the System file. It may be inside a folder on a hierarchical file system (HFS) disk.

2. Open the resource window for the CURS resources. It contains a replica of each pointer in the file.

3. Double click the pointer you want to edit. A cursor-editing window opens.

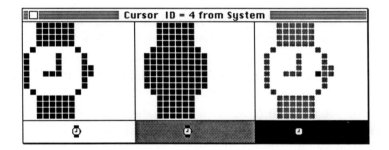

All pointers except the standard arrow are resources that you can edit in a ResEdit cursor-editing window. You can change both the pointer shape and the hot spot that links it to the mouse location.

The cursor-editing window has three editing panels: The left panel shows a magnified version of the icon, the center panel shows the optional mask (which affects the appearance of the pointer against non-white backgrounds), and the right panel shows the location of the hot spot. The window also shows the pointer against three background patterns.

The following table shows how a pointer's appearance is determined by the color—black or white—of each dot in the pointer itself, the color of each dot in the pointer's mask, and the color of the dots under the pointer. If all mask dots are white, for example, the pointer is completely transparent.

Color of Pointer Dot	Color of Mask Dot	Resulting Color
White	Black	White
Black	Black	Black
White	White	Same as background
Black	White	Inverse of background

Once you have located the pointer shape, you change it like this:

1. Edit the magnified pointer in the left panel as if it were in MacPaint's FatBits. Click on a black dot to make it white and on a white space to make a black dot.

2. If the center panel of the editing window is not blank, choose Data − >Mask from the Cursor menu. This creates a mask that shadows the pointer. You can also edit the mask using FatBits techniques.

3. In the right panel of the editing window, click the place where you want the hot spot. A black dot appears there.

4. Try out the new pointer by choosing Try Cursor from the Cursor menu. See how it looks over various background patterns and test the serviceability of the hot-spot location. If the pointer doesn't look right, edit it or its mask. If it doesn't have the right feel, change the location of the hot spot.

5. When you have finished editing, close the cursor-editing window.

6. Repeat steps 2 through 5 for each pointer you want to change in the file. Then close the System file window, answer Yes when ResEdit asks if you want to save the changes you just made, and quit ResEdit.

Many applications define special pointers, and a few even redefine the standard pointers in the System file. Therefore, you may have to look for CURS resources in application files rather than in the System file in order to find the pointer shape you want to change. The procedure for editing an application CURS resource is exactly as just described, except that in step 1 on the facing page, you open the application file instead of the System file.

Some applications don't use CURS resources to define their pointers. MacPaint, for example, uses a FONT resource. You can't change a pointer using the method described here unless it's a CURS resource.

KEYBOARD RESOURCES

The Dvorak layout

If you do a lot of typing on your Mac, you may be interested in trying the keyboard layout devised by Dr. August Dvorak for improved speed and accuracy. The Dvorak desk accessory, which is in the public domain, can switch the standard Mac QWERTY keyboard to a Dvorak layout and back. The keyboard layout remains in effect until you restart the Mac; changing disks or application programs has no effect. The standard Key Caps desk accessory shows which layout is active.

The Dvorak desk accessory does diverge from the original Dvorak layout in a few ways. For example, the desk accessory doesn't rearrange the top row of keys, whereas Dr. Dvorak's original layout changed the order of the numerals and symbols in the top row. Also, the Option or Option-Shift keys for special characters work the same as they do with the QWERTY layout.

You install the Dvorak desk accessory in your System files with Apple's Font/DA Mover program.

Reset from keyboard

If you're the kind of person who always seems to be groping along the left side of your Mac for the Reset button, you might like to move the reset function to the keyboard. No, there's no soldering to do, but you will have to write a machine-language program that instructs the Mac to reset itself when you press Command-Shift-0. Sound intimidating? Don't worry. Your job is easy, because the Mac does most of the work for you. When you press Command-Shift-*number,* the Mac looks in the System file for an FKEY resource whose ID number matches the number key you pressed. If it finds a matching resource, it runs the machine-language program code contained in the resource.

The program code that resets the computer consists of one machine-language instruction: the RESET instruction. So all you have to do is create the new FKEY resource and type the four-character code for the RESET instruction (4E70) into it. You can do this easily with the ResEdit program. Here's how:

1. Start ResEdit, insert a copy of the startup disk you want affected by the keyboard reset, and find and open the System file, all as described in "The ResEdit program." The System file may be inside a folder on a hierarchical file system (HFS) disk. Open the resource window for the FKEY resources.

2. There should be two FKEY resources listed in the resource window, one with ID number 3 and the other with ID number 4. Create a new FKEY resource by choosing New from the File menu. An FKEY-editing window opens, with a text insertion point flashing inside a box labeled *Data*.

3. To write the machine-language program, type *4E70* (don't press Return).

4. Choose Get Info from the File menu and, in the information window that opens, change the resource ID number to 0. Also, click the Purgeable option to give the Mac maximum flexibility in memory management.

5. Close the information window, the FKEY-editing window, and the System-file window. Answer Yes when ResEdit asks if you want to save changes.

6. That's all there is to it, so you can now quit ResEdit.

The Command-Shift-0 reset only works if the FKEY 0 resource is installed in the System file currently in use. It won't work after a catastrophic failure when an application locks up, the pointer freezes, or the screen goes haywire.

Warning: Don't habitually reset the computer as a shortcut to quitting and shutting down in an orderly fashion. Otherwise you'll sooner or later corrupt a disk and perhaps lose documents and applications in the bargain.

MENU RESOURCES

Adding Command-key shortcuts

Command-key shortcuts for menu choices are great timesavers, but some application programs don't have enough of them. You can add your own Command-key shortcuts, or change existing ones, using the ResEdit program as follows:

1. Start ResEdit, insert a copy of the disk containing the application for which you want to create Command-key shortcuts, and open the application file all as described in "The ResEdit program." The System file may be inside a folder on a hierarchical file system (HFS) disk. Open the resource window for the MENU resources.

2. Each menu is a separate resource whose ID number indicates its location on the menu bar. ID number 1 is the Apple menu, ID number 2 is usually a File menu, and so on. Double click the ID number of the menu for which you want to create Command-key shortcuts, and a menu-editing window opens.

Menu contents are MENU resources that are stored in an application file. You can edit them with the ResEdit program to add Command-key shortcuts, change wording, alter text style, or add icons.

3. Make sure you've got the right menu by checking the title in the box labeled *title*. If you've missed the mark, close the editing window and repeat step 2.

4. Use the scroll bar to find the command you want; its name will be displayed in a box labeled *menuItem*.

5. Continue scrolling until you see the box labeled *key equiv*. In this box, enter the character that, in combination with the Command key, will be the shortcut for the selected command.

6. Repeat steps 4 and 5 for each Command-key shortcut you want to create or edit in the same menu.

7. If you want to work with another menu in the same application, go back to the MENU resource window and repeat from step 2.

8. When you have finished editing menus in this application, close the application's file window and answer Yes when ResEdit asks whether you want to save your changes.

Command-key shortcuts must be unique within an application; you should not try to use one Command-key shortcut for more than one menu command in the same program. When used in combination with the Command key, shifted keys are considered the same as unshifted keys. Hence *q* and *Q* are the same, and so are = and +. For consistency among applications, use uppercase letters in Command-key shortcuts.

It's best to avoid Command-*number* combinations, since Command-Shift-*number* combinations are reserved for ejecting disks, recording screen snapshots, and so on. If you run out of uppercase letters when creating your Command-key shortcuts, use Command-Option with uppercase letter or symbol keys.

Menu wording and style

While you're using the ResEdit program to create or edit Command-key shortcuts as just described, you can also change the menu title and the menu items. In ResEdit's menu-editing window, they appear in the boxes labeled *title* and *menuItem*. Use standard text-editing methods to change the contents of these boxes.

The menu title is always displayed in plain style. The menu items, though, can be displayed in any combination of bold, italic, underline, outline, shadow, condensed, and extended styles. You can select style attributes for each menu item individually while you are otherwise editing the menu with ResEdit. Here's how:

1. In the menu-editing window, scroll beyond the *menuItem* box until you can just see several pairs of buttons, each pair labeled with the name of a different style.
2. To select a style, click the button labeled *1*. To deselect a style, click the button labeled *0*.

Incidentally, the pair of buttons labeled *ignored* is, in fact, ignored; whichever of the two buttons you click, it has no effect.

Menu icons

Very few application programs use icons in menus, probably because the icons take up so much space. But any menu item can have an icon. It appears to the left of the menu-item text, or by itself if there is no text.

The icons used in menus are ICON resources. The icon for a particular menu item is identified in a MENU resource by a number equal to the ICON resource ID number minus 255. For example, an icon whose ICON resource ID number is 256 has an icon number of 1 in a MENU resource. The icon number in the MENU resource must be between 1 and 255 (an icon number of 0 means the menu item has no icon), so only those icons with ICON resource ID numbers between 256 and 511 may appear in menus. Therefore the first task to accomplish in adding an icon to a menu is to define the icon as an ICON resource with an ID number between 256 and 511. You can do this using ResEdit as follows:

1. Start ResEdit, insert a copy of the disk containing the application to whose menu you want to add an icon, and open the application program file, all as described in "The ResEdit program." The file may be inside a folder on a hierarchical file system (HFS) disk.

2. If the application has no ICON resource type, choose New from the File menu. In the dialog box that appears, type *ICON*. A blank ICON resource window opens. Skip to step 5.

3. If the application does have an ICON resource type, double click it while pressing the Option key. A general-format resource window opens, listing resource ID numbers currently used by ICON resources. Make a note of the resource ID numbers between 256 and 511 that are already in use, and close the resource window.

4. Double click the ICON resource type (this time without pressing the Option key). A resource window opens, showing pictures of the existing ICON resources.

5. To create a new icon, choose New from the File menu. A blank icon-editing window appears. Skip to step 8.

6. To use an existing icon as is or to edit one, click it to select it and choose Duplicate from the Edit menu. A copy of the icon appears in the ICON resource window.

7. If you want to use the duplicate icon as is, skip to step 9. To edit the duplicate icon, double click it and an icon-editing window opens. The ID number in the title bar should be different from the original icon's ID number. If they're the same, you've opened the original instead of the duplicate, so close the editing window and try the other icon.

8. Edit the icon as if it were in MacPaint's FatBits. Click on a black dot to make it white and click on a white space to make a black dot. Close the editing window when you finish editing.

9. Click the icon you want to use in the menu to select it, and choose Get Info from the File menu. An information window appears.

10. Change the ID number to some unused ID number between 256 and 511, and close the information window, the ICON resource window, and the application file window. Answer Yes when ResEdit asks you whether you want to save your changes.

After preparing the ICON resource, you have to enter the icon number, which is the resource ID number minus 255, in the MENU resource. Menu editing with ResEdit is described in "Adding Command-key shortcuts" on page 93. After opening the MENU resource window and then the menu-editing window for the menu in which you want the icon, scroll through the editing window until you find the menu item next to which you want the icon to appear. The icon number goes in the box labeled *icon,* located just below that menu item's title.

DIALOG- AND ALERT-BOX RESOURCES

Displaying longer Get Info comments

The Finder's Get Info command, which is on the File menu, displays a dialog box that reports various facts about an application, document, or folder icon. In addition, it provides space for you to type comments about the icon in your own words. The comments can be as long as five lines, but you can only see three lines at a time.

The Get Info dialog box itself is a DLOG resource. The items in it—text, icon, text-editing area, and so on—comprise a DITL (dialog item list) resource. You can edit these resources with the ResEdit program to enlarge both the dialog box and the area provided for comments. First you need to locate the Get Info DLOG resource and its contents, as follows:

1. Start ResEdit, insert a disk with a copy of the Finder, and open the Finder. It is usually inside the System Folder on a hierarchical file system (HFS) disk. Then open the resource window for the DLOG resources, all as described in "The ResEdit program."

2. Find the DLOG resource whose ID number is 192 and double click on it. A dialog-editing window opens, titled *Dialog ID = 192 from Finder*.

Dialog boxes, such as the Finder's Get Info dialog box, are DLOG resources that you can edit in a ResEdit dialog-editing window. To resize a dialog box, drag its bottom right corner. You can also drag the dialog box to a new location, but application programs often ignore the location set in the DLOG resource and display the dialog box elsewhere.

3. Double click anywhere inside the miniature Get Info dialog box. An editing window opens for DITL resources. Drag this editing window up by its title bar so you can see its lower edge.

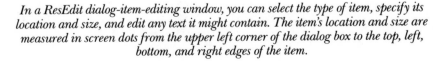

The items in a dialog box—buttons, text, text-editing areas, and so on—
are DITL resources that you can reposition and resize in a ResEdit
dialog-item-list-editing window.

The text-editing area reserved for Get Info comments appears as a rectangle at the bottom of the DITL-editing window. Although you could resize the text-editing area by dragging the rectangle's bottom right corner, it's easier and more accurate to specify a new size numerically, as follows:

1. Double click inside the text-editing rectangle. A window opens in which you can edit one dialog item.

In a ResEdit dialog-item-editing window, you can select the type of item, specify its
location and size, and edit any text it might contain. The item's location and size are
measured in screen dots from the upper left corner of the dialog box to the top, left,
bottom, and right edges of the item.

2. Change the number in the box labeled *bottom* from 204 to 236. This will make the comments rectangle 32 dots taller, which is the amount needed for two more lines of Chicago 12 text. Then close the dialog-item-editing window and the dialog-item-list-editing window.

3. Back in the dialog-editing window, lengthen the miniature Get Info dialog box by dragging its bottom right corner straight down far enough to accommodate the newly lengthened comments rectangle.

4. After adjusting the length of the Get Info dialog box, close the dialog-editing window, the DLOG window, and the Finder window. Answer Yes when ResEdit asks whether you want to save your changes.

Editing alert boxes

From a resource point of view, alert boxes and dialog boxes are very similar. In fact, some alert and dialog boxes look very much alike. So it should come as no surprise that alert boxes are usually defined by resources that you can edit with the ResEdit program.

Alert boxes themselves are ALRT resources, which you edit exactly like DLOG resources. The items in alert boxes are DITL resources, which you edit the same as DITL resources used for dialog boxes.

Experimenting with dialog and alert box changes

Because you can edit resources, you have a great deal of control over the appearance of dialog and alert boxes. However, dialog and alert boxes are not solely defined by resources: Application programs can and do alter them on the fly. If their alterations overlap changes you have made with ResEdit, ugly may be too polite a word to apply to the result. Hence, you should experiment with dialog and alert box changes on a copy of the application program or System file, and should not put the redesigned dialog or alert box into service until you have thoroughly tested all aspects of it in action.

Before changing a dialog or alert box, make sure you are editing the right ALRT, DLOG, or DITL resource. For example, many application programs contain custom Open and Save As dialog boxes that will override those resources in the System file. So before blithely editing either of these System-file resources, you should check every application you plan to use with the System file. If you find equivalent resources in the applications, you must edit them, too; otherwise the unedited application versions will override the edited System-file versions.

Application resources may not have the same resource ID numbers as the System-file resources they replace. For example, the resource ID number for the standard Open dialog box is −4000, for both DLOG and DITL resources. MacWrite uses the standard Open dialog box from the System file, but the Font/DA Mover program uses ID number 300 for its custom Open dialog box.

Some of the changes you can make with ResEdit to ALRT, DLOG, and DITL resources are almost sure to cause problems, unless you also rewrite the application program that uses them. You'd be wise to heed these warnings:

☐ Never remove items from a dialog or alert box.

☐ Never change an item in a dialog or alert box from one type—button, check box, static text, CNTL resource, user item, and so on—to another.

☐ Don't use the Send to Back or the Bring to Front command in the DITL menu, which appears when a dialog-item-list-editing window is active. Those commands can disrupt the way the dialog or alert box works.

☐ Don't edit or remove text such as ^0 or ^1 that you find in a dialog-item-list-editing window. These markers are destined to be replaced by meaningful text when a program that uses them is run.

☐ When editing some DITL resources, choosing Full Window from the DITL menu enlarges the editing window considerably. The enlarged window may be so large that you have to drag it around to see it all. You may find items at the extreme edges of an enlarged dialog-item-list-editing window. Such items are invisible when used in a dialog or alert box, unless the application that uses them makes them visible by relocating them while it is running. Don't move these "invisible" items.

PRINTING RESOURCES

Custom paper sizes

Two or three of the five paper sizes offered in the Page Setup dialog boxes of most application programs are of no use to most Mac users. Not many people use both US Letter and A4 Letter, for example. The five paper sizes are specified in the PREC resource 3 in the ImageWriter file, so with ResEdit you can change them to the sizes you use most frequently.

ResEdit versions 1.0D7 and above allow you to define your own resource-editing templates similar to the built-in templates for menus windows. The templates are TMPL resources in the ResEdit file. You define a template for PREC resource 3 as follows:

1. Start ResEdit, insert a disk containing a copy of ResEdit, find and open that copy of ResEdit, and open the resource window for the TMPL resources, all as described in "The ResEdit program."

2. Choose New from ResEdit's File menu. A template-editing window opens, showing only a line of five asterisks. In this window, you will create a template that describes the structure of PREC resource 3 by listing the items it contains in the order they occur.

```
┌──────────────────────────────────────────────────────────┐
│ ▣▢▦▦  TMPL "PREC" ID = 27858 from ResEdit 1.0D7 ▦▦  │▲│
│ *****                                                    ├─┤
│ Label      ┌──────────────────────────────────────────┐  │ │
│            │ # Sizes                                  │  │ │
│            └──────────────────────────────────────────┘  │ │
│ Type       ┌────────┐                                     │ │
│            │ DWRD   │                                     │ │
│            └────────┘                                     │ │
│ *****                                                    │ │
│ Label      ┌──────────────────────────────────────────┐  │ │
│            │ Height #1                                │  │ │
│            └──────────────────────────────────────────┘  │ │
│ Type       ┌────────┐                                     │ │
│            │ DWRD   │                                     │ │
│            └────────┘                                     │ │
│ *****                                                    │ │
│ Label      ┌──────────────────────────────────────────┐  │ │
│            │ Width #1                                 │  │ │
│            └──────────────────────────────────────────┘  │ │
│ Type       ┌────────┐                                     │ │
│            │ DWRD   │                                     │ │
│            └────────┘                                    ├─┤
│ *****                                                    │▽│
└──────────────────────────────────────────────────────────┘
```

The TMPL resources in ResEdit contain templates for editing resources. You can create a template for any resource that doesn't already have one, such as the ImageWriter file's PREC resource 3.

3. To add an item to the template-editing window, select the line of asterisks by clicking it, and choose New from ResEdit's File menu. Two boxes, labeled *Label* and *Type,* appear below the asterisks you selected, and another line of asterisks appears at the bottom of the window. In the Label box, you enter a word or short phrase that describes the item. Then, in the Type box, you enter a four-letter code that identifies the type of item. A PREC resource 3 has two types of items, DWRD and PSTR. DWRD is a decimal number (not hexadecimal) from 0 to 65535. PSTR is a string of characters that ResEdit invisibly prefixes with the string length.

4. The first item in PREC resource 3 is the number of page sizes to be displayed in the Page Setup dialog box. It's a type DWRD item. So, type something like *# Sizes* in the first Label box and *DWRD* in the first Type box.

5. The next 12 items in PREC resource 3 are the paper dimensions. They're also type DWRD items. Select the bottom line of asterisks and choose New 12 times from the File menu. In the 12 new Label and Type boxes, enter *Height #1, DWRD, Width #1, DWRD,* and so on through *Width #6, DWRD.*

6. The last six items in PREC resource 3 are the paper-size names. Add another six new items to the end of the template, and enter labels such as *Name #1, Name #2,* and so on. The names are all type PSTR items.

7. Carefully check the labels and types you have entered. Then close the template-editing window. The as yet unamed TMPL resource you just created is selected in the list of TMPL resources. Name it by choosing Get Info from ResEdit's File menu and typing PREC in the space provided for the name. Notice that ResEdit has supplied a unique resource ID number in the space below the name.

8. Close the information window, the TMPL window, and the ResEdit window. Click Yes when ResEdit asks whether you want to save the changes you just made.

9. Quit ResEdit.

To change the page sizes listed in the Page Setup dialog box:

1. Start the copy of ResEdit in which you created the new template, insert a copy of the disk containing the ImageWriter file whose page sizes you want to change, and find and open that ImageWriter file. The file may be inside a folder on a hierarchical file system (HFS) disk. Then open the resource window for the PREC resources, all as described in "The ResEdit program."

2. There are several PREC resources. Double click the one whose ID number is 3. An editing window opens, showing all the items in the PREC resource 3 displayed according to the template you created.

3. Use standard editing methods to change the number of page sizes, the page-size measurements, and the page-size names. Page size is expressed in increments of $\frac{1}{120}$-inch, so you must multiply all dimensions by 120 before typing them. For example, 11 inches is entered as 1320.

After making changes, check them thoroughly before placing the new version of the ImageWriter file into service. Not all paper sizes work with all applications. For example, MacWrite's 1-inch-minimum left margin makes it hard to use small sizes of paper effectively.

Custom paper sizes for one application

The Page Setup dialog box normally contains the paper sizes specified in the ImageWriter file, but any application can substitute its own sizes and have them displayed in the dialog box, instead. The sizes specified by PREC resource 4 in an application file override the sizes specified by PREC resource 3 in the ImageWriter file. If you want to use nonstandard paper sizes with a particular application, you can use the ResEdit program to add a PREC resource 4 to an application file by copying, renumbering, and editing the PREC resource 3 from the ImageWriter file. Here's how:

1. Start ResEdit, insert a disk that contains any ImageWriter file, and open the ImageWriter file. The file may be inside a folder on a hierarchical file system (HFS) disk. Then open the resource window for the PREC resources, all as described in "The ResEdit program."

2. Select the PREC resource with ID number 3 in the ImageWriter window and choose Copy from the Edit menu.

3. Open the application file by double clicking on its name in the disk window. A window opens, listing the resources in the application. If you need to switch disks in order to open the application file, you can eject a currently inserted disk by closing its disk window.

4. Choose Paste from the Edit menu to add PREC resource 3 to the application file.

5. Double click on the PREC resource. Another window opens, listing PREC resources by number. If there is already a PREC resource 4, then select PREC resource 3, choose Clear from the Edit menu, and skip to step 7.

6. Select PREC resource 3 and choose Get Info from the File menu. In the window that opens, change the ID number to 4, then close the window.

7. Quit ResEdit. A dialog box asks if you want to save your changes; answer Yes.

After adding PREC resource 4 to the application file, you change the paper sizes it specifies to suit your needs for that application. Do this using ResEdit in the manner described for PREC resource 3 in "Custom paper sizes."

Printing

Printing is a common concern of most applications. What's true in MacWrite about reductions and enlargements, wrinkled paper, print quality, disk workspace, and ImageWriter versus LaserWriter also applies to MacDraw, Microsoft Excel, and scores of other applications. These are the topics covered in this chapter.

CONTROL

Printer buffers and spoolers

When printing, the Macintosh stands idle much of the time because it outputs information much faster than the printer can print it. For more efficient use of your Mac, you can attach a device between it and the printer to act as a reservoir for the information waiting to be printed. This frees your Mac to get on with other tasks.

One kind of device, called a printer buffer, accepts information from the Mac at a fast rate, stores it in its own memory, and sends it out as the printer is ready for it. The more memory the buffer has, the more information it can store.

A small printer buffer is built into the ImageWriter itself. (If you watch carefully when printing a MacPaint document, you can see the effects of the buffer: The ImageWriter continues for several seconds after MacPaint returns to the drawing window, printing the information that the Macintosh has passed to its buffer.) But this buffer is not large enough to make an appreciable difference in the Mac's efficiency, so you may want to buy an accessory printer buffer that contains more memory than the buffer built into the ImageWriter. If you have an ImageWriter II, you can attach a small buffer inside the printer, or you can buy larger external buffers that work with nearly any printer. They include the Universal Printer Buffer from Jonathan Freeman Designs and the Transet 1000 from Hayes Microcomputer Products.

A printer buffer reduces the wait while printing but does not eliminate it. If the document being printed is larger than the printer buffer, the Mac must eventually slow down and trickle information into the buffer at the same rate at which the printer empties the buffer. A delay also occurs as the Mac prepares each page for printing. This delay is longer for best-quality printing than for faster-quality, and some application programs are faster at preparing pages for printing than others. You may not notice this delay because buffers have a sort of flywheel effect, smoothing out the surges of printer and disk activity, so that the Mac and the printer don't have to wait on one another.

Another kind of device that can free up the Mac is a program called a print spooler. Some hard-disk drives, such as Tecmar's MacDrive or Personal Computer Peripherals' MacBottom, contain built-in print spoolers that use the hard disk as a printer buffer. The spooler stores printer-bound information on an unused part of the hard disk and sends the information to the printer on demand.

You can also buy print-spooler software as a separate option. For example, MacServe, from Infosphere, allows you to print documents and continue working on other documents in the same application.

Unattended chain printing

Would you like to print several documents in succession, without having to give the Print command for each one? The Finder can instruct an application program to print a series of documents directly from a directory window, a folder window, or the desktop. All you do is select the documents you want printed (by dragging a selection rectangle around their icons or by holding down the Shift key as you click their icons one at a time) and choose Print from the Finder's File menu.

The Finder starts with the selected icon nearest the upper left corner of the window or desktop, and continues from left to right and top to bottom. For each selected icon, the Finder opens the appropriate application and tells it to print the document. The documents you select for printing can be from different applications. The only requirement is that the application needed to print each document must be present on one disk whose icons are currently on the desktop.

For example, suppose you have two disk icons currently on the desktop: a MacWrite/MacPaint disk in the internal drive and a documents-only disk in the external drive. With this arrangement, you could print a group of MacWrite documents, a group of MacPaint documents, or a mixture of both types of documents.

In contrast, suppose you have three disk icons on the desktop: a MacWrite disk in the internal drive, a documents-only disk in the external drive, and a MacPaint disk that's been ejected from the internal drive. With this arrangement, you could print a group of MacWrite documents or a group of MacPaint documents, but not a mixture of both types. Here's why. Suppose a MacPaint document were the first to be printed. After printing it, the Mac would display only two disk icons on the desktop, one for the MacPaint disk and the other for the documents-only disk. The MacWrite disk would have been ejected so that you could insert the MacPaint disk, and the MacWrite icon would have disappeared from the desktop after MacPaint was opened. The Finder would then continue chain-printing until it encountered the first MacWrite document. Then, since it could no longer locate MacWrite, it would have to stop.

Resetting margins for reductions or enlargements

When you specify a reduction or enlargement for either the ImageWriter or LaserWriter printer, most applications reduce or enlarge the margins right along with the document. If you want unscaled margins, you must adjust them manually.

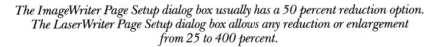

The ImageWriter Page Setup dialog box usually has a 50 percent reduction option.
The LaserWriter Page Setup dialog box allows any reduction or enlargement
from 25 to 400 percent.

Some applications, such as Microsoft Word, File, and Microsoft Excel, automatically adjust both the right and left margins so that the document spans the page. With these applications, you need to change the margins only if you want to enlarge or reduce them. Other applications, such as MacWrite, ThinkTank, and MacDraw, automatically adjust the left margin but not the right; you must do it manually. For example, in MacWrite you must drag the right margin marker in all formatting rulers before printing.

It's not always possible to set the right margin so that the document prints across the whole page. For example, the 7 inches between right and left margins allowed in MacWrite's formatting rulers normally span the page, but shrink to 3½ inches when reduced by 50 percent.

Removing blank pages

Blank lines at the end of a text document sometimes cause the printer to "print" a blank page after the last page of the document. A manually inserted page break at the end of a text document has the same effect. You can avoid these blank spaces at the end of the document by removing all unnecessary white space or page breaks. Just drag across the whitespace to select it and press the Backspace key.

Other types of documents may also have useless page breaks that cause blank pages. When you enlarge objects in a MacDraw document, for example, MacDraw automatically expands the size of the drawing so that it covers more pages. If you later shrink the objects, MacDraw does not automatically reduce the size of the drawing. To eliminate the blank pages that result, use the Drawing Size command in the Layout menu.

Spreadsheet documents may also have useless page breaks. Most spreadsheet programs allow you to set page breaks manually by selecting a cell and choosing a command. Multiplan and Microsoft Excel, for example, create a page boundary above and to the left of the selected cell when you choose Set Page Break from the Option menu. If you have too many manually set horizontal page breaks, you can remove them by selecting any cell in the row below the page-boundary line and choosing Remove Page Break from the Options menu. Similarly, you can remove a manually set vertical page break by selecting any cell in the column to the right of the page-boundary line and choosing Remove Page Break from the Options menu.

Eliminating blank rows and columns

Spreadsheet programs normally print a full page of rows and columns, even if the spreadsheet being printed occupies only the top left corner. Usually you can eliminate blank rows at the bottom and blank columns to the right using one of the following:

☐ The Print dialog box may contain an option to print just selected cells. Multiplan, for example, has this option.

☐ You may be able to designate a print area. In Microsoft Excel, for example, you select the area you want to print and then choose Set Print Area from the Options menu.

☐ Almost all programs let you set your own page boundaries and print only the pages you specify. In Multiplan and Microsoft Excel, for example, you select the cell below the bottom row and to the right of the rightmost column of the area you want printed, and choose Set Page Break from the Options menu. Then you specify a range of pages in the Print dialog box to exclude the blank pages below and to the right of the manually set page boundaries.

Printing nonadjacent spreadsheet pages

In Multiplan and Microsoft Excel, you can print several nonadjacent pages with one Print command. Your spreadsheet must be organized vertically into one-page sections. To suppress printing of a particular page, you temporarily set all the column widths in that section to zero.

PROBLEMS

My printer is battery-powered

Because the clock battery in the Macintosh maintains information about which printer is in use and to which port it is connected, the printer may stop working if the battery runs low. If that happens, turn off the Mac and remove the battery. Wait five or ten minutes, and then turn it back on and leave it on until you have a replacement battery. In the meantime, the Mac will use electricity from the power cord to maintain the clock, printer, and port information.

Only U

Under certain circumstances your ImageWriter may suddenly start printing the letter *U* over and over. You can turn off the printer to stop the annoying *U* characters, but your screen will soon go into slow motion as a result. Don't despair. Quit the application you're using and shut down the Mac. While you're doing that, you can keep up the screen speed by occasionally turning the printer on and off quickly.

This behavior may occur when you try to print on an ImageWriter after using a startup disk that was set up for the LaserWriter, with AppleTalk connected. You need not actually have printed anything on the LaserWriter.

The AppleTalk setting in the Control Panel is not affected by changing application programs, switching disks, shutting down, pressing the Reset button, or turning off the Mac. You must use the Control Panel desk accessory to change the AppleTalk setting. If your Control Panel does not include a setting for AppleTalk, the startup disk has an old version of the desk accessory. Use the Installer program, which is on the System Tools disk that comes with the Mac Plus and Mac 512K Enhanced.

Garbage in the middle of the page

When the ImageWriter pauses midpage and then prints garbage, it may mean that the Mac sent the ImageWriter too much information at once. The ImageWriter is supposed to signal when its built-in printer buffer becomes full, and the Mac is supposed to heed the signal and stop sending. This communication process, called handshaking, fails if the ImageWriter doesn't send the signal or if the Mac doesn't receive it. If the Mac keeps sending information when the printer is busy, the information gets garbled and the ImageWriter starts printing garbage.

There are two possible causes of handshaking problems: a wrong setting on the ImageWriter and a missing wire in the printer/Mac connecting cable. In order for the ImageWriter to send its busy/ready signals, switch 3 of switch assembly SW2 must be set to the open position. So first check the switch assembly, which is located under the front cover of the ImageWriter. If the switch is set correctly, then the problem is in the cable that connects the Mac to the ImageWriter. The wire that runs between pin 2 on a Mac Plus plug or pin 7 on a Mac 512K plug and pin 2 on an ImageWriter II plug or pin 20 on an ImageWriter plug is used exclusively for the busy/ready signal. Some cables, including the first 3000 ImageWriter to Mac 512K cables manufactured by Apple, do not have a wire connecting those pins, and may even lack the pins. If the wire is missing, the Mac cannot tell whether the printer is busy or ready, and may send information too rapidly. Sorry, but the only thing to do is buy or make a new cable.

Pin-feed paper wrinkles

If pin-feed paper wrinkles as it goes through your ImageWriter, the paper-feed lever is probably set in the friction-feed position. While you can get away with cross-feeding for a few pages, eventually the paper starts to drift sideways in the friction-feed mechanism while the pin-feed sprockets try to keep it on track. So make sure the paper-feed lever is flipped to the pin-feed position before you start printing a multiple-page document on pin-feed paper.

First line on page compressed?

The ImageWriter may compress the line being printed on pin-feed paper when the perforation at the top of the page passes under the pinch rollers. On an original ImageWriter, this occurs in the top ½ inch of the page, and as a result is only visible when the No Gaps Between Pages option has been selected in the Page Setup dialog box. On an ImageWriter II, the problem occurs about 1 inch from the top of the page and the results may be visible with normal gaps between pages.

Line compression is less likely if there is an even, gentle tension on the paper coming out of the printer. Try attaching a clothespin or other light weight to the outgoing paper as it falls over the back of the printer. Sometimes switching to a different weight of paper eliminates the squashed line. If all else fails, use single sheets instead of pin-feed paper.

Compressed lines may also be caused by using pin-feed paper in an Image-Writer with the paper-feed lever in the friction-feed position. Flipping the paper-feed lever may eliminate the problem.

Burping to take up the slack

Even when the ImageWriter's paper-feed lever is set correctly, the first line of a document may be squashed or stretched in height. To reduce the chance of this happening—especially if you have just torn off some paper—"burp" the ImageWriter by turning it off and on again. Burping takes up the slack in the gears.

Solving print-time system errors

If a system-error alert box appears while you are printing a document, try printing smaller sections by specifying page ranges in the Print dialog box. If you are able to print most of the document but have trouble with one page, it's possible an unprintable character has infiltrated the document. You may be able to print a troublesome page of text in draft quality and spot the characters that have gone bad. If so, delete the text around the bad characters and retype from the draft-quality printed page. Then try printing again.

When best and faster quality don't work...

If nothing happens when you try to print a document in best or faster quality on an ImageWriter, the application disk is probably locked. The locked disk prevents the application program from saving images of the printed pages on disk, a necessary intermediate step for most applications when printing in faster or best quality. Unlocking the application disk usually solves the problem. If it doesn't, unlocking all the disks you are currently using should do the trick.

Draft printing on the ImageWriter does not require images of the printed pages to be saved on disk, so you can usually print in draft quality when all disks are locked.

APPEARANCE

Achieving the best results in best quality

To achieve the best results with best-quality printing, the Mac uses a font that is double the size to be printed. The double-size font is then reduced 50 percent before printing. For example, the Mac needs Geneva 20 for best-quality Geneva 10 printing.

Before you print a document in best quality, make sure the double-size font is available. If necessary, use the Font/DA Mover program to copy a missing size into the System file, which is generally on the application disk.

Printing better draft-quality documents

The ImageWriter uses its own nonproportional font for draft-quality printing. To match the word spacing of the Mac's proportional fonts, the printer inserts unsightly gaps between the draft-quality words. You can eliminate the gaps by changing the entire document to a nonproportional font, such as Monaco 12, before printing it in draft quality.

In addition, Microsoft Word can use the ImageWriter as a generic printer for fast, decent-looking draft-style output. Proceed as follows:

1. Make sure the icon named Typewriter, which comes on the Microsoft Word master disk, is on the same disk as the Microsoft Word program you're using for printing. On a double-sided disk, hard disk, or other disk that uses the hierarchical file system (HFS), the Typewriter icon must be in the same folder as Microsoft Word.

2. Choose Printer Setup from Microsoft Word's File menu. In the dialog box that appears, select Typewriter as the type of printer and 12 as the pitch. Click OK.

3. Choose Preferences from the Edit menu and select the Display as Printed option. Click OK. Microsoft Word temporarily substitutes the Dover 10 font throughout your document, so you can review paragraph formatting onscreen before printing.

4. When you're ready to print, choose Print from the File menu. You can specify a page range, number of copies, and type of paper feed, but you have no choice of print quality.

If the Dover font is not in the System file, New York or Geneva is used for display. When reviewing the document in step 2, you can change the font, size, or style of any text. Italic, outline, and shadow styles are not displayed on the screen or printed, nor are any font or size changes. These unseen changes are made to the file, however, and will appear if you reverse either step 2 or step 3.

The choices you make in the Printer Setup and Preferences dialog boxes are semipermanent. Neither closing the document window, quitting Microsoft Word, nor shutting down the Mac (in an orderly manner) has any effect on them. In order to subsequently print any Microsoft Word document in faster or best quality, you must reselect the ImageWriter in the Printer Setup dialog box.

ImageWriter print-quality problems

The original ImageWriter has trouble printing certain patterns—especially the standard gray desktop pattern—evenly. The ImageWriter II has less trouble.

A number of factors contribute to the problem, including the type of paper you use, the method of paper feed, and the alignment of the print head. Try a heavy paper with a rough finish. Move the pin-feed sprockets off to the side and try pin-feed paper with the paper-feed lever in the friction-feed position. Or try a combination: Feed pin-feed paper through the sprockets and put the paper-feed lever in the friction-feed position. But only print two or three pages at a time this way, because the friction-feed and pin-feed mechanisms get out of sync after about three pages and the paper may wrinkle.

Unfortunately, there's little you can do about print-head alignment. Sometimes removing and reinstalling the head helps; the procedure for the original Image-Writer is described on page 28 of the ImageWriter user's manual.

Improving the quality of pictures printed outside MacPaint

MacPaint pictures inserted into MacWrite text often look worse on paper when you specify best-quality printing than when you specify faster-quality printing. Neither version looks as good as MacPaint's final-quality printing. This discrepancy occurs because MacPaint and MacWrite do not use the same method to prepare the image of a page for the printer.

MacWrite uses the standard ImageWriter file, which is usually located in the System Folder, and the QuickDraw procedures built into the Mac's ROM to prepare the image of the printed page. When you choose best quality for a MacWrite document, text is printed using a 50 percent reduction of a font that is twice the displayed point size. The result is denser, darker, and more fully formed than faster-quality print.

However, graphics created in MacPaint, which are called bitmap images, generally look worse if they are doubled and then reduced. Each dot in the original bitmap image would end up expanded to a cluster of four dots in the printed image. An original ImageWriter can't print such a dense image well, because its dots are larger than the space between them. For example, a gray pattern would end up black. To prevent loss of detail, MacWrite, and other applications that use the ImageWriter file, normally thin the expanded bitmap image by removing three of the dots in each cluster of four. This is preferable for most bitmap images, though the thinned graphics do come out lighter than the unthinned text.

In contrast, MacPaint has its own special programming that smooths and enhances the image when you choose Print Final. Since this programming is part of MacPaint itself and is not contained in the QuickDraw procedures or the ImageWriter file, it is not available to another application such as MacWrite.

There are some bitmap images that look better without thinning. Application programs can choose not to thin a specific bitmap image, but few programs use this capability. There's a desk accessory, called FixPic, that you can use to modify a MacPaint graphic that you've cut or copied to the Clipboard but haven't yet pasted into another type of document, so that it will not be thinned. FixPic, written by Michael A. Casteel, works with MacWrite and Microsoft Word, but does not work with MacDraw.

For a solution that works with all applications, replace your original ImageWriter with an ImageWriter II. It prints smaller dots, so the Mac does not thin bitmap images that are to be printed best quality.

Correctly proportioned MacPaint pictures

Do MacPaint pictures seem to be stretched vertically when printed as part of other types of documents? You can print correctly proportioned pictures from programs such as MacDraw, MacWrite, and Microsoft Word by doing the following:

1. Before printing, choose Page Setup from the File menu.
2. In the dialog box that appears, select Tall Adjusted orientation.

The normal Tall orientation results in a horizontal dot density of 80 dots per inch. Tall Adjusted orientation results in 72 dots per inch, the same as MacPaint.

Tall Adjusted does have some side effects, however. The whole document—text as well as pictures—is widened by about 13 percent on the printed page. For example, text that was supposed to take 5¾ inches will take 6½ inches, instead. The expanded text that results from selecting Tall Adjusted orientation is somewhat lower in quality than the normal text you get with Tall orientation. The degree of difference in quality depends on the font, size, and quality (best or faster) you choose. By the way, Wide orientation has the same proportions as Tall Adjusted.

Wide documents

To produce certificates and other documents wider than an 8½- by 11-inch piece of paper on a typewriter, you simply insert the paper crosswise. With the Mac, the Page Setup dialog box in most applications offers a page-orientation option that has the same effect. You feed the paper in normally and the printer prints sideways.

MacPaint does not use the Page Setup dialog box. To print a MacPaint document sideways, you must draw it sideways. Any part of a MacPaint drawing that can only be created upright, such as text, can be selected with the selection rectangle and then rotated sideways by choosing Rotate from the Edit menu. You can also use the Paint Cutter or Paint Doctor program, or the ClickArt Effects desk accessory, to rotate a drawing after creating it. Resist the urge to turn your Mac on its side, or you'll block its cooling vents and make it overheat.

MANAGING DISKS

Why disks fill up while printing

With some applications, printing an entire document in standard or high quality on an ImageWriter may require as much as twice the amount of disk space needed to save the document. The extra disk space is used to store an image of every printed page. Other applications prepare and print one page image at a time, and therefore require only enough disk space to save the entire document and store the image of the page about to be printed.

If there is not enough disk space available, a message appears during preparation of the page images advising you that the disk is full. The message may be specific, such as Microsoft Word's *Not enough disk space to print current page,* or it may be vague, such as MacDraw's *The print command was not completed.*

Draft-quality printing on the ImageWriter does not require extra disk space, because the preparation of page images is not necessary for printing. Likewise, printing on the LaserWriter does not require extra disk space, since each page image is prepared in the LaserWriter's memory.

Working around full disks

If you get a disk-full message during printing, what do you do? Here are some techniques to try:

- [ ] Many applications look for space only on the disk that contains the System file. So you must move the document you want to print to a disk that contains only documents and remove it from the System disk. (With some applications, notably MacDraw, the application program must also be moved to the document disk.)

- [ ] If the document is already on a document disk, move it to a blank disk. A few applications, such as Microsoft Word, are smart enough to look for disk space on any disk available, not just the application or System disk.

- [ ] Move the application program to the document disk and remove it from the System disk.

- [ ] Make more space available on the System disk by using the Font/DA Mover to remove unneeded fonts and desk accessories from the System file.

- [ ] Print the document a few pages—or even one page—at a time.

- [ ] Use a hard disk.

Most of these methods involve freeing up disk space. How much space is enough? The answer varies depending on the application doing the printing and the complexity of the document being printed. MacWrite and Microsoft Word, for example, need about 6K per page for pages that contain only text. A page containing a simple picture requires about 8K, while a page containing an extremely complex picture can require up to 32K of free disk space. MacDraw can be even greedier than MacWrite or Microsoft Word. A MacDraw document containing lots of MacPaint-style pictures may require 70K or more to print one page at a time.

As a rule of thumb, 30 to 50K of free space on the disk that contains the application program is enough. But be prepared to set aside more if your experience shows that it's needed.

No extra disk space for MacPaint printing

Unlike most application programs, MacPaint does not pause before printing to prepare an image of the page. Why? Because no single MacPaint document ever occupies more than one page and MacPaint always knows what that page looks like. Thus there is no need to prepare a page image for printing.

THE IMAGEWRITER

Faster Faster quality

When you select Faster print quality in the Print dialog box, the ImageWriter's bidirectional printing capability is normally suppressed to improve quality. On an ImageWriter II, you can sacrifice some quality for bidirectional speed by pressing the Caps Lock, Shift, and Option keys while you click OK in the Print dialog box. Some ImageWriter IIs are adjusted well enough for satisfactory bidirectional faster-quality printing. Bidirectional printing stays in effect until you change startup disks, restart, or press the Command key while clicking OK in the Print dialog box.

Avoiding paper curl

Paper that sits in the ImageWriter for a couple of hours, wound around the platen, acquires a permanent curl. You can avoid the curling by rolling the paper back just far enough to turn on the ImageWriter's red Paper Error light. At that point, the paper clears the platen but is still engaged in the pin-feed sprockets. Remember to roll the paper forward again before printing.

Aligning paper to print with no gaps between pages

Ordinarily, you load paper into the ImageWriter so that the top edge of the paper is about ½ inch above the print head, putting the top edge of the paper just above the place where the pressure rollers contact the platen.

Application programs normally consider the top ½ inch of every page an unprintable area. Selecting the No Gaps Between Pages option in the Print dialog box allows printing in the top ½ inch of the page, but requires somewhat different paper handling.

- ☐ On an original ImageWriter, load hand-fed paper with the pressure rollers pulled back and the top edge of the paper even with the top of the print head. The entire page is then printed with the pressure rollers back.

- ☐ On an ImageWriter II, use the Form Feed/Paper Load button to load hand-fed paper, and then roll the paper back ¹⁄₁₆ inch, so it's even with the top of the hole located to the left of the print head in the clear plastic guide.

- ☐ Load continuous paper as usual, with the top edge nearly even with the top of the pressure rollers. Then, if the first page of the document contains something to be printed in the top ½ inch of the page, the Mac rolls the first sheet of paper forward until the print head is even with the perforation between sheets, and prints the first page of the document on the second sheet of continuous paper. The first sheet of paper is wasted. However, if there is nothing to print in the top ½ inch of the first page, printing begins immediately and the first sheet is not wasted.

No cure for no-gaps glitch

When you print without gaps between pages on the ImageWriter, a slight imperfection may appear about ½ inch below the top of some pages. This glitch occurs if the paper buckles slightly as the perforation rolls through the pressure rollers. The design of the ImageWriter's paper-feed mechanism causes the problem, so there's not much you can do about it except try different weights and kinds of paper or use hand-fed paper.

Unavoidable page breaks

With some odd sizes of paper it's impossible to completely eliminate breaks between pages. Selecting the No Gaps Between Pages option in the Page Setup dialog box forces the height of the page image to be a multiple of eight dots, which equals ⅑ inch. If the paper size, as selected in the Page Setup dialog box, is not a multiple of eight dots high, the paper size and page size cannot match. A mismatch causes a very thin gap (less than eight dots) at the bottom of every page. All of the standard paper sizes—US Letter, US Legal, A4, and International Fanfold—are an even multiple of eight dots high.

Switch settings

The ImageWriter has two sets of small switches, labeled *SW1* and *SW2*, that are located under the front cover. On an original ImageWriter, they are near the right front corner; on an ImageWriter II, they are near the left front corner. Ostensibly, these switches control page size, text size, foreign character set, and several esoteric options. In fact, the SW1 settings are not critical since Mac programs can and do override all of them. However, if the SW2 settings are wrong, the ImageWriter may refuse to print, or may print gibberish. Here are the correct settings:

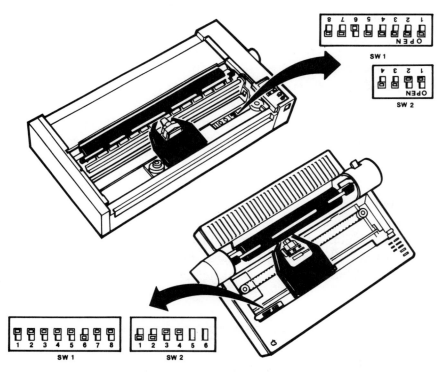

Standard settings for the switches on an original ImageWriter (top) and on an ImageWriter II (bottom). On the ImageWriter II, switches 5 and 6 of SW2 are set at the factory and shouldn't be changed.

The LaserWriter fonts look crowded on screen, and may look a bit crude if the sizes you're using aren't installed in the System file. Don't let the crowded, crude display bother you; Helvetica, Times, Courier, and other LaserWriter fonts actually used for printing are stored in the LaserWriter itself and always print beautifully.

Line-length differences

The LaserWriter expands the screen width by 10 percent. Some applications adjust for the difference, while others do not. For example, a line that measures 6 inches long on a MacWrite formatting ruler actually prints 6.6 inches long on a LaserWriter. To print a 6-inch MacWrite line on a LaserWriter, you must set the margins for a 5½-inch line. Instead of adjusting the margins, you could specify a 90 percent reduction in the Page Setup dialog box, but that would shrink the height as well as the length.

Unlike MacWrite, Microsoft Word adjusts the formatting ruler for you, so that its measurements are true for the ImageWriter or the LaserWriter. However, if you switch printers using the Chooser or Choose Printer desk accessory after starting Word, you must also choose Page Setup from the File menu and click OK in the dialog box (no changes are required in the dialog box) in order to get Word to change the ruler dimensions to match the printer change.

Font-size differences

LaserWriter fonts are smaller than similar screen fonts. Thus, a document takes less room on the page after you change it from a screen font such as New York to a LaserWriter font such as Times. You have to change tabs, spacing, page breaks, and font size to compensate.

Call me Ishmael. Some years ago—never mind how long precisely— having little or no money in my purse, and nothing particular to interest me on shore, I thought I would sail about a little and see the watery part of the world. It is a way I have of driving off the spleen, and regulating the circulation. Whenever I find myself growing grim about the mouth; whenever it is a damp, drizzly November in my soul; whenever I find myself involuntarily pausing before coffin warehouses, and bringing up the rear of every funeral I meet; and

Call me Ishmael. Some years ago—never mind how long precisely—having little or no money in my purse, and nothing particular to interest me on shore, I thought I would sail about a little and see the watery part of the world. It is a way I have of driving off the spleen, and regulating the circulation. Whenever I find myself growing grim about the

Text printed in New York 12 on an ImageWriter (right) takes considerably more room on the page than the same text printed in Times 12 on a LaserWriter (left). Similar differences exist between Geneva and Helvetica and between Monaco and Courier.

Automatic font substitution

When printing on a LaserWriter, you do not have to manually change the text in your document to a LaserWriter font. If you select the Font Substitution option in the Print dialog box, the LaserWriter automatically uses Times for New York, Helvetica for Geneva, and Courier for Monaco.

However, the Font Substitution feature does not compensate for the fact that LaserWriter fonts are smaller overall than their screen counterparts. Instead it adjusts the space between letters, words, and lines in order to match the line breaks and number of lines per page that you see on the screen. As a result, text looks spread out on the page.

Call me Ishmael. Some years ago—never mind how long precisely—having little or no money in my purse, and nothing particular to interest me on shore, I thought I would sail about a little and see the watery part of the world. It is a way I have of driving off the spleen, and regulating the circulation. Whenever I find myself growing grim about the

The Font Substitution option in the LaserWriter Print dialog box automatically replaces a screen font such as New York with an equivalent LaserWriter font such as Times. It adjusts the spacing between letters, words, and lines to maintain fidelity with the screen.

LaserWriter fonts onscreen

Even after converting a document to LaserWriter fonts such as Times and Helvetica, what you see on the screen is not quite what you get on the LaserWriter. How could it be? The LaserWriter composes text from dots that are less than one-quarter the size of screen dots. As a result, the LaserWriter fonts must be rounded to the nearest whole screen dot for display on the screen.

The dot-size differences make the enhanced LaserWriter font styles you see on the screen vary tremendously from the same thing printed on a LaserWriter. The LaserWriter's diminutive dots allow more subtle enhancements than do the screen's bulky dots.

Helvetica 12 oblique (italic)
ABCDEFGHIJKLMNOPQRSTUVWXYZ
abcdefghijklmnopqrstuvwxyz
$1234567890

Helvetica 12 oblique (italic)
ABCDEFGHIJKLMNOPQRSTUVWXYZ
abcdefghijklmnopqrstuvwxyz
$1234567890

Helvetica 12 bold
ABCDEFGHIJKLMNOPQRSTUVWXYZ
abcdefghijklmnopqrstuvwxyz
$1234567890

Helvetica 12 bold
ABCDEFGHIJKLMNOPQRSTUVWXYZ
abcdefghijklmnopqrstuvwxyz
$1234567890

Helvetica 12 Shadow
ABCDEFGHIJKLMNOPQRSTUVWXYZ
abcdefghijklmnopqrstuvwxyz
$1234567890

Helvetica   12   Shadow
A B C D E F G H I J K L M N O P Q R S T U V
W X Y Z
a b c d e f g h i j k l m n o p q r s t u v w x y z
$ 1 2 3 4 5 6 7 8 9 0

Times 12 italic:
ABCDEFGHIJKLMNOPQRSTUVWXYZ
abcdefghijklmnopqrstuvwxyz
$1234567890

Times 12 italic
ABCDEFGHIJKLMNOPQRSTUVWXYZ
abcdefghijklmnopqrstuvwxyz
$1234567890

Times 12 bold
ABCDEFGHIJKLMNOPQRSTUVWXYZ
abcdefghijklmnopqrstuvwxyz
$1234567890

Times 12 bold
ABCDEFGHIJKLMNOPQRSTUVWXYZ
abcdefghijklmnopqrstuvwxyz
$1234567890

Times 12 Shadow
ABCDEFGHIJKLMNOPQRSTUVWXYZ
abcdefghijklmnopqrstuvwxyz
$123456789

Times   12   Shadow
A B C D E F G H I J K L M N O P Q R S T U V W
X Y Z
a b c d e f g h i j k l m n o p q r s t u v w x y z
$ 1 2 3 4 5 6 7 8 9

With LaserWriter fonts, what you see onscreen (left) is not quite what you get in print (left). The screen can only approximate with its big dots what the LaserWriter prints with its small ones.

Avoiding slow printing

The LaserWriter takes much longer to print some documents than it does to print others. There are things you can do to cut down on printing time. When printing any type of document:

☐ Print a multiple-page document all at once, not a page at a time. The Laser-Writer does a lot of time-consuming preparation at the beginning of every print run.

When creating any document that contains text, not including text that's part of a MacPaint image:

☐ Use LaserWriter fonts rather than screen fonts. Screen font definitions must be loaded from the FONT resources on the Mac, but the LaserWriter fonts are built in.

☐ If you do use screen fonts, avoid large, heavy ones such as Athens, London, and Venice. The LaserWriter takes an extraordinarily long time to print a page that contains these fonts.

☐ Don't change fonts frequently in the document. The LaserWriter builds each character to be printed either from its built-in font definitions or from the font definitions in FONT resources. It keeps characters it builds in its memory for reuse. When the font changes, it must clear its memory and build each character in the new font from scratch.

When creating a MacDraw document or other object-oriented graphics document:

☐ Avoid patterns other than black, white, and the standard grays. The LaserWriter has built-in definitions for those patterns, but others must be constructed from scratch.

Printing envelopes

Envelopes can be fed manually and printed one at a time on a LaserWriter. Here's how:

1. Choose Page Setup from the File menu and select the sideways printing orientation.
2. Set up the address in the top left corner of the page, about 3½ inches from the left edge and 2 inches from the top. Don't forget to allow for the page margins when you place the address.
3. Choose Print from the File menu and select Manual Feed as the paper source. Click OK. The LaserWriter may print a page of instructions that explain how to feed paper manually.
4. Tuck the flap of the envelope out of the way, inside the envelope.
5. Wait for the yellow light on the front of the LaserWriter to glow steadily. Then hold the envelope face up and place it at the top of the LaserWriter's manual-feed tray, so that it is just under the roller inside the printer.
6. After a few seconds, the LaserWriter realizes something is under the roller, grabs the envelope, and draws it in.

Labels and other small items can also be handled in the same manner as envelopes. However, the LaserWriter cannot print any closer than ½ inch from any edge.

Word processing

*If you're like most Mac users, you do some writing
with your Mac. You may do other things
with it too, but you probably at least write
an occasional letter with a word-processing
application such as MacWrite or Microsoft Word.
On the surface, word-processing applications are
about as easy to use as an electric typewriter.
Just beneath the surface, though, are dozens of
powerful features that let you work more efficiently.
This chapter discloses methods you might not
discover in the normal course of using your word-
processing application for selecting text, getting
around a document, editing, dealing with graphics
in text, formatting, and more.*

GETTING AROUND

Finding the insertion point

When you scroll back and forth in a large Microsoft Word document to review your work, it's easy to lose track of the insertion point. To bring the part of the document that contains the insertion point back into view, type a letter—any letter. Then, if necessary, press Backspace to delete the letter.

Although this technique also works in MacWrite, there's an easier way to locate the insertion point in a MacWrite document: Pressing the Enter key scrolls the document to show the insertion point without your having to make any changes.

Keyboard navigation

The thought of selecting an insertion point or some text with a mouse rankles many accomplished typists. They would prefer to keep their hands on the keyboard. Microsoft Word allows you to move the insertion point or cursor, scroll the document, and select text—all from the keyboard. Pressing the Command and Option keys turns the right side of the keyboard into a directional control pad. While holding those keys down, pressing O moves the insertion point up one line, L moves it right one character, the Comma moves it down one line, and K moves it left one character. Adjacent to those four keys are four more that move in the same direction as their neighbors, but a greater distance: Command-Option-P moves the insertion point up one page, Command-Option-Semicolon moves right one word, Command-Option-Period moves down one page, and Command-Option-J moves left one word. If you hold down the Shift key along with the Command and Option keys, Microsoft Word selects text as you move the insertion point. Pressing the Quote key while holding down Command-Option intensifies the action of the next control-pad keystroke. For example, pressing Command-Option-Quote followed by Command-Option-K moves the insertion point to the left end of the line.

In MacWrite, there is no way to move the insertion point or select text with the keyboard.

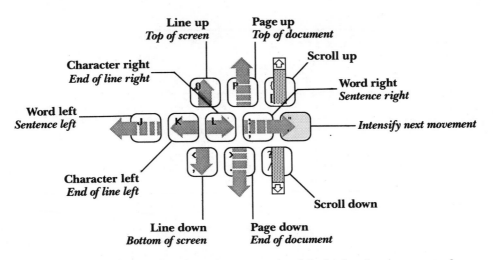

In Microsoft Word, holding down the Command and Option keys lets you move and select text from the keyboard without using the mouse.

Place markers

Finding a particular passage of text in a large document using nothing but the scroll bar is a chore. Some word-processing programs will, on command, bring into view a place you have previously marked in the document. Although neither MacWrite nor Microsoft Word has this feature, you can fake it. Here's what you do:

1. Type unique character combinations, such as *$1*, *$2*, and so on, at the points in the document that you want marked.

2. Locate the markers later using the Find command (from the Search menu).

Don't forget to remove the markers when you finish editing the document.

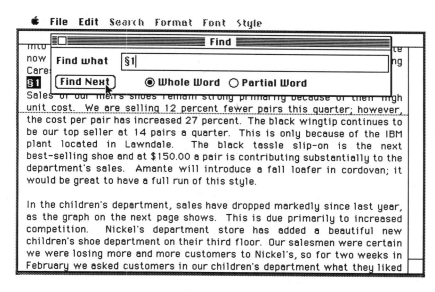

Use unique characters as place markers in long documents, then locate them quickly with the Find command.

SELECTING

Selecting words

To quickly select a whole word, point at it and double click the mouse button. If you hold down the mouse button on the second click, you can drag the pointer to select text in whole-word increments.

Double clicking selects words differently in MacWrite and Microsoft Word. MacWrite does not select the blank space after a word, but Microsoft Word does.

Selecting lines

To select text a line at a time in a MacWrite document, place the pointer in the left margin, hold down the mouse button, and then drag the pointer up or down in the margin. As you drag, lines of text are highlighted.

To select text a line at a time in a Microsoft Word document, place the pointer in the left margin (it changes to the shape of an arrow pointing to the right). To select just one line, click the mouse button once. To select more than one line at a time, hold down the mouse button and drag up or down in the margin.

In MacWrite or Word, you can drag the pointer past the top or bottom edge of the window to scroll the document and automatically select more lines as it scrolls.

Selecting sentences

In Microsoft Word, you can speedily select a sentence by holding down the Command key and clicking on any part of the sentence. To select several sentences, hold down the Command key, press the mouse button, and drag. Once you start dragging, you can release the Command key. You can also extend a selection by sentences: Use the scroll bar to locate the sentence to which you want to extend the selection, press the Command key, and click anywhere in the sentence.

MacWrite has no method for quickly selecting an entire sentence. You must place the pointer at one end of the sentence, hold down the mouse button, and drag the pointer to the other end of the sentence. Alternatively, you can place the pointer at one end of the sentence and click the mouse button, then place the pointer at the other end of the sentence and hold down the Shift key while you click the mouse button again.

Selecting phrases

You may find it easier to select phrases by dragging backward—right to left, and up—from the end of the phrase to its beginning. Your eye is already at the end of the phrase after reading from right to left, and it's easier to start there and drag backward than to look back and drag forward.

Selecting paragraphs

To select a whole paragraph in a MacWrite document, place the pointer in the left margin next to the first line, hold down the mouse button, and then drag down the margin until the pointer is next to the line after the end of the paragraph. This method ensures that the selection includes the invisible return character that marks the end of the paragraph.

With Microsoft Word, place the pointer in the left margin next to any line of the paragraph and double click the mouse button. If you hold down the mouse button on the second click, you can select adjacent paragraphs by dragging the pointer up or down.

Selecting large blocks of text

To select a large block of text in both MacWrite and Microsoft Word, click an insertion point at one end, use the scroll bar to bring the other end into view, and press the Shift key while clicking an insertion point there. This method is faster than forcing either program to scroll automatically by dragging past the window boundaries.

Selecting the entire document

To select an entire MacWrite document, proceed as you would with any other large block of text: Click at one end of the document, scroll to the other end, and then hold down the Shift key while clicking again. With Microsoft Word, place the pointer in the left margin next to any line, hold down the Command key, and click the mouse button.

EDITING

Saving often to avoid clogging memory

During a Microsoft Word editing session, the Mac's memory can become clogged with fragments of added, deleted, and changed text. Performance suffers and eventually this message appears: *Session too long: low on memory. Save your document before continuing.* These symptoms are common after a massive text replacement using the Change command, for example, or after a change in tabs that affects many paragraphs simultaneously.

You can forestall the low-on-memory syndrome by saving often. Just press Command-S whenever you pause to ponder.

Efficient correction while typing

As you type, it is easiest to erase a mistyped word or two with the Backspace key. Mouse methods for text removal may be more powerful, but moving your hands away from the keyboard may interrupt your typing flow.

Restoring backspaced text

In MacWrite, if you use the Backspace key to erase a word or phrase character by character and you later change your mind, you can press Command-Backspace to restore the text, even if you have typed something else or moved the insertion point in the interim. This technique restores up to 49 characters, one at a time. However, if you highlight the word or phrase and press Backspace just once to erase it, pressing Command-Backspace will not restore it.

Pressing Command-Backspace will not restore erased text in Microsoft Word.

Replacing text directly

To replace text, select the old and type the new. The selected text is automatically deleted when you start typing. There's no need to press Backspace first.

Recycling deleted text

Today's trash may be tomorrow's treasure, so don't hastily condemn the sentences and paragraphs you delete to oblivion. Instead, cut and paste them to a recycling bin, perhaps at the end of your document, beneath a line of asterisks. You can also store scraps in the Scrapbook, but you may find that method too slow unless you have a hard disk or RAM disk. In Microsoft Word, you can open a new, untitled window to hold discarded text. Don't delete the leftovers permanently until you have finished the final editing on the document.

Evaluating phrasing options

Trying to decide which of two phrasings works better in a certain passage? In both MacWrite and Microsoft Word, the following method lets you see first one passage, then the other, in context:

1. Type one alternative, select it, and type the other.
2. Deliberate.
3. Choose Undo or press Control-Z, the shortcut for the Undo command. The first alternative reappears.
4. Deliberate.
5. Undo again. The second alternative reappears.
6. Repeat steps 2 through 5 until you either make a decision or fall asleep.

Quick moves and copies

Microsoft Word versions 1.05 and above let you move or copy selected text from one place in a document to another without using the Cut, Copy, or Paste command. Here's how you do it:

1. Select the text you want to move or copy.
2. If necessary, scroll the new location into view.
3. To copy the selected text, hold down the Option key, press the mouse button, drag the insertion point to where you want the selected text copied, and then release the mouse button. (You may release the Option key once you start dragging the pointer.) To move the selected text rather than copying it, press Shift-Option rather than Option by itself.

Holding down Option or Shift-Option when you press the mouse button changes the behavior of the insertion point. Instead of selecting text as you drag, the insertion point follows the pointer. This method works between two windows containing the same document, but not between two windows containing different documents.

Removing double spaces

After a lengthy editing session, your document may be sprinkled with double spaces between words. While these gaps won't stop the earth from rotating, they're ridiculously easy to eliminate with the Change command, so why put up with these blemishes? Get rid of them like this:

1. In Microsoft Word, select the entire document by pressing the Command key and clicking with the pointer anywhere in the left margin (no need to do this in MacWrite).
2. Choose Change from the Search menu and, in the dialog box that appears, type two spaces in the Find What field and one space in the Change To field. Naturally, the spaces you type are indistinguishable from the blank space already in the dialog box, but they are there nonetheless.
3. Click the Change All or Change Selection button. In MacWrite, you must then click OK to acknowledge that you realize Change All cannot be undone. This limitation does not apply in Microsoft Word.

Note that if you have indented your paragraphs, aligned columns in tables, or done any other text placement by typing spaces instead of using tabs or indentation markers in formatting rulers, this method for removing double spaces ruins your paragraph indentation, column alignment, and so forth.

Save typing time

Save time by devising standard abbreviations for long or complicated words and phrases, and using them throughout a document. After you have finished typing your document, use the Change command (from the Search menu) to replace each abbreviation in turn with its proper expansion. Instead of using the Change command to expand abbreviations in batches in Microsoft Word, you can use the glossary to expand each abbreviation right after typing it.

Try to pick unique abbreviations that won't appear in the middle of regular words. For example, you might decide to use //ne for *Nebuchadnezzar,* but you wouldn't want to choose *ne,* because the *ne* in the word *prune* would then be expanded to *pruNebuchadnezzar.* Alternatively, to guard against unwanted expansion of embedded occurrences of an abbreviation, select the Whole Word option in the Change dialog box before clicking the Change All or Change Selection button. Or in Microsoft Word, click the Change Then Find button to expand an abbreviation or click the Find button to skip an abbreviation. If necessary, undo the change by pressing Command-Z.

Using multiple windows when editing documents

While you are editing, Microsoft Word's multiple-window capability can help you reduce clutter, avoid unintentional changes, and keep the original text intact until you finish revising. Instead of trying out changes directly on the original document, open a new window for use as an editing scratch pad. (Resize and move the windows so that the original window fits above the editing window; the lower window's title bar and the upper window's scroll bar can overlap.) Copy text from the original window, paste it into the new window, and experiment. When you finish revising one section, cut it from the editing window, paste it into the original document, and save the original.

All character formatting done in the editing window is transferred when you paste. If you paste whole paragraphs, the paragraph formatting is also transferred, but transferred words and sentences match the paragraph formats of their destinations. Numbered footnotes in the original and the revision are renumbered automatically when you paste.

Although MacWrite doesn't have multiple windows, you can use a desk accessory, such as MockWrite or Notepad + (which is part of SideKick), as an editing scratch pad. However, these desk accessories do not allow you to do any character or paragraph formatting, so you have to format your changes after pasting the edited text into the MacWrite window.

PICTURES IN TEXT DOCUMENTS

Precise picture pasting

Copying a picture from MacPaint into MacWrite or Microsoft Word should be a simple task—a matter of cut- or copy-and-paste. But sometimes where the picture ends up in the text document seems to be controlled by mysterious, supernatural forces. In fact, three things determine a picture's initial position:

☐ The location of the insertion point in the text document determines where the picture will be inserted. If the insertion point is at the beginning of a line, the picture goes on that line. Otherwise the picture goes on the line below. In either case, any text that follows the insertion point becomes a new paragraph below the picture.

☐ Both Microsoft Word and MacWrite always place a picture flush against the left margin.

☐ A picture that seems off-center in Microsoft Word or away from the left margin in MacWrite has extra white space around it. MacWrite and Microsoft Word treat the whole picture—surrounding white space included—as an indivisible unit. The extra white space results from selecting too large an area with the selection rectangle in MacPaint. To avoid excess white space, always select with the lasso.

The insertion-point location and margin settings similarly affect the initial position of pictures copied from MacDraw, Microsoft Chart, and other drawing programs. Extra white space is not a factor here though, because drawings from these applications never have extra surrounding white space.

Moving pictures up and down

After pasting a picture into a MacWrite or Microsoft Word document, you can move the picture up or down by removing or adding lines above it.

Moving pictures sideways

A picture in a MacWrite or Microsoft Word document can be dragged left or right as far as the margins allow. Here's how:

1. Select the picture by clicking anywhere on it. A selection box appears around the picture, showing just how much white space is actually part of it. Be careful not to type anything or brush the keyboard while a picture is selected, because the typing will replace the picture. Should this happen accidentally, immediately choose Undo from the Edit menu.

2. Place the pointer over any border of the selection box (but avoid the three black squares on the bottom border). The pointer changes shape from an I-beam to an arrow.

3. With the mouse, drag the selection box right or left to the place where you want the picture.

4. Release the mouse button. The picture jumps inside the selection box at its new location.

If the margins keep you from moving the picture as far to the right or left as you'd like, adjust them. In MacWrite, insert a formatting ruler above the picture and move its margin markers. Don't forget to insert another formatting ruler below the picture to reset the margins for the text following the picture. In Microsoft Word, select the picture, choose Show Rulers from the Edit menu, and change the margin markers.

Resizing pictures

To stretch or shrink a picture in a MacWrite or Microsoft Word document, you can use the three black squares that appear on the bottom border of every selection box. Follow these steps:

1. Place the pointer over one of the squares and drag it with the mouse. As you drag, the selection box changes size.

2. Release the mouse button when the selection box is the size you want the picture to be. The picture changes its proportions to fit the box's new size and shape. You can undo the size change by choosing Undo from the Edit menu.

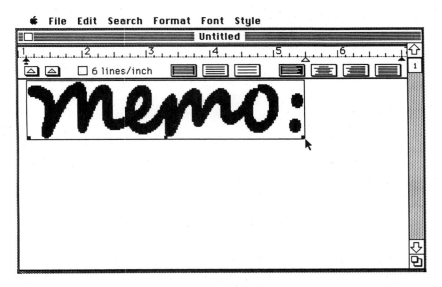

Pictures in MacWrite and Microsoft Word documents can be resized by dragging the small black squares on the bottom border of the selection box.

Microsoft Word has an alternate method of resizing, as follows:

1. After selecting the picture, press Command-Shift-Y.

2. Type a number from 0 to 9 to indicate the new picture size. The number 9 produces a picture 90 percent the size of the original, 8 produces one 80 percent as large, and so on. The number 0 restores a reduced picture to its original size.

CHARACTER FORMATTING

Extra space after italics

Italic text has its place in an otherwise Roman (plain) text paragraph: It is most often used for book titles, technical terms, and foreign-language phrases. But with normal spacing, italic text often collides with the Roman text that follows it. To prevent such character collisions, type an extra blank space after the last italic letter.

Do not add extra space after italics in a document you plan to print on a LaserWriter, however. Unlike the screen and the ImageWriter, which fabricate italics by slanting Roman fonts, the LaserWriter has special italic fonts designed to fit seamlessly with their Roman counterparts.

Nonproportional spacing

Proportionally spaced fonts predominate on the Mac. In the Chicago, Geneva, and New York fonts, for example, an *m* is wider than an *l*. You cannot turn off proportional spacing with those fonts. If you want nonproportional spacing, you will have to use a monospaced font, such as Monaco, Dover, Washington D.C., or Courier. If the monospace font of your choice is not listed in MacWrite's Font menu or Microsoft Word's Character Formats dialog box, use the Font/DA Mover program to install it.

Hard Spaces

Normal blank spaces, which you type by pressing the Spacebar, are considered soft places in a paragraph, where lines can be broken to fit the margins. Sometimes you may want to prevent a line from breaking on certain spaces—when typing formulas and equations, for example. In those places, press Option-Spacebar to type a hard, nonbreaking space.

You can use hard spaces anywhere you can use normal spaces, including dialog boxes. In Microsoft Word, pressing Command-Spacebar also produces a nonbreaking space in regular documents, but does not work in dialog boxes.

One cautionary note: With a proportionally spaced font (Geneva, New York, Times, Helvetica, and so on), a hard space is twice the width of a normal space. With a monospaced font (Monaco, Courier, and so on), hard spaces are the same width as normal spaces.

Using style to create visual separation

Some people like to separate different elements of a document with a line of asterisks, hyphens, underscores, lowercase *o*'s, periods, colons, solid dots (press Option-8), or other characters. The Mac's different character formats—bold, italic, underline, outline, and shadow—permit a great many variations on the standard line of characters. For example, an underlined underscore produces a double horizontal line.

Keystroke		Style	
*****	Shift-8	*****	Outline
------	Hyphen	------	Shadow
_____	Shift-Hyphen	_____	Underline
000000	0	*000000*	Italic, Outline
....	Period	....	Outline
:::::::::::::::	Colon	:::::::::::::::	Italic, Shadow
•••••	Option-8	ooooo	Outline
++++++	Option-/	++++++	Bold, Italic
◇◇◇◇◇	Shift-Option-V	◇◇◇◇◇	Bold, Outline

Combine characters and styles for visual separation.

Double subscripts and superscripts

Formulas and equations that require double subscripts (that is, subscripts of subscripts) and double superscripts can easily be created in MacPaint and copied into a text document. But the desired results can also be obtained directly in MacWrite and Microsoft Word.

Special subscript and superscript fonts contain letters and numerals that are raised above or below the standard position of characters on a line. When you use these fonts with the Subscript or Superscript style, you get double subscripts and superscripts. The Dayton Fonts, from Plugh, Inc., include subscripts and superscripts, ornamented Greek and English alphabets, a square-root toolkit, fraction connectors, dots, integrals, sums, large brackets, and other symbols used in equations. SciFonts, from Paragon Courseware, inclues 12-point regular, 9-point superscript, and 9-point subscript fonts of the standard English alphabet and Arabic numerals, the Greek alphabet, and mathematical symbols, plus a 12-point cursive English font. All these fonts can be installed in any System using the Font/DA Mover, and work equally well with MacWrite and Microsoft Word.

Copying character attributes

Choosing fonts, sizes, and styles from menus gets tedious in no time. Using keyboard shortcuts saves work, if you can remember the right keystroke for the attribute you want. In Microsoft Word, you need only use the keyboard shortcut once for each combination of font, size, and style in a document. After that, you can copy the attributes from an already formatted character, as follows:

1. Select the text you want to format.
2. Locate any character that has the combination of attributes you want to copy and place the pointer over it. You can scroll the document if necessary; the text you selected in step 1 need not be visible.
3. Press Command-Option while you click on the character you found in step 2.

With Word version 1.05 or above, you can copy character attributes across a split window but not between two different windows.

LINE FORMATTING

New line, same paragraph

Ordinarily, the wordwrap feature automatically starts a new line when your typing reaches the right margin. At times you may want to start a new line before reaching the right margin, without starting a new paragraph. In Microsoft Word, you type Shift-Return to start a new line. MacWrite, on the other hand, has no new-line feature.

Custom line spacing

Standard line-spacing options may not provide enough flexibility for all occasions. You can add height to a line without otherwise affecting it by changing the font size of any blank space on the line. The larger the font size, the taller the blank space, and therefore the more space there will be above the letters on the line. Giving the blank space the Outline or Shadow style increases its height even more. Even choosing a different font for the blank space can affect the line height. Here is a list of the heights in screen dots of several fonts at different sizes:

| | Font Sizes | | | | | |
Font	9	10	12	14	18	24
Chicago			15			
New York	12	12	15	17	21	26
Geneva	12	12	15	18	22	28
Monaco	11		15			
Toronto	12		15	17	23	29
Athens					22	
Los Angeles			14			28
Dover		12	12			

Enlarging a blank space also makes it wider, not just taller. This side effect is invisible if you enlarge the blank space at the end of the line. Remember, however, that later editing may move the enlarged blank space away from the end of the line or even down to the next line, necessitating a new round of fine-tuning. Also, if the blank space at the end of the line is too close to the right margin, enlarging it may have no effect, and MacWrite may not even let you select it.

Don't bother figuring font sizes of blank spaces in Microsoft Word. You can directly set the line spacing used in each individual paragraph to any number of points, any fraction of an inch, or any fraction of a centimeter. (A point equals $1/72$ inch, or about the size of one screen dot.) Use the Formats command in the Paragraph menu.

How MacWrite treats hyphens

Hyphenated words and phrases occur frequently in English writing. MacWrite, unlike Microsoft Word, treats these as an indivisible entity. It keeps an entire hyphenated compound word on one line, because it does not consider a hyphen a legitimate place to automatically break a long line. Thus, if one of the following terms did not fit at the end of a line, MacWrite would wrap the whole thing around to the next line:

aide-de-camp	much-loved
daughter-in-law	namby-pamby
ex-husband	president-elect
half-baked	quasi-judicial
helter-skelter	self-restraint
higgledy-piggledy	10-meter
hocus-pocus	touch-me-not
hurdy-gurdy	vice-president
jack-o'-lantern	white-faced
matter-of-fact	wishy-washy

✕ You can trick MacWrite into breaking a line at a hyphen by typing a blank space after the hyphen. The extra space is invisible while it is at the end of the line. Just remember that later editing may move the extra space away from the end of the line, where it will become visible.

Using optional hyphens

Microsoft Word breaks a line at the hyphen in a compound word or phrase, but keeps unhyphenated long words intact. For example, if the word *anthropomorphism* does not fit at the end of a line, the entire word is put at the beginning of the next line.

You can show Microsoft Word where a long word may be divided by pressing Command-Hyphen to type an optional hyphen. When a word that contains optional hyphens occurs at the end of a line, Microsoft Word tries to divide the word at one of them and, if successful, shows a hyphen. Otherwise, optional hyphens are invisible. To save time typing, put long words with optional hyphens in the glossary.

When lines won't center

Are centered lines in your MacWrite document off-center? You probably have blank spaces at the beginning or end of the lines. Here's how you can remove them:

1. Select leading spaces by dragging the pointer from the first word on the line toward the left margin, as shown in the next figure. Press Backspace.

2. Select trailing spaces by dragging the pointer from the last word on the line toward the right margin. Press Backspace.

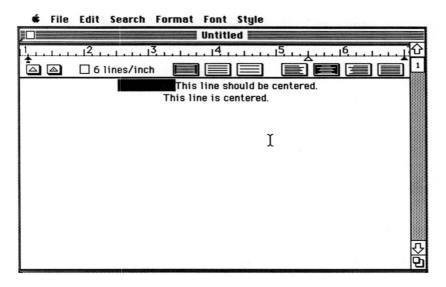

In MacWrite, extra blank spaces at the beginning or end of a centered line throw the line off-center.

Reliable column alignment

Have you ever spent hours carefully lining up lists and columns with blank spaces, only to have a change of font, size, or style throw everything off? If so, you are a victim of proportional character width. Spacing over with the Spacebar may work fine on a typewriter, where all characters have the same width, but characters in the Mac's proportional fonts have very different widths. When you factor in the complications caused by different fonts and different styles, accurate alignment with blank spaces becomes virtually impossible.

For reliable alignment of lists and tables in MacWrite and Microsoft Word documents, you must use tabs, not blank spaces. Unlike blank spaces, the location of tab markers in formatting rulers is unaffected by your choice of font, size, or style.

PARAGRAPH FORMATTING

MacWrite ruler specifications

The following restrictions apply to the markers in a MacWrite formatting ruler:

- ☐ The maximum right margin is 8 inches.
- ☐ The minimum left margin is 1 inch.
- ☐ The smallest adjustment interval for all markers is $\frac{1}{16}$ inch.
- ☐ Margin markers must be at least 2 inches apart.
- ☐ The indent marker must be at least 1 inch from the right-margin marker.
- ☐ No tab markers are allowed left of the left-margin marker or right of the right-margin marker.
- ☐ Tab markers must be at least $\frac{3}{16}$ inch from margin markers.
- ☐ Tab markers must be at least $\frac{3}{16}$ inch apart.
- ☐ The maximum number of tab markers per ruler is 10.

✳ Speedy changing of the formatting ruler

Every time you make a change to a MacWrite formatting ruler, you must wait while the change is applied to all the text between that formatting ruler and the next one. The more text there is, the longer you have to wait. If you are making several changes to the same ruler, having to wait between each change can be pretty annoying.

✳ You can cut your waiting time to virtually nothing by temporarily inserting a formatting ruler immediately below the one you are changing. Here's what you do:

1. Click an insertion point at the beginning of the line below the ruler you plan to change.
2. Choose Insert Ruler from the Format menu, so that you now have a pair of rulers.

3. Make all your changes to the top ruler of the pair. MacWrite does not make you wait between changes while it adjusts the text below the pair of rulers, because the bottom ruler temporarily governs the text's format.

4. Remove the temporary bottom ruler by clicking on it and pressing the Backspace key. MacWrite makes all the changes at once.

Eleventh MacWrite tab marker

When the indentation marker is to the left of the left margin marker in a MacWrite formatting ruler, pressing the Tab key on the first line of a paragraph advances the insertion point to the left margin marker. The presence of other tab markers does not affect this feature, so the left margin marker effectively becomes an eleventh tab marker.

Avoiding too many MacWrite paragraphs

With version 4.5 of MacWrite, heavily formatted MacWrite documents, especially those with lots of short paragraphs, are apt to display the message *Too many paragraphs for this document!* This is because this version counts paragraphs in order to keep track of a document's size. (Earlier versions of MacWrite—versions 2.2 and below—do not count paragraphs.) By counting paragraphs instead of characters, as most other word-processing programs do, MacWrite version 4.5 can scroll through a long document more quickly.

The program allows you to create a document with 500 paragraphs on a 128K Mac and 2047 paragraphs on a 512K Mac, marking every return character and formatting ruler as a paragraph. Since it considers single lines and even blank lines to be paragraphs, you can imagine how quickly these limits are reached in documents that contain many one-line paragraphs: television, stage, radio, and movie scripts, for example.

You can avoid the *Too many paragraphs...* message in some documents by ending paragraphs with tabs instead of carriage returns. For paragraphs whose first lines are not indented, follow these steps:

1. Place the indentation marker over the left margin marker, place a decimal tab as near the left margin as you can, and remove all other tab markers.

2. To end a paragraph, press the Tab key instead of the Return key.

3. Now type the next paragraph. Text emerges from the left of the decimal tab until it hits the left margin, after which it emerges from the right.

If one of the first three or four characters in a paragraph is a period, you must end the paragraph before it with a carriage return, not a tab. Otherwise the period throws off the alignment of the paragraph.

For paragraphs with indented first lines, follow these steps:

1. Place the indentation marker over the left margin marker and place a regular tab marker at the point to which you want the first line indented.
2. To end a paragraph, press the Tab key instead of the Return key.
3. Type the next paragraph. Text emerges from the right of the regular tab.

If you wish to type an occasional flush-left paragraph, such as a heading, end the paragraph before it with a carriage return, not a tab.

In documents that already have tab markers in their formatting rulers, you may have to type more than one tab to start a new paragraph. In documents with text justified at both margins, you must end paragraphs with carriage returns; the tabbing methods just described will not work.

Flush headings, indented paragraphs

Creating a MacWrite document that has headings flush with the left margin and indented paragraphs is simple if you use enough formatting rulers. A ruler before every heading sets up the flush-left condition and another ruler after the heading sets the indented-paragraph condition. But formatting rulers visibly clutter up the document and they chew up memory and disk space. You can reduce the profusion of formatting rulers with the strategic use of tabs. Here's how:

1. In the formatting ruler above the first heading, place a decimal tab as close to the left margin as possible.
2. Set the indentation marker for the amount of indentation you want on the first line of every regular paragraph.
3. When you're ready to end the last paragraph before a new heading, press the Tab key instead of the Return key. Remember, MacWrite considers a blank line a paragraph. So if you want a blank line between the paragraph and the heading, press Return and then press Tab.
4. As you type the heading, text emerges from the left of the decimal tab until it hits the left margin, after which it emerges from the right.

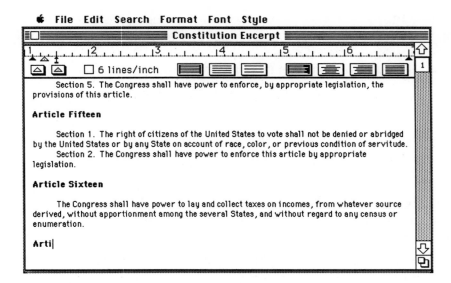

It takes only one formatting ruler with a decimal tab to set up flush-left headings and indented paragraphs, provided you press Tab, not Return, to end the last paragraph before a heading.

The decimal-tab method does not work if there is a period near the beginning of the heading, since the period lines up at the decimal tab, thus pulling the leftmost part of the heading away from the margin. The following method is a bit more complex than the decimal-tab method, but it works for headings with periods near the left margin:

1. In the formatting ruler above the first heading, place a regular tab as close to the right margin as possible.

2. Set the indentation marker for the amount of indentation you want on the first line of every regular paragraph.

3. When you're ready to end the last paragraph (or blank line) before a new heading, type tabs to advance to the rightmost tab marker. Then advance to the end of the line by typing a couple of blank spaces: two spaces for 12-point or larger text, four spaces for 9- or 10-point text.

4. Now type the heading. Text emerges from the right, at the left margin.

Both of these methods work with all types of alignment—left, right, centered, and justified.

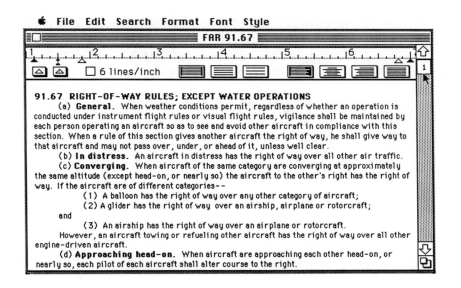

This MacWrite formatting ruler gives indented paragraphs when you press Return, and flush-left headings with periods near the left margin when you press Tab twice and type a couple of blank spaces.

Mixing indentation in MacWrite correspondence

Either of the methods just described for mixing flush-left headings and indented paragraphs works well for correspondence in which the address, salutation, and complimentary close are all flush left but where the body paragraphs are all indented. Just use tabs to start new flush-left lines or paragraphs and carriage returns to start new indented paragraphs.

Invisible MacWrite formatting rulers

In MacWrite, outlines and other documents with several paragraph styles— different margins, tabs, indentations, and so forth—require lots of formatting-ruler changes. To eliminate the tedium of constantly inserting and adjusting new rulers, or of scrolling through the document in search of an existing ruler to copy, why not keep a set of preformatted rulers at the end of your document? When you need to change paragraph formats, you copy the appropriate ruler from the end of the document and paste it above the paragraph to be formatted.

Don't worry about the set of rulers taking up too much valuable screen space
and slowing down the display speed as you type. Those problems disappear if you
hide the rulers. But how do you select and copy an invisible ruler? You give it a visible
name, as follows:

1. Choose 9-point text and type a line of hyphens to separate the main document from the set of rulers. Press Return twice at the end of the line.

2. Insert a formatting ruler (choose Insert Ruler from the Format menu) and
   adjust it for the first paragraph style. Then type a descriptive name for the
   ruler you have just set up and press Return twice.

3. Repeat step 2 for each additional paragraph style.

4. Choose Hide Rulers from the Format menu.

To copy a ruler, you select the blank line above the appropriate ruler name at the
end of the document and choose Copy from the Edit menu, or press Command-C.
Then you can paste the copied ruler—still invisible—ahead of the paragraph to be
formatted in the main document. The best place to paste the invisible ruler is over
the entire blank portion at the end of the line below which you want the format
change. To do this, drag the mouse from the end of that line to the left margin
on the line below it, and then paste.

```
 ♦  File  Edit  Search  Format  Font  Style
┌──────────────────────────────────────────────────────┐
│ □ ▤▤▤▤▤▤▤▤▤▤▤▤▤▤▤▤ Faraday Outline ▤▤▤▤▤▤▤▤▤▤          │
├──────────────────────────────────────────────────────┤
│ Series I                                         ⇧    │
│         § 1. On the Induction of Electric Currents    │
│         § 2. On the Evolution of Electricity from Magnetism  │ 1 │
│         § 3. New Electrical State or Condition of Matter │
│         § 4. Explication of Arago's Magnetic Phenomena │
│ Series II                                              │
│         § 5. Terrestrial Magneto-electric Induction    │
│         § 6. General Remarks and Illustrations of the Force and Direction of │
│                   Magneto-electric Induction           │
│ Series III                                             │
│         § 7. Identity of Electricities Derived from Different Sources │
│             I. Voltaic Electricity                     │
│             II. Ordinary Electricity                   │
│             III. Magneto-electricity                   │
│             IV. Thermo-electricity                     │
│             V. Animal Electricity                      │
│                                                        │
│ -------- Preset formatting rulers reside below, on blank lines above names -------------- │
│                                                        │
│ 1st level                                              │
│ ▬▬▬▬▬▬▬▬▬▬▬▬▬▬▬▬▬▬▬▬▬▬▬▬▬▬▬▬▬▬▬▬▬▬▬                     │
│ ]       2nd level                                ⇩    │
│                                                        │
│         3rd level                                ⊡    │
└──────────────────────────────────────────────────────┘
```

Hidden MacWrite formatting rulers can be copied from the end of a
document and pasted where you need them, provided you type a visible description
below each invisible ruler.

About Microsoft Word's formatting rulers

Formatting rulers in Microsoft Word cannot be cut, copied, and pasted the way they can in MacWrite. In Microsoft Word, a formatting ruler is automatically attached to every return character. If you move or remove a paragraph's return character, you also move or remove its formatting ruler.

For example, if you paste one paragraph (A) into the middle of a differently formatted paragraph (B), Word changes the format of the first part of paragraph B to match the format of paragraph A. To put it another way, the first part of paragraph B becomes the first part of paragraph A. To copy just the text from paragraph A, and not the format, exclude the return character at the end of paragraph A when you select it.

Similarly, unintentional changes to a paragraph's format occur if you accidentally remove the return character at the end of the paragraph. Use caution when selecting text at the end of a paragraph to avoid unintentionally including the return character in the selection.

Return characters are normally invisible, but you can see them if you choose Show ¶ from the Edit menu.

Copying paragraph formats

Once you set up a paragraph format—tabs, margins, indentation, spacing, and alignment—in a Microsoft Word document, the format is retained as you continue typing. Each time you press the Return key to start a new paragraph, the paragraph format is automatically copied from the preceding paragraph. But what if you want to change the paragraph format for one paragraph and then revert to a format used earlier for the next paragraph? Changing the format for each paragraph by adjusting formatting rulers and choosing commands from menus is too much work. And using keyboard shortcuts only saves time if you can remember the right keystrokes for the attribute you want.

In Microsoft Word, you need to use those methods only once for each paragraph format you set up in a document. After that, you can copy the format from any existing paragraph, as follows:

1. Select the paragraph you want to format.
2. Locate any paragraph that has the format you want to copy. You can scroll the document if necessary; the paragraph that you selected in step 1 need not be visible.

3. Place the pointer in the left margin alongside the paragraph you found in step 2. The pointer shape becomes an arrow pointing to the right.

4. Press Command-Option while you click next to the paragraph whose format you want to copy.

With Microsoft Word version 1.05 or above, you can copy paragraph formats across a split window but not between two different windows.

PAGE HEADERS AND FOOTERS

Retrieving MacWrite header and footer windows quickly

After you open MacWrite's header or footer window, you can return to the main document window by clicking anywhere on it. The header and footer windows remain on the screen but are hidden beneath the document window. You can retrieve the header or footer window by clicking at the extreme right edge of the screen. To display the header window, click alongside the document window's title bar; to display the footer window, click alongside the document window's scroll bar.

You may not be able to retrieve the header and footer windows in the manner just described if you have moved any of the windows from their standard positions (by dragging their title bars). Also, you will be unable to retrieve them in that manner if you explicitly closed them (by clicking their close boxes or choosing Close from the File menu while they are active).

Header and footer experiments

To experiment with headers and footers in MacWrite, set up the screen so the header, footer, and document windows are all visible. Then, as you change the header or footer, you can see how it affects the document. Here's the procedure:

1. Shrink the document window so that it occupies the upper half or so of the screen.

2. Open the header or footer window, shrink it to about half its initial size, and drag it below the document window.

3. Create an experimental header or footer in its window.

4. To see how the experimental header or footer looks, click on the document window. If necessary, scroll to the nearest page break.

5. Repeat steps 3 and 4 until you like the way the header or footer looks in the document.

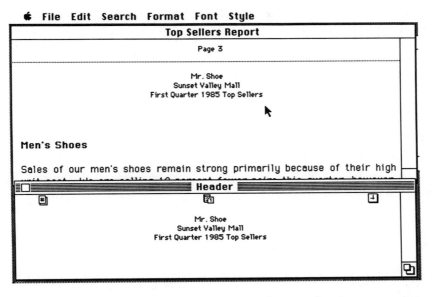

Experiment with headers and footers in MacWrite by arranging the screen so the header or footer window is visible at the same time as the document window.

Formatting header and footer page number, date, and time

In MacWrite, the font, style, and size of the page number, date, and time icons in the header and footer windows are determined by the attributes of the first character typed in the window. If the window is empty except for the icons, assign the attributes as follows:

1. Type a blank space in the upper left corner.

2. Select the space and, from the Font and Style menus, choose the attributes you want for the page number, date, and time.

This trick won't let you specify a different style for each icon, so if, for example, your document requires bold page numbers and underlined dates, you might consider putting the page numbers in the footer window and the date in the header window, or vice versa.

Putting text next to pictures in headers and footers

Although MacWrite won't let you type next to a picture in a document window, you can position the page number, date, and time icons next to a picture in the header and footer windows. You may even put the icons on top of a picture.

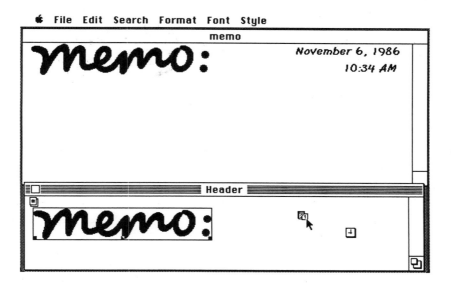

The page number, date, and time icons in MacWrite's header and footer windows can be placed next to or on top of a picture.

When to leave out the date icon

Don't use MacWrite's date icon in the header or footer windows of a letter or other document that carries a fixed date. MacWrite always replaces the icon with the current date, rather than the date on which you printed or saved the document. Typing the date may seem like more work now, but in three weeks, when you re-open the document to see exactly when you sent the letter, you'll be glad you didn't use the date icon.

Suppressing a MacWrite header after the first page

Eliminating the header from the first page of a MacWrite document is easy: You just choose Title Page from the Format menu. Achieving the opposite effect— eliminating the header from all but the first page—is more difficult. You must print the document in two stages: First, you print the first page of the document with the header visible; then you print the remaining pages of the document with the header hidden. Follow these steps:

1. Make the header visible by choosing Display Headers from the Format menu.
2. Print only the first page by choosing Print from the File menu and entering a page range from 1 to 1.
3. Hide the header by choosing Remove Headers from the Format menu.
4. Print the remaining pages by choosing Print from the File menu a second time and entering a page range from 2 to 999.

Why would you want to bother with this cumbersome procedure? If you wanted to print a letterhead at the top of the first page of your letter, for example, it might seem simpler to put it directly at the top of the document. Then you'd use the header window to restate the name of the recipient and print the page number and date on following pages, using the Title Page command from the Format menu to keep the header off the first page. However, this "simpler" approach would require that you type the date on the first page and in the header. You wouldn't be able to use the date icon in the header window unless the date on which you printed the letter coincided with the date you typed on the first page of the letter.

Changing the page-number font in Microsoft Word

Microsoft Word's automatic page-numbering feature, which you select in the dialog box displayed when you choose Division from the Document menu, always uses the New York 12 font. If you want a different font or special style, you have to set up your own page numbering in a running-head paragraph. Here's how:

1. Type the word *page* in your running-head paragraph in the location where you want the page number to appear. (This is a placeholder for the actual page number, which will be inserted at the time of printing.)

2. Press Command-Backspace, causing Microsoft Word to look up *page* in the glossary and replace it with its expansion *(page)*.

3. Select the word *(page)* and use the Character menu to set the font, style, and size you want for page numbers.

When you print the document, Microsoft Word replaces the word *(page)* with the correct page number in your chosen format. Note that you must expand *page* to *(page)* using the glossary; typing *(page)* directly does not work.

FOOTNOTES AND REFERENCES

Using Notepad as a footnote repository

MacWrite does not automatically position and number footnotes or references, but you can do it yourself with the aid of the Notepad desk accessory. Here's how:

1. After opening your MacWrite document, get out the Notepad and drag it by its title bar to the bottom of the screen.

2. Click on the document window. The Notepad should be just visible at the bottom of the screen, sticking out beneath the document window.

3. Type your document. When you encounter a footnote, bring out the Notepad by clicking on the edge that sticks out beneath the document window, and type the footnote on the Notepad. Start the footnote with the next footnote number. When you return to your main document, be sure to add the footnote number to it (use superscript style if you like).

4. When you have finished typing and editing your document, cut and paste the footnotes from the Notepad to the main document, either at the end of each page or at the end of the document, whichever your style dictates. If you like, you can select each footnote number in turn and make it superscript style.

The standard Notepad desk accessory has a limited capacity. For heavily annotated documents, you may need a more capacious repository for your footnotes or references, such as the MockWrite or Notepad + desk accessories.

FORMATTING DOCUMENTS

Creating wide MacWrite documents

The standard width of a MacWrite document is 5⅞ inches. By widening the document window and adjusting the margins, you can increase that width to 6¼ inches and still see the whole document. Here's what you do:

1. Set the left-margin marker and, if you want, the indentation marker at the 1-inch mark.

2. Drag the document window to the left slightly, but leave a narrow gap between its left edge and the left edge of the screen.

3. Widen the document window by dragging its size box to the right as far as possible. The document window partially hides the scroll bar, but the scroll bar still works.

4. Set the right-margin marker at the 7¼-inch mark.

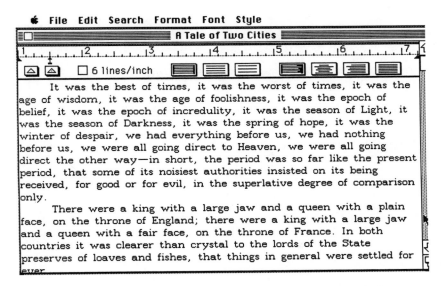

The MacWrite document window can be adjusted to display all of a
6¼-inch-wide document.

Creating even wider MacWrite documents

Hidden on the right of every MacWrite document is another inch or so of usable space. Displaying the hidden space only requires a couple of mouse moves:

1. Drag the document window by its title bar an inch to the left.
2. Widen the window by dragging its size box as far to the right as possible.

Having displayed the hidden part of a wide document, how do you make use of it? Unfortunately, there is no way to take advantage of the extra width gracefully—at least, not while you are actually creating a document. MacWrite lacks a horizontal scroll bar and does not automatically scroll from side to side as you type. To see the hidden part of a wide document, you must drag the window to the side. This procedure is so cumbersome that you're better off typing, editing, and proofing your document with narrower margins. Then, just before printing, widen the window and reset the right margin at the 8-inch mark in the formatting rulers.

```
  File   Edit   Search   Format   Font   Style
================= A Tale of Two Cities =================
....|....3....|....4....|....5....|....6....|....7....|....8
ines/inch

e best of times, it was the worst of times, it was the age of
: the age of foolishness, it was the epoch of belief, it was the
ulity, it was the season of Light, it was the season of
as the spring of hope, it was the winter of despair, we had
ire us, we had nothing before us, we were all going direct to
ire all going direct the other way—in short, the period was so
isent period, that some of its noisiest authorities insisted on its
 for good or for evil, in the superlative degree of comparison

ire a king with a large jaw and a queen with a plain face, on
ingland; there were a king with a large jaw and a queen with
 the throne of France. In both countries it was clearer than
ords of the State preserves of loaves and fishes, that things in
ittled for ever.
e year of Our Lord one thousand seven hundred and
ipiritual revelations were conceded to England at that favoured
```

A MacWrite document can be up to 7 inches wide, though using the last ¾ inch on the right is not easy.

Widening the top and bottom margins in MacWrite

The normal top and bottom margins in a MacWrite document are ½ inch and ¼ inch, respectively. If you want larger margins on every page, add blank lines to the header and footer windows.

The header and footer windows each hold up to six return characters, or a total of seven lines. If you need taller margins, remember that you can use formatting rulers in the windows to set line spacing. You can also change the font, size, and style of each line to fine-tune its height.

Accommodating printed letterheads

When typing a letter that will be printed on letterhead stationery, you must plan for the space taken up by the letterhead. You could ignore the problem as you type and take care of it when you print, by cranking the stationery through the printer until the letterhead is above the print head. However, this method makes it hard to tell when you have typed more than will fit on one page. Depending on the length and format of your letter, you can do one of the following instead:

- ☐ If your letter is only one page long, the easiest and most reliable method of accommodating a letterhead in MacWrite is to insert the appropriate number of blank lines above the text of the letter.

- ☐ If your MacWrite letter runs to more than one page and you want the top margin to be the same on all the pages, insert blank lines in the header window.

- ☐ If your MacWrite letter will be more than one page long and subsequent pages will have a different top margin from the first page, first insert the number of blank lines necessary to accommodate the letterhead above the text of the letter. Then insert blank lines in a header window and choose Title Page from the Format menu to print the blank header on all pages but the first.

- ☐ For a Microsoft Word letter, change the top margin in the Page Setup dialog box to the distance from the top of the page to where you want the first line of the letter printed. If you need to allow extra space for a wider margin at the top of the first page of a multiple-page letter, type blank lines at the beginning of the letter.

- ☐ When you print the letter, feed each sheet of paper through the printer until its top edge lines up with the top of the paper bail.

Starting a new page

The method for starting a new page in MacWrite is obvious: Choose Insert Page Break from the Format ruler. The method in Microsoft Word is less obvious but just as easy: Press Shift-Enter.

Removing a MacWrite page break

MacWrite has no special command for removing a page break inserted by an Insert Page Break command. To delete one, do this:

1. Select the blank space at the end of the page by placing the pointer just above the dotted line that marks the page boundary and clicking once.
2. Press Backspace or use the Cut command.

If the Mac beeps when you try to select the blank space in step 1, it means the page break occurred naturally due to the length of the document, including the size of the header and footer. Natural page breaks cannot be removed, only artificial ones.

You can delete any blank lines that remain after removing a page break by dragging the pointer across them and pressing Backspace.

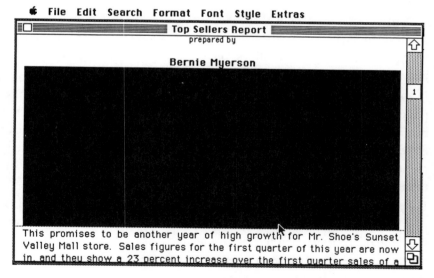

An artificial page break in a MacWrite document can be selected by clicking once just above the page boundary's dotted line.

Removing a Microsoft Word page break

To remove a page break set by pressing Shift-Enter in a Microsoft Word document, double click anywhere on the dotted line that marks the artificial page break and press the Backspace key.

Top-to-bottom centering

MacWrite has no command to vertically center text on a page, but you can do it yourself by adding the right number of blank lines above the text. Here's one approach:

1. Remove extra blank lines above and below the text to be centered.
2. Below the text, press Return repeatedly until a page break appears, counting the number of times you press Return.
3. Press Backspace half the number of times you pressed Return.
4. Select all the remaining blank lines below the text.
5. Cut the selected lines and paste them above the text.
6. If more text follows on another page, insert a page break below the centered text.

Creating document templates

Unless every document you create is different, you will save time in the long run if you sort your documents by type and make a preformatted template for each category. This is how you create a template:

1. Choose New from the File menu.
2. Set up formatting rulers, headers, footers, and other paragraph and document formatting.
3. Choose the font, size, and style you wish to start the document with.
4. Enter any text that will appear in every document of this type.

5. Insert any pictures that will appear in every document of this type.
6. Save the document using a suitable generic name, such as *Letter, Envelope,* or *Label.*

The next time you want to create a new document, instead of using the New command, open the appropriate template document. To avoid accidentally overwriting the original template with your new document, immediately use the Save As command and give the document its own name.

Envelope addressing

Usually, the business letters you type have the address of the recipient at the top of the first page. Why type this address again for the envelope? Instead, you can copy the address to a separate "page" at the end of the letter and print using the Cut Sheet or Hand Feed option. After typing the letter, follow these steps:

1. Select all lines of the address at the beginning of the letter and choose Copy from the Edit menu.
2. Scroll to the end of the letter, click an insertion point, and start a new page there for the envelope. In MacWrite, choose Insert Page Break from the Format menu. In Microsoft Word, press Shift-Enter.
3. Get ready to format the address. In MacWrite, choose Insert Ruler from the Format menu. In Microsoft Word, choose Show Ruler from the Edit menu.
4. Press Return seven times in order to create seven blank lines at the top of the envelope.
5. Choose Paste from the Edit menu, putting a copy of the address on the new page.
6. Drag the indentation marker to about the 3½-inch mark on the ruler. In Microsoft Word, you must select the entire address before dragging the marker. The copied address will shift to the right, lining up with the new position of the marker.
7. Change the size of the address to 12 or 14 point if you prefer, even if the letter itself uses a smaller size.

The document is now set up to print the address on a separate page. If you need to, you can now go back and change the letter without affecting the position or accuracy of the address that will be printed on the envelope.

When you print the letter, be sure to select the Cut Sheet or Hand Feed option. As you print, a dialog box advises you each time you must insert another sheet of paper into the printer. After you have printed the last page of the actual letter, put an envelope in the printer instead of a sheet of paper.

You may have to experiment at first in order to get the address positioned where you want it on the envelope. Adjust the left/right alignment of the envelope in the printer, the indentation-marker position in the formatting ruler, and the number of blank lines between the formatting ruler and the address.

Envelope addressing: Another method

The method for addressing envelopes just described does not work well if the document uses headers or footers, because they are printed on the envelope as well as on the pages of the letter. If you have headers or footers in your letter, you can still print the recipient's address on the envelope by copying the address from the letter to a separate document, as follows:

1. Print the letter.
2. Select all lines of the address at the beginning of the letter and choose Copy from the Edit menu.
3. Close the letter document and create a new document for the envelope (in Microsoft Word, you need not close the letter document before opening a new one).
4. Get ready to format the address. In MacWrite, choose Insert Ruler from the Format menu. In Microsoft Word, choose Show Ruler from the Edit menu.
5. Press Return seven times in order to create seven blank lines at the top of the envelope.

6. Choose Paste from the Edit menu, putting a copy of the address in the new document.

7. Drag the indentation marker to about the 3½-inch mark on the ruler. In Microsoft Word, you must select the entire address before dragging the marker. The copied address will shift to the right, lining up with the new position of the marker.

8. Change the size of the address to 12 or 14 point if you prefer, even if the letter itself uses a smaller size.

9. Print the envelope.

Note that steps 3 through 8 here are the same as steps 2 through 7 in the previous method of envelope addressing.

You may wish to save the envelope document as a template. The next time you need to address an envelope, you open the template, select the old address, and paste the new address in its place. In Microsoft Word, you should paste the new address below the old address, copy the paragraph format from the old address as described in "Copying paragraph formats," on page 153, and then remove the old address.

Return addresses for envelopes

Your best bet if you want a return address on a standard, number 10 (business-size) envelope is a rubber stamp or printed stationery. You can use the ImageWriter to print a return address, but it is hard to print closer than ½ inch from the top edge. And with MacWrite you can't print the address less than ¾ inch from the side of the envelope unless you fold the envelope first. (With Microsoft Word, you can get closer to the side.)

If you're determined to try printing the return address, proceed as described in either of the two tips on envelope addressing, substituting the return address for three or four of the seven blank lines at the top of the envelope. The return address and the recipient's address require different indentation-marker settings, so you'll need two sets of formats (or tabs). Position the indentation marker for the return address as far to the left as possible, and that for the recipient's address at about the 4-inch mark.

CONVERTING DOCUMENTS

Removing unwanted return characters

Documents imported from other computers often have a return character at the end of each line, making each line act like a separate paragraph. Although you can laboriously weed out the extra return characters one at a time with the Backspace key, why not use Microsoft Word's Change command to eliminate them all in a few seconds? (Sorry—this can't be done in MacWrite.) First, you replace the blank line that occurs after every real paragraph with an unusual combination of characters you are certain doesn't appear anywhere in the document. Next, you replace all the remaining return characters in the document—the extra returns at the end of each line—with spaces. And finally, you change the unusual combination of characters that you inserted after every real paragraph back to return characters. It takes a lot longer to explain than to do, as you'll see if you follow these steps:

1. Select the entire document by pressing Command and clicking anywhere in the left margin.

2. Choose Change from the Format menu and, in the dialog box that appears, tell Word to find $^\wedge p^\wedge p$ and change it to an unusual combination of characters, such as @@@. Then click Change All.

3. Choose Change again, and in the Change dialog box tell Word to find $^\wedge p$ and change it to one blank space (hit the Spacebar once). Then click Change All.

4. Choose Change a third time, and in the Change dialog box tell Word to find @@@ (or whatever you used in step 2) and change it to $^\wedge p^\wedge p$. Click Change All one last time.

In Microsoft Word's Change and Find dialog boxes, the symbol $^\wedge p$ stands for a return character. Using $^\wedge p^\wedge p$ for the Find What string assumes that the blank lines after each real paragraph contain exactly one blank space. If the blank lines in your document have more spaces or no spaces, you will have to type a different number of blank spaces between the two $^\wedge p$ symbols in step 2. Use the Show ¶ command in the Edit menu to reveal paragraph marks and blank spaces.

Using MacLink to convert from WordStar or Multimate

Almost all word-processing programs allow the same types of formatting variations, such as boldface text, variable margins, and page headers. However, WordStar accomplishes that formatting one way on an IBM PC and MacWrite does it another way on the Macintosh. If you simply transfer a WordStar document to the Mac and open it with MacWrite, it will be full of strange characters—the result of MacWrite's misinterpreting the WordStar formatting conventions.

MacLink, a communications program designed specifically for transferring documents between the Macintosh and the IBM PC, can translate formatted WordStar or Multimate documents into formatted MacWrite documents, and vice versa.

Converting from ThinkTank to Microsoft Word

Suppose you have prepared an outline with ThinkTank and you now want to dress it up or flesh it out with Microsoft Word. You use the Open command in Microsoft Word's File menu to open the ThinkTank outline, but the outline looks odd: Attached to each line at the left margin is a prefix, such as *.HEAD0 +*. How do you clean up the mess? To transform the odd-looking document into a conventional outline, follow these steps:

1. Before you start to tinker, use the Save As command to save a copy of the outline as a Microsoft Word document—under a different name—and close the original ThinkTank document.

2. Select the entire document (press the Command key and then click in the left margin).

3. Set tabs every ½ inch or so across the document (use the Tabs command in the Paragraph menu).

4. Select and delete the prefix *.HEAD0 +*, together with all the blank spaces that follow it. (The prefix is next to your summit headline, which you may now wish to center and embellish.)

5. Choose Change from the Search menu. In the dialog box that appears, tell Word to find *.HEAD 1 ?* . (Don't forget the initial period and each of the blank spaces; choose Show ¶ from the Edit menu to see exactly how many spaces there are.) Then tell Word to change the Find What string to nothing. Click Change Selection and *voila!* All your main headings are now flush against the left margin.

6. Choose Change again and modify the Find What string to *.HEAD 2 ? .* Tell Word to change the string to its symbol for a tab character: *^t.* Click the Change Selection button (the entire document should still be selected from step 4), and all your second-level headings are indented to the first tab marker.

7. Now choose Change again and tell Word to replace *.HEAD 3 ?* with *^t^t.* Click Change All and all your third-level headings are indented to the second tab.

8. Continue as in steps 5, 6, and 7, modifying the Change dialog box to replace each additional heading level with one more tab-character symbol than the previous level.

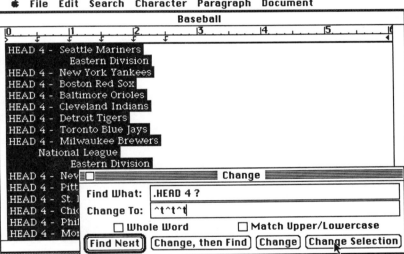

Although you can open ThinkTank outlines directly in Microsoft Word, you must replace the odd-looking prefixes with tab characters in order to restore proper indentation.

If an outline heading is too long for one line, it will automatically wrap around to the next line, with the wrap starting at the left margin. You may wish to adjust the left margin for runover lines, so that they line up with the appropriate tab.

If you typed text windows in ThinkTank 512, when you open the outline in Word, the text in the windows remains flush against the left margin and a return character is embedded at the end of each line. You should remove all return characters except the last one in each paragraph, and you may wish to adjust the margin and indentation settings as well. Make these and any other changes just as you would with any other Microsoft Word document.

Incidentally, Microsoft Word treats pictures in a ThinkTank document as text. The result is lots of gibberish instead of pictures. Each picture begins with *.pict* and ends just before *.HEAD.* You'll have to clear out the gibberish between these markers and copy the pictures from ThinkTank to Word using the Edit menu's Cut and Paste commands, perhaps using the Scrapbook desk accessory or the Switcher program.

Graphics

Thanks to MacPaint and MacDraw—and your own creativity—you'll never produce dull documents again. You can learn a lot about these applications by experimenting, but if you want to get right down to the business of creating art, the tips in this chapter will get you started fast.

SELECTING

Selection rectangle or lasso?

MacPaint has two tools for selecting parts of a drawing: the selection rectangle and the lasso. The selection rectangle, sometimes called the marquee, selects every dot (black or white) within a rectangular region. Typically, this means an object is selected along with some surrounding white space. If you copy an object selected by the selection rectangle and paste it over a larger object or background pattern, the selected surrounding white space is pasted, too.

The lasso selects the black dots it encircles and, if some of the selected black dots completely enclose a region, any white dots inside the region are also selected. The end result is that the lasso selects objects without extra surrounding white space. If you copy a lassoed object and paste it over a larger object or background pattern, only the selected object is pasted.

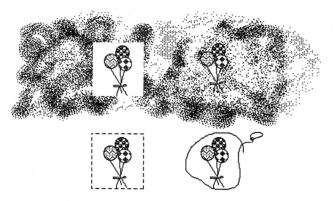

The selection rectangle includes extra white space around an object,
but the lasso does not.

The Trace Edges, Flip Horizontal, Flip Vertical, and Rotate commands in the Edit menu can be used only with objects selected by the selection rectangle.

Tightening the noose

Don't bother completely encircling objects as you select them with the lasso. Instead, drag the "rope" three-quarters of the way around the objects and release the mouse button. MacPaint takes the rope straight back to your starting point for you, and then tightens the noose.

Selecting large MacPaint areas

It's impossible to cut or copy an area of a MacPaint document that's larger than the drawing window, at least using MacPaint itself. However, several desk accessories and independent application programs can copy or cut larger pieces. This list shows how large an area the following four products can select:

	Type	**Width × height (inches)**
Art Grabber	Desk accessory	8.00 × 10.00
QuickPaint	Desk accessory	7.05 × 4.34
Paint Cutter	Application	8.00 × 10.00
PaintMover	Application	8.00 × 10.00

Centering a MacDraw object

Instead of adjusting the scroll bars to center a selected object in the MacDraw window, choose Reduce and then Enlarge from the Layout menu. If you're already using a reduced view, select Enlarge and then Reduce.

Selecting multiple MacDraw objects

When you want to make the same change to several objects in a MacDraw document, select all the objects first and make the change once. To select multiple objects, hold down the Shift key as you click on them one by one.

If you need to select more than half the objects in a document, it's faster to select them all and then exclude the ones you don't want selected. Here's how:

1. Choose Select All from the Edit menu, or press Command-A.
2. Hold down the Shift key as you click on the objects you don't want selected.

Selecting a group of MacDraw objects

Selecting an entire group of adjacent objects in a MacDraw document relies on a familiar Mac technique: dragging a selection rectangle. You do it like this:

1. Imagine a rectangle around the group of objects.
2. Place the pointer at one corner of the imaginary rectangle and press the mouse button. The pointer changes to the shape of a pointing hand.
3. Drag to the diagonally opposite corner of the imaginary rectangle. A selection rectangle appears.
4. When the selection rectangle encloses all the objects, release the mouse button. The selection rectangle disappears, leaving all the objects it enclosed selected.

The selection rectangle must completely enclose every object you want selected. If an object you thought you had enclosed is not selected, try again with a different shape or size selection rectangle. Or add objects to the group selection by holding down the Shift key while you click on them one by one. (You can also use this method to deselect objects without deselecting the whole group.)

Missing MacDraw handles

MacDraw marks the corners of selected objects with small black boxes, called handles. However, when you select two or more identical objects that exactly overlap, all their handles are invisible. If this happens, how can you work with them, either as a group or singly?

To treat the objects as a group:

1. Choose Group from the Arrange menu.
2. Proceed as if you were working with one object.

To treat the objects singly, you'll have to separate them, like this:

1. Select the topmost object by clicking on it, then drag it aside.
2. Repeat this step with the next object.

Later, you can restack the objects by selecting them all and aligning them on left/right centers and top/bottom centers.

DRAWING TOOLS

Constraining MacPaint and MacDraw tools

With most MacPaint and MacDraw tools, pressing the Shift key before you start to draw restricts the tool's freedom of movement. For example, the Shift key restricts the line-drawing tool so that it will draw only a line that goes up, down, sideways, or on a 45-degree diagonal. Similarly, the Shift key restricts movement of a MacPaint object selected with the selection rectangle or the lasso to a vertical or horizontal direction. In MacDraw, pressing the Shift key contrains movement of a selected object to a vertical, horizontal, or 45-degree diagonal direction.

Left	Tool	Tool	Right
Selected object can be moved vertically or horizontally only	(lasso)	(selection rectangle)	Selected object can be moved vertically or horizontally only
Scrolls up/down or right/left only	(hand)	A	No effect
No effect	(paint bucket)	(spray)	Sprays up/down or right/left only
Brushes up/down or right/left only	(brush)	(pencil)	Draws line up/down or right/left only
Draws line up/down or right/left, or at 45-degree diagonal only	(line)	(eraser)	Erases up/down or right/left only
Draws square only	(rectangle)	(filled rectangle)	Draws square only
Draws rounded-corner square only	(rounded rect)	(filled rounded rect)	Draws rounded-corner square only
Draws circle only	(oval)	(filled oval)	Draws circle only
No effect	(heart)	(filled heart)	No effect
Draws polygon with vertical, horizontal, or 45-degree diagonal sides only	(polygon)	(filled polygon)	Draws polygon with vertical, horizontal, or 45-degree diagonal sides only

The Shift key restricts freedom of movement for most MacPaint tools. MacDraw tools are similarly constrained.

In MacPaint, you must press the Shift key before you start to use a tool or move a selected object, but you can release it once you begin: The Shift key's effect lasts until you release the mouse button. If you happen to start moving in the wrong direction, choose Undo and try again.

Customizing MacPaint's brush shapes

Who could ask for more than 32 brush shapes for MacPaint's paintbrush tool? Anyone who wants any shape other than a square, circle, straight line, or dot, that's who! If you count yourself among this group, you'll be glad to learn that MacPaint's brush shapes are in fact part of a special "font" and, as such, they are resources that you can edit with Apple's resource-editor program, ResEdit (this works with version 1.0D5, but not with versions between 1.0D7 and 1.0D 12). First you need to locate the font, as follows:

1. For safety, make a copy of your MacPaint disk. Experiment on the spare copy, never on the original.

2. If you have only one disk drive, remove all icons except MacPaint and the System Folder from the disk window. Then copy ResEdit onto the disk.

3. Start ResEdit. A small window appears for each disk currently inserted. Each window lists the names of all the applications and documents on that particular disk. For double-sided disks and other disks that use the hierarchical file system (HFS), folders are also listed.

4. Find MacPaint (it may be inside a folder on an HFS disk) and double click on it. Another small window opens, listing all of MacPaint's resources by their four-letter names.

5. Find the resource named FONT and double click on it. Yet another small window opens, listing the names and ID numbers of the fonts contained in MacPaint.

6. MacPaint should have only one font, named *12*. Double click on it. A large font-editing window opens; you may have to drag it by its title bar to see all of it.

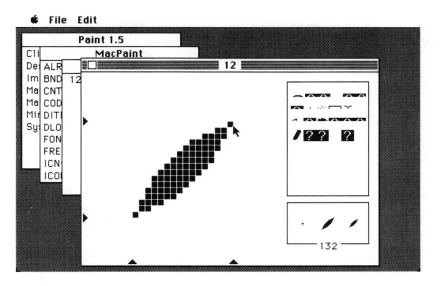

MacPaint's brush shapes are part of its private "font," called font 12, and you can edit them using the ResEdit program's font-editing features.

ResEdit's font-editing window has three parts. A box in the upper right corner displays a sample of the font. With conventional fonts, the sample is *The quick brown fox jumped over the lazy dog,* but with MacPaint's font 12, the sample is unintelligible. Near the middle of the window is an enlargement of the character currently selected for editing.

The selected character appears in its actual size inside a selection rectangle near the bottom right corner of the window. Beneath the selected character is the ASCII code number assigned to the character. Characters with adjacent code numbers flank the selected character. Character code numbers range between 0 and 256. In a conventional font such as Geneva, code 65 is assigned to capital *A*, 66 to *B*, and so on. In MacPaint's font 12, the code numbers are interpreted as tools, as cursors, and as brush shapes. MacPaint's brush shapes have code numbers between 120 and 151. The large black square shape (code number 120) defines the shape and size of the eraser tool too, so don't change it unless you want a different eraser shape. You may edit the tools and cursors with code numbers outside the brush-shape range, but doing so has no effect in most cases.

To change a brush shape, you select an existing shape and then edit it using FatBits techniques. For each brush shape you want to change, follow these steps:

1. In the bottom right corner of the editing window, select the brush shape you want to change. To scroll rapidly through the shapes, drag the selection rectangle right or left. Scroll one shape at a time by clicking beside the selection rectangle.

2. In the middle of the text-editing window, edit the enlargement of the shape as if it were in MacPaint's FatBits. Click on a black dot to make it white and on a white space to make a black dot. (The maximum size of a brush shape is 16 dots high by 16 dots wide.) At any time during the editing, you can revert to the last saved version of MacPaint's resources by choosing Revert from ResEdit's File menu.

3. When you have finished making changes, choose Quit from ResEdit's File menu. ResEdit asks if you want to save the changes you just made; click Yes or No.

After quitting, you'll want to use the Finder to rename this custom version of MacPaint so that you don't confuse it with the regular version.

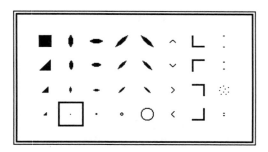

If none of MacPaint's 32 brush shapes is quite what you need, create your own using the ResEdit program.

Borderless MacPaint shapes

To draw borderless rectangles, ovals, freehand shapes, and polygons, select the dotted line at the top of the line-width palette in the bottom left corner of the MacPaint screen.

Self-closing polygons and freehand shapes

Connecting the last side of a MacPaint polygon to the starting point takes a sharp eye and steady hand, or some cleanup with the eraser after the fact. The same difficulty arises when drawing freehand shapes. MacPaint will draw the last side of a filled polygon if you double click at the end point of the next-to-last side. Likewise, it will close a freehand shape by drawing a straight line from the point at which you release the mouse button to the starting point of the shape.

How to activate FatBits precisely

To activate MacPaint's FatBits magnifier over a particular part of the drawing window, use the Command key in conjunction with the pencil tool. Simply select the pencil tool, press the Command key, and click on the part of the picture you want magnified.

Using tools in FatBits

Most tools function normally in FatBits. Although they are not themselves magnified, their effects usually are. For example, the spray-can and paintbrush pointers appear in their normal size, but they paint with magnified ink. In contrast, the eraser not only appears unmagnified, it also erases an unmagnified swath. Watch the small inset window in the upper left corner of the drawing window to see the actual effect of the tool you're using.

You can use the selection rectangle or lasso in FatBits to precisely select a very small area of your picture.

Be careful with the paint can in FatBits. If there's a gap in the boundary of a shape you're filling, the pattern will leak out across the entire drawing window, not just the portion currently visible in the FatBits window. You may not notice the extent of the damage until you've left FatBits, by which time it's too late to choose Undo.

Switching to the grabber

To scroll another part of your picture into view when using MacPaint's pencil tool, you can switch temporarily to the grabber just by pressing the Option key. This technique is particularly useful with FatBits.

Brush-mirrors symmetry

MacPaint's brush mirrors make it easy to draw symmetrical objects. But it's hard to draw a symmetrical object that converges at the center unless you start on the axis of symmetry. Finding the axis empirically can be aggravating, but not if you take advantage of the Undo feature, as follows:

1. Choose Brush Mirrors from the Goodies menu and select the brush shape and brush-mirror axes you want to use. Click OK.
2. Estimate the location of the axis of symmetry in the drawing window and click there. If, for example, you have selected two or more axes, you must estimate the location of the center of the drawing window and click there. One or more pairs of dots appear, bracketing the axis or axes.
3. Center the pointer by eye between all the dots. Do not click.
4. Without moving the mouse, undo the dots by pressing Command-Z or the Tilde key.
5. Hold down the mouse button and create the desired brush-mirrors pattern.

Double-click shortcuts in MacPaint

By double clicking on the selection rectangle, grabber, paintbrush, pencil, eraser, or any pattern, you can shortcut the more time-consuming mouse actions listed here:

	Selects entire drawing windows		**Engages/Disengages FatBits**
	Shows entire page		**Erases entire drawing window**
	Chooses brush shape		**Selects (any pattern) for editing**

Reusing the same MacDraw tool

After you draw an object—a line, rectangle, rounded-corner rectangle, oval, curve, freehand shape, or polygon—MacDraw versions 1.7 and 1.9 select the standard arrow-shaped pointer so you can move or resize the object you drew. If you would rather draw another similar object, you must reselect the tool you used. You can either click on the tool in the tool rack in the usual way, or you can press the Command key and click anywhere in the drawing window.

LINES AND CURVES

Patterned lines

If you press the Option key as you start to draw a line in MacPaint, the line is drawn in the currently selected pattern. You may release the Option key once you start to draw the line. The same trick works for MacPaint's other drawing tools: the rectangle, rounded-corner rectangle, oval, freehand shape, and polygon.

Dotted and dashed MacPaint lines

The dotted line in MacPaint's line-width palette and the dashed line in MacDraw's Lines menu do not produce dotted and dashed lines. They are used for drawing borderless filled shapes.

You can get dotted and dashed lines by using any of the other line widths with an appropriate pattern. In MacPaint, first choose the line width and pattern, and then hold down the Option key as you draw. In MacDraw, choose the line width and pattern—before or after drawing—from the Pen and Lines menus.

The spacing of the dots and dashes and the length of the dashes that make up the line depend on the pattern you choose and the angle of the line. For example, any pattern made up of horizontal lines produces a dotted vertical line. For a dotted horizontal line, you must use a pattern made up of vertical lines.

With some patterns, the position of a line affects how it looks. To understand why, you need to think about how patterns are defined and used. Each pattern is defined by an 8- by 8-dot square. As you draw, the patterned squares are laid end to end like floor tiles. A line one dot wide uses $\frac{1}{8}$ of each patterned square, so a single pattern may produce differently patterned lines, depending on where the lines fall in the 8- by 8-dot square. For example, the gray diamond pattern can produce several varieties of dotted and dashed lines or no line at all, depending on where on the screen you draw them.

❖ ░░░░░░░░░░░░░

Dotted and dashed lines can be produced by using an appropriate line width and pattern. The same pattern produces differently patterned lines, depending on the angle and location of the line.

When you need smooth MacPaint curves

For a smooth curve in MacPaint, you can lasso part of a circle or oval and drag it into position.

PATTERNS AND FILLING

Using transparent (watercolor) paint

MacPaint normally draws and fills with opaque paint that covers objects underneath. If you hold down the Command key as you draw, MacPaint uses transparent paint that blends with objects underneath like a watercolor wash. The Command key has this effect on the paintbrush and spray can, on patterns inside filled shapes, and when you hold down the Option key, on lines and shape borders, too. The Command key does not affect the paint can.

Screening with MacPaint patterns

It's impossible to produce a true gray color on the Macintosh screen, but you can simulate shades of gray with a technique used in the publishing industry. Black-and-white books and newspapers often contain photographs and other illustrations that seem to have been printed in shades of gray. To get the apparent gray tones, the printing trade photographs the original illustration through a mesh screen, breaking the continuous gray color into a pattern of closely spaced black dots on a white background. Where the dots are large, the image looks dark gray, and where the dots are small, the image looks light gray. The result is called a halftone. Dot spacing in a normal halftone screen is regular, but other screens can be used for special effects.

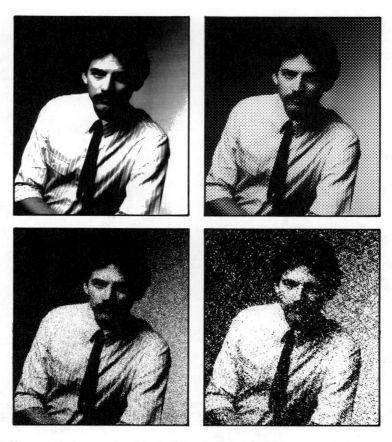

Halftone variations rendered by the following special-effect screens (clockwise from top left): horizontal line, normal halftone, mezzotint, and random line.

If you are willing to give up detail for startling results, you can get the effect of special halftone screens with MacPaint patterns. Here's how:

1. Use the selection rectangle to select the object to be screened and choose Invert from the Edit menu.

2. Select the filled-rectangle tool, the no-border line width, and the pattern you want to use for screening.

3. Hold down the Command key and draw a rectangle on top of the inverted object.

4. Select the inverted, screened object with the selection rectangle and choose Invert from the Edit menu.

For special-effect screens in MacPaint, invert an object, draw over it with transparent paint, and invert it again.

Saving custom MacPaint patterns

Spend as long as you like creating a custom MacPaint pattern palette. You won't lose it when you quit if you save the current document before quitting. MacPaint saves the current pattern palette along with the current document, and uses that palette when you open the same document later.

You can use this feature to override MacPaint's standard selection of patterns. Simply save your custom pattern palette with a blank document and open that document instead of choosing New when you want to start a new picture. Use Save As, not Save, the first time you save your picture, to give the document its own name. Otherwise the document containing the picture replaces the blank document.

Picking up MacPaint patterns

Instead of recreating dot by dot a custom pattern that appears in the drawing window but not in the pattern palette at the bottom of the screen, you can copy the pattern from the drawing window to the pattern palette. Here are the step-by-step instructions:

1. Use the grabber tool or Show Page command to manuever the drawing so that the pattern you want to put in the palette appears in the right half or bottom third of the drawing window.

2. In the palette, double click the pattern swatch you want to replace with the pattern from the drawing window. A pattern-editing window appears.

3. Point at the pattern you want to copy from the drawing window and click the mouse button. The center of the arrow, not the tip, determines which pattern is picked up.

4. Click OK to install the pattern in the palette.

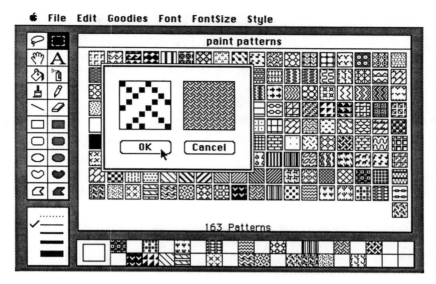

You can copy a pattern from the drawing window to the pattern-editing window by pointing at it and clicking.

Transferring patterns between MacPaint drawings

Using the pattern-pickup technique described in "Picking up MacPaint patterns," you can replace a pattern in one picture's pattern palette with a custom pattern from another picture. Follow these steps:

1. Open the document that contains the pattern you want to copy, and find or create a swatch of the pattern in the drawing window.

2. Copy part of the pattern from the drawing window to the Clipboard and close the drawing window.

3. Open the destination document, locate an empty spot in it, and paste the imported pattern swatch there. For best results, the pattern should be in the right side or bottom of the drawing window.

4. Activate the pattern-editing window by double clicking on the pattern you want to replace in the pattern palette, then pick up the imported pattern by clicking on it in the drawing window.

If you want to copy several patterns from the same document, maneuver them into a group and copy the whole group to the Clipboard in step 2. (Don't worry about clobbering the picture; remember you can always choose not to save these changes when you close the document.) When you paste into the destination document, the whole group of patterns appears in the drawing window. Repeat step 4 for each pattern you want to pick up.

Creating a MacPaint pattern library

Copying a pattern from one MacPaint picture to another is easy, but finding a particular pattern is difficult unless you know where to look. To reduce the confusion, create a pattern library in the Scrapbook or a MacPaint document dedicated to that purpose. Each time you create a custom pattern, copy a small swatch of it to the Scrapbook or your pattern-library document. If the library document fills up, start another. When you need to copy a pattern, you need to search only through your library, not through every document you've ever created (and bothered to save).

LaserWriter gray tones

Since the Mac cannot display true shades of gray, it must fake them with patterns of black and white dots. The illusion of middle gray tones on the screen is fairly convincing, but light and dark grays are less so. To fool the eye, dot distribution must be smooth, but a few coarse dots sparsely sprinkled on a contrasting background on the Mac screen can only approximate light and dark shades of gray.

Much smoother dot distribution is possible on the LaserWriter, where dots are one-quarter the size of screen dots. As a result, gray patterns from MacDraw's Fill and Pen menus look different displayed on the screen than printed on the Laser-Writer. The transition from one shade of gray to the next is much subtler on the LaserWriter, giving you smoother shading but also making patterns on things like graphs less distinguishable. These effects are also apparent in other applications that produce MacDraw-type drawings, such as Microsoft's Chart and Excel.

With MacPaint, the gray patterns you use in a picture do not change when you print them on a LaserWriter. When you draw or paint with patterns in MacPaint, they become an inseparable part of the overall picture. The LaserWriter sees the whole MacPaint picture as one unit, and cannot treat selected parts of it in any special manner.

Filling around an object

Filling inside an object is easy: Use the paint can in MacPaint and the Fill menu in MacDraw. Filling around an object isn't much harder. Here's the procedure:

1. In MacPaint, you must select the object with the lasso and copy it to the Clipboard. This step is unnecessary in MacDraw.

2. Next, draw a filled object the size and shape you want the background around the object to be. The filled object obscures the original object. If you want the surrounding area to be borderless, choose either the dotted line in MacPaint's border-width palette or the dashed line in MacDraw's Line menu.

3. In MacPaint, paste the original object on top of the one you just drew. In MacDraw, choose Send to Back from the Arrange menu.

Customizing MacDraw patterns

In MacDraw, you have 36 patterns available in the Pen and Fill menus for drawing or filling objects. MacDraw versions 1.7 and 1.9 do not let you customize the patterns available in these menus. However, since MacDraw's patterns are resources, you can edit them with Apple's resource-editor program, ResEdit (version 1.0D5 or above), as follows:

1. For safety, make a copy of your MacDraw disk. Experiment on the copy, never on the original.

2. If you have only one disk drive, remove all icons except MacDraw and the System Folder from the MacDraw disk window. Then copy ResEdit onto the disk.

3. Start ResEdit. A small window appears for each disk currently inserted. Each disk window lists the names of all the applications and documents on that particular disk. For double-sided disks and other disks that use the hierarchical file system (HFS), folders are also listed.

4. Find MacDraw (it may be inside a folder on an HFS disk) and double click on it. Another small window opens, listing all of the resources in MacDraw by their four-letter names.

5. Find the resource named *PAT#* in the MacDraw window and double click on it. A small window titled *Pattern Lists* opens, showing a dozen of the patterns contained in MacDraw.

6. Double click anywhere on the patterns. A small pattern-editing window opens. At the bottom of the editing window are three patterns. The one currently selected for editing has a selection rectangle around it. A larger sample of the selected pattern appears in the upper right part of the window, and an enlargement of the pattern appears in the upper left corner of the window.

7. Select the pattern you want to change. You can scroll rapidly through the patterns by dragging the selection rectangle right or left, or you can scroll one pattern at a time by clicking beside the selection rectangle.

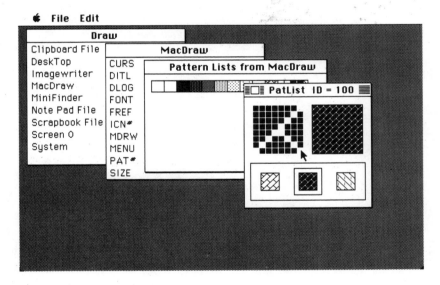

The patterns in MacDraw's Fill and Pen menus are resources that you can edit using the ResEdit program's pattern-editing features.

8. Edit the enlargement of the selected pattern as if it were in MacPaint's pattern-editing window. Click on a black dot to make it white, and click on a white space to make a black dot. You cannot make a pattern larger than eight dots high by eight dots wide. At any time during editing, you can revert to the last saved version of the MacDraw resources by choosing Revert from ResEdit's File menu.

9. When you have finished making changes, choose Quit from ResEdit's File menu. ResEdit asks if you want to save the changes you just made; click Yes or No.

10. After quitting, you'll want to use the Finder to rename the custom version of MacDraw to distinguish it from the regular version.

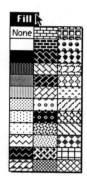

If none of MacDraw's 36 patterns is quite what you want, create your own using the ResEdit program.

The changes you make to MacDraw patterns affect both new and old documents, occurring retroactively in old documents when you open them. The changes are not permanent, however. You can always re-edit the patterns with ResEdit, or reopen old documents with a version of MacDraw that has different patterns.

SHADOWS

Using Trace Edges for shading in MacPaint

Ordinarily, MacPaint's Trace Edges command (from the Edit menu) outlines everything you select with the selection rectangle. If you press the Shift key as you choose Trace Edges, or press Command-Shift-E, you get an outline with a shadow on the right and bottom edges. The difference between using Trace Edges with the Shift key and using it without is similar to the difference between the outline and shadow text styles.

Making shadows

You can add a shadow to any object in a MacPaint picture by using the lasso and the Edit menu, as follows:

1. Lasso the object and choose Copy from the Edit menu, putting a copy of the object on the Clipboard.
2. With the object still lassoed, select a dark pattern for the shadow from the pattern palette and choose Fill from the Edit menu.
3. Choose Paste from the Edit menu to get a copy of the original object from the Clipboard.
4. Drag the copy of the original object over the filled object, leaving just a shadow showing on two adjacent sides.

In MacDraw, you can use a similar technique, except that you don't need to use the Clipboard:

1. Select the object and choose Duplicate from the Edit menu.
2. Choose a dark pattern for the shadow from the Fill menu.

3. Choose Send to Back from the Arrange menu.

4. If necessary, select the original object and choose a nontransparent pattern from the Fill menu.

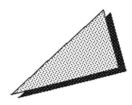

It is easy to add shadows in MacPaint or MacDraw.

LABELS AND OTHER LETTERING

Civilizing MacPaint typing with Note Pad

MacPaint was never meant to be a word processor, but at times you will want to include text in a picture. Since MacPaint has no word-wrap feature, you must keep your eye on the screen as you type and press the Return key when the line you're typing gets too long. Editing is simple, but tedious, consisting of backspacing and retyping. The Note Pad desk accessory is much more civilized, so why not type and edit small amounts of text there, copy the finished text to the Clipboard, and paste it into MacPaint? Be sure to copy from the Note Pad, not cut, so that if necessary you can go back to the Note Pad, edit the text, and paste it again into MacPaint.

Changing the style of text copied to MacPaint

If you copy a text selection from the Note Pad, MacWrite, Microsoft Word, or another word processor onto the Clipboard and then paste it into MacPaint, the text arrives in MacPaint's standard font, style, and size. While the transplanted text is still selected, you can easily change any of those text attributes. Simply choose the attributes you want from the MacPaint menus. You can also change the text's alignment, using the Align Left, Align Center, and Align Right commands in the Style menu.

The dimensions of the selection rectangle into which you paste the text from the Clipboard determine the left, right, top, and bottom margins for the text. When you change the font size or reshape the selection rectangle, the lines of text are reformed automatically to fit within the left and right borders of the selection rectangle. If there is too much text to fit in the rectangle, the excess is chopped off at the bottom, though you can retrieve it by choosing a smaller font size or by stretching the selection rectangle.

There are limitations to the formatting you can do in MacPaint, however. Since the text attributes you choose in MacPaint affect all the selected text, you can't mix fonts, sizes, and styles in the same selection. Also, it is difficult to duplicate the margins, indentation, and tab formatting of a full-fledged word-processing program by adjusting the size of the selection rectangle.

When you want more style...

You can use the Mac's screen snapshot feature to import elaborately formatted text into MacPaint from a word processor such as MacWrite or Microsoft Word without losing the formatting. The text must be copied one screenful at a time and cannot be changed in MacPaint. Here are the steps:

1. Open the word-processing document, scroll the formatted text you want to copy into view, and press Command-Shift-3 to take a snapshot of the screen. The snapshot is saved as a MacPaint document on the same disk as the application program (MacWrite or Microsoft Word) under the name *Screen 0.*

2. Quit the word-processing program. Start up MacPaint, select the text you need from the *Screen 0* document, cut the selection to the Clipboard, and paste it into the final MacPaint document.

If the formatted text is too long to fit on a single screen, you can scroll the next piece of text into view and take another snapshot. When you press Command-Shift-3 again, another MacPaint document, named *Screen 1,* is recorded. You can take up to ten snapshots, named *Screen 0* through *Screen 9,* at a time. A beep when you press Command-Shift-3 means the disk is too full to record another snapshot.

Mixing MacPaint text attributes

Is there an easy way to mix text attributes in MacPaint? If you make changes to the font, size, or style of a piece of text, all the text is affected. You cannot selectively change the style of just a portion of the text. Clicking another insertion point does allow you to change text attributes without affecting the text you've already typed, but it's hard to properly align the insertion point with existing text. Using MacPaint's grid feature helps you position it on the same line, but doesn't help you as far as even spacing between words is concerned.

The answer is to press the Enter key before choosing a different font, size, or style. Attributes of previously typed text are unchanged, but any new text you type has the new attributes and is perfectly aligned with text you were typing when you pressed Enter. You can press Enter as many times as you like while typing a text passage. However, be aware that you can only backspace as far as the last place where you pressed Enter.

Typing text over patterns in MacPaint

Typing directly over a patterned area of a MacPaint picture leaves a white border around the text. To eliminate the surrounding white space, type the text in a vacant area of the picture, lasso it, and drag it over the patterned area. If the patterned area is dark, type the text in outline or shadow style to make it stand out more. If the patterned area or the text is especially large, you may have to type the text in a remote part of the picture (or even a scratch picture), then lasso it, cut it to the Clipboard, and finally paste it into place over the patterned area.

As you drag the text over the patterned area, you'll notice that the hollow parts of letters such as *O* and *e* are filled with white. You can fill those voids with the paint can; FatBits may be helpful in this endeavor.

Creating compact shadow and outline text

If you want a more compact outline-style text than you can obtain with MacPaint's regular Outline option (from the Style menu), select plain text with the selection rectangle and use the Trace Edges command. If you hold down the Shift key while you choose Trace Edges, or press Shift-Command-E, you get a compact shadow-style text.

Normal:	Lafayette, we are here.
Outline:	**Lafayette, we are here.**
Shadow:	**Lafayette, we are here.**
Trace Edges:	**Lafayette, we are here.**
Trace Edges, with Shift:	**Lafayette, we are here.**

MacPaint's Trace Edges command yields compact outline- and shadow-style text.

Ultrabold

Many commercial typefaces come in an "ultrabold" or "heavy bold" weight that is even larger than the regular bold available on the Mac. You can create ultrabold lettering in MacPaint as follows:

1. Choose Outline, and optionally Bold, from MacPaint's Style menu before you type the text.

2. After typing, use the paint can to fill the hollow letters with black or a dark pattern. For small sizes and italics, you may have to do the filling in FatBits.

3. Use the pencil in FatBits to clean up the notches in letters such as *a, e, h, i, n, r, s,* and *T.*

New York Globe

New York Globe

Ultrabold style can be simulated in MacPaint by filling outline-style letters with the paint can and touching up in FatBits.

Patterned MacPaint text

One way of creating fancy titles in a MacPaint document is to change ordinary black text into patterned text. Just lasso the text, click the pattern you want in the pattern palette, and choose Fill from the Edit menu.

White text

Two of the Mac's text styles, outline and shadow, allow you to create white text against a black or patterned background. The procedure is similar in MacPaint and MacDraw:

☐ In MacPaint, choose Outline or Shadow, and optionally Bold, from the Style menu and type the text. Then lasso the text and drag it over the patterned background. Or draw an unfilled shape around the text and, using the paint can, fill it with any pattern.

☐ In MacDraw, type the text (or select some existing text) and choose Outline or Shadow, and optionally Bold, from the Style menu. Then choose a background pattern from the Fill menu. Or drag the text over a patterned object and, if necessary, choose Bring to Front from the Arrange menu.

Mixing MacDraw text attributes

MacDraw treats text typed together as a single object that must have the same font, size, and style attributes. If you want some parts to have different attributes, you must type them separately, choose their attributes, and position them over gaps you have left in the main text.

As you get each insert positioned correctly, group it together with the main text. To do that, hold down the Shift key while you click on the main text and the insert, thereby selecting both, and then choose Group from the Arrange menu. When you finish, you'll be able to move the group of text pieces as a single object, without disturbing the relative positions of the inserts.

MacDraw superscripts and subscripts

MacDraw's Style menu does not include superscript or subscript, but you can fake them with the same technique just described for mixing text attributes. Use a small type size for the superscripted or subscripted text and, when you drag it over the main text, position it slightly above or below the standard line. Don't forget to group the superscript or subscript with the main text by selecting both and choosing Group from the Arrange menu.

Converting MacDraw captions to paragraphs

There are two types of text in MacDraw. When you click a text insertion point using MacDraw's text tool, which has an I-beam-shaped pointer, and then type, you create caption text. Caption text appears on one line unless you start a new line by pressing the Return key. In contrast, when you select an object, such as a rectangle, and then type, you create paragraph text. Line breaks occur automatically in paragraph text so that it fits within the imaginary rectangle that bounds the selected object in which you type it.

Text pasted into a MacDraw document from another application appears as caption text. You can convert it, or any other caption text, to paragraph text as follows:

1. Select the text tool (the I-beam-shaped pointer) by clicking on the T in the tool rack at the left side of the drawing window, and then triple click anywhere on the caption to be converted. (Double clicking selects one word; triple clicking selects the entire caption.)

2. Copy the caption to the Clipboard by choosing Copy from the Edit menu or by pressing Command-C.

3. Draw or select a rectangle and type a few letters to be used as a disposable paragraph. Do not select the text tool or click the mouse button for any other reason before typing the temporary text. Your typing appears inside the rectangle as paragraph text.

4. Select the text tool again and triple click anywhere on the temporary text you just typed inside the rectangle.

5. Replace the selected temporary text with the caption text from the Clipboard by choosing Paste from the Edit menu or by pressing Command-V.

When MacDraw text won't align...

When the Align Objects command won't align caption text with other objects, it may be because there are blank spaces at the beginning of the text. To see the true size of a piece of caption text, select it by clicking on it with the arrow-shaped pointer. Remove extra blank spaces by selecting them with the text tool and then either choosing Clear from the Edit menu or pressing the Backspace key.

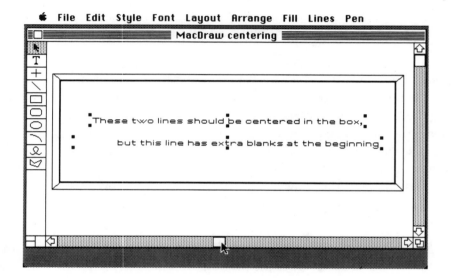

Text with extra blank spaces at the beginning is impossible to align using the Align Objects command in MacDraw's Command menu.

ERASING AND REMOVING

Erasing with the Backspace key

To erase an object you don't want to use again, select it and press the Backspace key. Backspace, like the Clear command in the Edit menu, does not put the selected object on the Clipboard. Thus, you can use it to erase without disturbing the Clipboard.

Detailed erasing in MacPaint

MacPaint's paintbrush tool makes a good eraser. Just pick a pattern to match the background and paint over unwanted parts of a picture. For detail work, select a small brush shape (after choosing Brush Shape from the Goodies menu or double clicking on the paintbrush in the tool rack).

Erasing lines in MacPaint

You can erase black lines by filling them with white paint from MacPaint's paint can. But be ready to undo: If the lines you're erasing touch another part of the picture, it will be erased too!

Erasing with MacPaint rectangles

Use a borderless white rectangle to erase large swaths across the MacPaint drawing window. As you draw the rectangle, you can adjust its size and shape without permanently erasing what it covers. When its size and shape are just right, release the mouse button to finalize the erasure.

Massive MacPaint erasures

You can erase large sections of a MacPaint document from the Show Page view. To be safe, save your document just before erasing from Show Page. Erasures done in Show Page cannot be undone, and the lack of detail makes it easy to erase erroneously. If you save first, you can always use the Revert command to undo.

None of the tools or menus is available in the Show Page view, but you can slide everything on the page to a new position. Just place the pointer outside the dotted-line rectangle and drag. To erase, simply slide part or all of the picture off the page and click OK.

Hiding objects with MacDraw masks

There is no way to erase part of an object in MacDraw, but you can hide part of one object with another. The object that does the hiding is called a mask. A mask can be any simple object—a rectangle, oval, freeform shape, polygon, and so on—or it can be a composite of several simple objects. Once a mask is in place, you should select it and the object it covers and then choose Group from the Arrange menu, so both objects will be treated as one.

MOVING AND COPYING

Constraining movement

By selecting part of a MacPaint picture with the lasso or selection rectangle and then dragging it with the pointer, you can move it any direction. This freedom of movement is often an advantage, but not when you're trying to move one part of a picture parallel with another to keep the parts aligned. You can keep the parts parallel, however, if you constrain the movement to a horizontal or vertical direction by pressing the Shift key before you start to drag the pointer. Once you start to drag, you can release the Shift key. You can't change direction once you start dragging, so be ready to undo and start over if you find yourself heading the wrong way.

You can also constrain movement in MacDraw. If you press the Shift key after you start to drag an object, MacDraw keeps the object aligned with its initial location, either on a vertical, horizontal, or 45-degree diagonal line, whichever is closer.

Making the MacPaint pointer less obtrusive

Does the arrow-shaped pointer get in the way when dragging a small lassoed object in MacPaint? Once you have used the lasso to select an object inside the drawing window, you can place the pointer out of the way near the edge of the window and still drag the object wherever you need it. Try this:

1. After lassoing, move the lasso-shaped pointer toward the left edge of the window. As the pointer approaches the edge, it becomes an arrow.

2. The instant the pointer changes to an arrow, stop, press the mouse button, and drag the selection by remote control. For best results, position the pointer exactly over the left edge of the drawing window before you press the mouse button and drag. If you accidentally move the pointer too far before pressing the mouse button, the remote-control feature does not work. If you don't move the pointer far enough and press the mouse button while it is still lasso-shaped, the lassoed object is deselected.

Making foreground objects appear transparent

Sometimes when you drag one object over another, you will want the background object to show through the voids in the foreground object. For example, the eyes on a face should show through when you give the face a pair of glasses.

To achieve this transparency in MacPaint, you must make sure none of the voids in the foreground object is completely enclosed before you lasso and drag it. Otherwise the lasso selects the voids as white spaces and they end up obscuring the background object. Proceed as follows:

1. Create a temporary path from each void to the outside edge of the foreground object. For example, you would need to cut the frames of the glasses before lassoing them.
2. Drag the object into place on top of the background object. The background object is able to fill the voids in the foreground object by flowing along the temporary paths.
3. Touch up the foreground object to remove the temporary paths.

MacPaint duplicates

To make several separate and complete copies of an object in MacPaint, select the object, hold down the Option key, and drag away a copy. Once you have started dragging, you can release the Option key. When you release the mouse button, the copy of the object is selected instead of the original. You can make another copy by again holding down the Option key and dragging the selected object.

MacPaint multiples

In MacPaint, dragging a selected object while holding down both the Command and Option keys creates continuous multiple copies of the selected object. The essential word here is continuous. If you drag the selected object slowly, each new copy overlaps most of the previous copy. If you drag quickly, the copies overlap less. If you drag erratically, you will get sporadic, out-of-sequence, chaotic fragments of the selection instead of multiple copies.

The line-width palette in the lower left corner of the screen also affects the amount of overlap, as you can see in the following figure. Less overlap occurs if you select one of the thicker line widths.

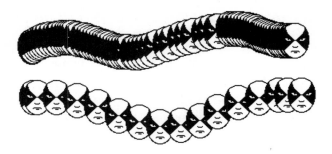

Dragging an object in MacPaint while holding down the Command and Option keys creates continuous multiple copies of the object. The speed at which you drag the object and the line width selected control the amount of overlap between copies.

Gauging movement of groups of objects in MacDraw

If you want to drag a group of objects in MacDraw, start by pointing to the component of the group that will best enable you to tell whether the group is correctly positioned in its new location. When you start to drag the group, a dotted-line rectangle that shows the group's overall size and location moves with the pointer. Inside the rectangle, an outline of the component at which you were pointing when you started to drag allows you to gauge how far and in which direction to move.

If you start by pointing at a piece of text, a freehand shape, or a polygon, MacDraw uses a rectangle that represents its overall size and position within the group selection. All other components are represented by their true outlines.

If you want to see MacDraw objects as you drag them...

If you want to see outlines of the MacDraw objects you are dragging, instead of the usual generic rectangle, hold down the Option key as you start to drag. All types of objects, including text, freehand shapes, and polygons, are represented by their true outlines.

Holding down the Option key continuously greatly slows the speed at which objects move on the screen, especially when you're dragging a complex object such as a smoothed polygon. To speed things up, just press the Option key when you want to take a reading on the exact location of the object or objects you are dragging, rather than continuously.

Equally spaced MacDraw duplicates

If you duplicate an object by choosing Duplicate from MacDraw's Edit menu or by pressing Command-D, MacDraw watches to see what you do next. If you move the copy of the object, MacDraw remembers where you moved it in relation to the original object. Then, if you use the Duplicate command again, MacDraw places the third object in the same position relative to the second object as the second is to the first. This makes it easy to create a series of equally spaced objects.

To take advantage of this feature, you must create the entire series of objects before doing anything else. If, for example, you draw a new object or select an existing one between uses of the Duplicate command, MacDraw forgets the relative position of the duplicated objects and cannot guarantee that any subsequent duplicates will also be equally spaced.

LAYOUT

MacPaint's grid feature

Ever wonder about the grid feature in MacPaint's Goodies menu? It's barely mentioned in the MacPaint user's manual, but it has several important uses.

Choosing Grid from MacPaint's Goodies menu imposes an invisible grid on the drawing window. Pointer movement for some tools is constrained to the grid lines, as if the drawing window were a piece of graph paper and the pointer could only move along the lines or jump from line to line. The invisible grid lines are eight dots apart, so the pointer moves eight dots at a time instead of one, making it easy to position parts of a picture by eye. The grid feature only affects the following operations:

- ☐ Selecting, dragging, and duplicating with the selection rectangle.
- ☐ Selecting a text insertion point with the I-beam pointer.
- ☐ Drawing straight lines.
- ☐ Drawing rectangles, rounded-corner rectangles, ovals, and polygons (but not freehand shapes).
- ☐ Dragging and duplicating an object selected by the lasso. However, the grid does not affect the process of selecting with the lasso.

Temporary alignment aids

You can draw temporary lines and rulers to make it easier to align and space objects. They are especially helpful in MacPaint, which has no built-in rulers or alignment commands.

Importing a ruler

MacPaint can't help you measure parts of your picture, but you can get around this deficiency by temporarily importing ready-made rulers from MacDraw. To display a copy of a MacDraw ruler, do this:

1. Start MacDraw and choose Show Rulers from the Layout menu. Change the ruler calibration if you like, using the Custom Ruler command in the Layout menu.
2. Scroll the MacDraw window to the upper left corner and take a snapshot of the screen by pressing Command-Shift-3.
3. Quit MacDraw, start MacPaint, and open the screen snapshot document, which is stored on the MacDraw disk under the name *Screen 0.*
4. Select the ruler and cut it to the Clipboard.
5. Paste the ruler into the Scrapbook for later use, or paste it directly into the MacPaint document where you need it.

You could import MacWrite's formatting ruler in a similar manner, but there's a drawback to using MacWrite's rulers: An inch on the MacWrite ruler measures 1.11 inches in MacPaint.

Rulers and coordinates

If you often create MacPaint pictures that need precise measurements, you'll be interested to know about a desk accessory called Rulers that displays rulers along the sides and bottom edges of the MacPaint picture window. Rulers, which is part of Accessory Pak I from Silicon Beach Software, offers a choice of three calibration scales: inches, centimeters, or pixels. A thin gray line in each ruler tracks the movement of the pointer in the MacPaint drawing window, letting you know precisely where you are, both vertically and horizontally.

The same software package also includes a desk accessory called Coordinates that displays the location of the pointer relative to the upper left corner of the screen (not the upper left corner of the drawing window). The pointer's coordinates are displayed at the right end of the menu bar. You can choose whether the coordinates are reported in inches, centimeters,or pixels.

Centering one object on another

The Align Objects command in MacDraw's Arrange menu makes it easy to center two or more objects on one another. Simply select both L/R Centers and T/B Centers in the Align Centers dialog box.

In MacPaint, you can't center several objects on one another in the same operation. However, you can center them, one at a time, in the middle of the drawing window. If you center them in order of size, starting with the largest, they will be coincidentally centered on each other.

To center an object in the drawing window, select it with the lasso, cut it, and immediately paste it.

Adjusting MacDraw's grid spacing

MacDraw's invisible grid makes it relatively easy to control the size and position of objects as you draw them, but if the grid lines are too widely spaced, you may not be able to accurately size and place objects. If this is the case, you may want to turn off the grid from the Layout menu or change its spacing.

The spacing of MacDraw's grid lines is determined by the number of minor divisions selected in the Custom Rulers dialog box. The more divisions, the less distance between the invisible grid lines. Initially, there are eight minor divisions, making the invisible grid lines ⅛ inch apart. Follow these steps to change the spacing:

1. Choose Custom Rulers from the Layout menu.
2. In the dialog box that appears, select the Custom option. The dialog box expands, revealing more settings.
3. Select the number of minor divisions you want and click OK.

Note that the MacDraw rulers might not show all the minor divisions you select. For example, if you set grid-line spacing at ⅟₃₂ inch, the rulers show minor divisions only every ⅟₁₆ inch. The finer grid lines are there, even though they're not marked on the rulers.

Finding a lost MacDraw object

Have you ever lost an object in MacDraw? Here are three ways to find a small object that is hidden behind a larger object:

☐ Select the object you can see and choose the None pattern from the Fill menu.

☐ Select the object you can see and choose Send to Back from the Arrange menu.

☐ Drag the object you can see off to the side.

MacDraw alignment rules

Ever wonder how MacDraw decides where to align objects when you use the Align Objects command? Here is a list of its rules:

Option	Aligns with
Left Sides	Left edge of leftmost object
Right Sides	Right edge of rightmost object
Tops	Top edge of topmost object
Bottoms	Bottom edge of bottom-most object
L/R Centers	Halfway between leftmost and rightmost objects
T/B Centers	Halfway between topmost and bottom-most objects

Aligning large MacDraw objects

To align objects that are too large to all fit in a MacDraw window at once, use a reduced view, as follows:

1. Choose Reduce or Reduce to Fit from the Layout menu.
2. Select the objects and then choose Align Objects from the Arrange menu.

RESIZING

New size and shape in MacPaint

You can stretch or shrink everything inside MacPaint's selection rectangle by dragging on or inside the flashing edge of the rectangle while holding down the Command key. To resize horizontally, drag from a side edge. To resize vertically, drag from the top or bottom edge. To resize both horizontally and vertically, drag from a corner. There will be some distortion of lines and patterns inside a resized selection rectangle, so be ready to undo should you dislike the results.

New size, same shape in MacPaint

You can keep the ratio of height to width constant while you stretch or shrink a MacPaint selection rectangle. Just hold down the Command and Shift keys as you start to drag a corner of the selection rectangle.

Using the three-finger stretch in MacPaint

It's possible to stretch just the middle of an object in MacPaint, so that the two opposite ends of the object are unchanged and parallel lines connect them. For example, a circle can be widened into a shape that has semicircular sides and straight top and bottom edges. Here's the general procedure:

1. Use the selection rectangle to select one end of the object: the left end if you want to stretch horizontally to the left, the top end if you want to stretch vertically upward, and so on.
2. Holding down the Command, Option, and Shift keys, drag the selection rectangle slowly in the direction of the stretch. As you drag, parallel lines appear in the wake of the selection rectangle.

If you drag too quickly, the parallel lines may be jagged. In that case, drag slowly back in the other direction, far enough to clean up the jaggedness, and then drag ahead again. This method has been dubbed the "three-finger stretch" by MacPaint's creator, Bill Atkinson.

In MacPaint, you can widen or heighten an object by selecting one side and using the
"three-finger stretch" (dragging while holding down Control-Option-Shift).

Combining the MacPaint grid with the three-finger stretch

Results of the three-finger stretch are unsatisfactory with patterned objects, because the pattern is disrupted. To maintain the pattern, make sure Grid is checked in MacPaint's Goodies menu.

Original   With grid off   With grid on

To retain pattern uniformity in a stretched MacPaint object, choose Grid from
the Goodies menu, select one end of the object, hold down Command-Option-Shift,
and then drag.

Automatically resizing while pasting in MacPaint

You can preset the size, shape, and location of an object you plan to paste into a MacPaint picture from the Clipboard. Before using the Paste command, draw a selection rectangle the size and shape you want the imported object to have and put the selection rectangle where you want the object to be. When you paste, MacPaint automatically resizes the contents of the Clipboard to fit within the selection rectangle.

Shrinking full-page MacPaint pictures

By applying the Mac's built-in screen-snapshot feature to MacPaint's Show Page view, you can reduce an 8- by 10-inch picture to 2⅔ by 3⅓ inches. Since the Show Page view compresses most of the detail out of a picture, this technique works best with large, simple drawings. To try out this technique, follow these steps:

1. Switch to the Show Page view by double clicking on the grabber or by choosing Show Page from the Goodies menu.

2. Drag the dotted-line rectangle in the Show Page view out of the way as much as possible and take a snapshot of the screen by pressing Command-Shift-3. The snapshot is saved on the MacPaint disk.

3. Cancel the Show Page view, close the picture window, and open the screen-snapshot document.

4. Find the reduced image of your full-page picture and touch it up as needed.

5. Select the reduced image with the lasso or selection rectangle and copy it to the Clipboard.

6. Close the drawing window, open the document into which you want to copy the reduced image, and paste.

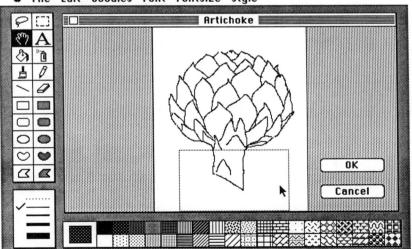

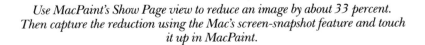

Use MacPaint's Show Page view to reduce an image by about 33 percent.
Then capture the reduction using the Mac's screen-snapshot feature and touch
it up in MacPaint.

Expanding drawing-window pictures to full-page

MacPaint's drawing window shows less than a third of the available drawing page. With moderate effort, you can enlarge a MacPaint picture from drawing-window size to full-page size. You work with the original picture a third at a time, from left to right, as follows:

1. Using the selection rectangle, select a third of the drawing window. For best results, the selection should be the full height of the drawing window and exactly one-third its width. The drawing window is 415 dots (5¾ inches) wide, so the selection should be 138 dots (1¹⁵⁄₁₆ inches) wide. (For help measuring in MacPaint, use the Rulers desk accessory, which is part of Accessory Pak I from Silicon Beach Software.)

2. Drag the selection to the middle of the screen. Because the drawing window is oriented horizontally and full pages are oriented vertically, choose Rotate from the Edit menu.

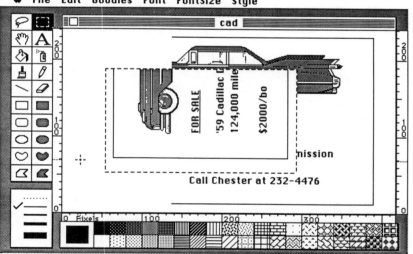

To enlarge a picture in MacPaint's drawing window to full-page size, first cut it vertically into thirds, then rotate each third, and save each third in the Scrapbook.

3. Cut the rotated selection to the Clipboard and then paste the clipping into the Scrapbook.

4. Repeat steps 1 through 3 for the remaining two thirds of the picture.

5. In the Show Page view, press the Shift key and drag the dotted-line rectangle to the top of the page. Click OK to return to the regular drawing window.

6. From the Scrapbook, cut the third of the original picture that was at the right side of the drawing window.

7. Select the entire drawing window by double clicking the selection rectangle tool in the tool rack to the left of the drawing window, then paste. MacPaint automatically resizes the clipping to fit the large selection rectangle.

8. Repeat steps 5 through 7 pasting the middle and left thirds of the original picture into the middle and bottom thirds of the page, respectively. Be sure to use the Shift key to prevent horizontal movement as you scroll the dotted-line rectangle vertically to a new position on the page. If necessary, you can use the grabber tool to precisely position the regular drawing window before selecting the entire window in step 7.

After pasting the pieces into position, you should save your work. Use the Save As command to save it under a different name. Then check for gaps between the middle third and the top and bottom thirds. Eliminate any gaps by lassoing the top and bottom thirds and dragging them toward the middle. If necessary, touch up jagged lines and blotchy patterns using any of MacPaint's tools and commands.

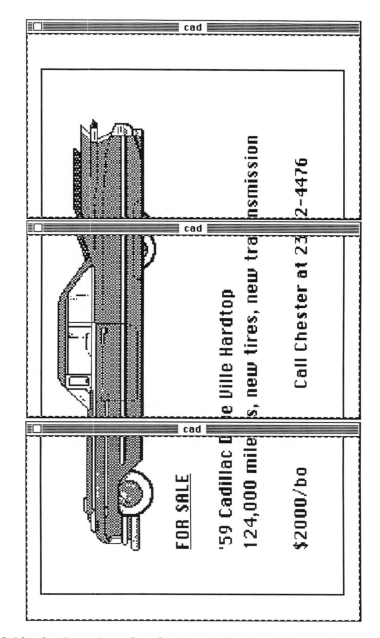

To finish enlarging a picture from drawing-window size to full-page size, paste each rotated third of the original picture into a third of the page. MacPaint will resize each segment automatically.

Enhancing MacPaint enlargements

The enlargements you produce in MacPaint by dragging a selection rectangle while pressing the Command key are pretty crude. You can touch them up with the paintbrush and other tools, but there is a more mechanical approach that yields good results with proportional enlargements that are some exact multiple—two, three, four, and so on—of the original. First you make the crude enlargement and then you thin its blocky texture, as follows:

1. Create a gauge for enlargement by arranging copies of the original side by side. For example, to triple the size of the object, arrange three copies of the original next to each other.

2. Select the leftmost original with the selection rectangle and proportionally enlarge it by pressing the Command and Shift keys as you start to drag the lower right corner. Continue to drag until the enlargement covers the rightmost copy of the original. The large, blocky dots in the enlargement should be uniform in size.

3. Start thinning by inverting the crude enlargement with the Invert command from the Edit menu. This yields a negative image of the crude enlargement.

4. Using a borderless filled rectangle with the third pattern from the left in the top row of the standard pattern palette, hold down the Command key and draw a transparent screen over the entire negative image.

5. Invert the negative image to get a light positive image. Save your work now so you can revert to this point later.

6. Now darken the light positive image by lassoing it, holding down the Option key, and dragging a copy one or two dots away. Release the mouse button without moving the mouse.

7. The light positive image is still selected. Darken it still more by holding down the Option key again and dragging another copy of the image a dot or two in another direction. Release the mouse button without moving the mouse.

8. Repeat step 7 until you get the look you want. You'll have to experiment. If you completely clobber the enlargement, the File menu's Revert command lets you go back to the single light positive image you saved in step 5, so you can begin darkening anew.

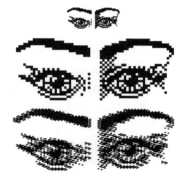

MacPaint's coarse enlargements can be enhanced without a lot of freehand touchup work, providing a smoother transition from black to white. (Eyes by Mark Stephen Pierce. Reproduced by permission from Art Grabber and Body Shop [Cambridge, MA: SPINNAKER Software Corp., 1986], Female Disguise Kit.)

Easy MacPaint enlargements

While it's possible to enlarge part of a MacPaint picture using MacPaint tools and commands, it's not always easy and the results can be somewhat crude. Another program, PaintMover by Bill Atkinson, can enlarge part of a MacPaint picture from 1 to 16 times. The maximum size of the enlargement is 8 by 10 inches, the same as a standard MacPaint document, and PaintMover restricts the size of the area being enlarged according to the magnification factor, so you know how large an area will fit on the 8- by 10-inch page. It optionally thins, smooths, or both thins and smooths the enlargement for better-looking results.

Creating jumbo MacDraw pictures with MacPaint components

Many individual MacPaint documents can be copied and pasted into one MacDraw document, creating one large picture. MacDraw can print the large picture full-size or half-size, using as many sheets of paper as necessary. You then tape together the sheets of paper to form the whole picture.

Each MacPaint picture must be transferred to the composite MacDraw document via the Clipboard. MacPaint's small drawing window forces you to chop each picture into as many as six pieces. Copying and pasting each piece separately takes forever unless you use the Switcher to switch between MacPaint and MacDraw. An alternative method is to copy all the pieces from the MacPaint picture to the Scrapbook, then copy the Scrapbook file, which is inside the System Folder, from the MacPaint disk to the MacDraw disk, and finally copy and paste the pieces from the Scrapbook to the MacDraw document.

Copying MacPaint pictures into MacDraw is much easier with the QuickPaint desk accessory from EnterSet, which allows you to copy fairly large pieces of any MacPaint document without quitting MacDraw. For the most efficient copying of full-width or full-height MacPaint pictures—up to 8 by 10 inches—use the Art Grabber desk accessory from SPINNAKER Software, or use the Paint Cutter program, which is part of Accessory Pak 1 from Silicon Beach, preferably with the Switcher.

You should paste the MacPaint pictures into MacDraw beginning with the top left section of the composite picture. MacDraw initially positions all pasted objects in the middle of the drawing window, but you can move them to align them properly. Before attempting to align objects, choose Turn Grid Off from the Layout menu, so the objects will not be forced to move in ⅛-inch increments.

Use the scroll bars to bring additional MacDraw document space into view in the drawing window. If you scroll to the right or bottom edge of the document and still need more space, choose Picture Size from MacDraw's Layout menu to enlarge the document.

Resizing or moving?

When moving, stretching, or shrinking a line or other object that extends out of the MacDraw window, it's difficult to tell whether you're changing its size or moving it. Choose Show Size from the Layout menu and watch the numbers as you manipulate the line. If they change, you're resizing the line, not moving it.

Precise enlargement and reduction

Scaling an object in MacDraw is easy, if you take advantage of the Show Size feature and use a temporary 1-inch square as a gauge. You can get reductions and enlargements accurate to the nearest whole percent or so by following these steps:

1. Choose Show Size from the Layout menu.
2. Draw a 1-inch square near the object to be scaled. Use the dimensions provided by the Show Size command to tell when the square is exactly 1 inch high and wide.
3. Select both the square and the object to be scaled.
4. Scale the square, and the other object along with it, by dragging one of the square's corner handles. Watch the square's dimensions as you drag. Stop dragging when both the height and width correspond to the percentage reduction or enlargement you want to obtain; for example, 0.50 for a 50 percent reduction or 2.00 for a 200 percent enlargement.
5. Cancel the current selection by clicking in any vacant area of the drawing window, then select the square and press the Backspace key to erase it.

CONSTRUCTING OBJECTS

Equilateral triangles

The following method for constructing an equilateral triangle in MacPaint makes use of three equal circles:

1. Draw a small circle and put a dot at its center. For best results, draw the circle with the grid feature activated and make the circle an even number of grid units in diameter.
2. Lasso the circle, hold down the Option and Shift keys, and drag a copy of the circle to one side so that it just touches the original circle.
3. With the duplicate circle still lassoed, hold down the Option key (but not the Shift key) and drag a copy of the circle to where it just touches the other two circles.
4. Erase the circles, leaving the center dots. Connect the dots using the polygon tool. The resulting triangle is equilateral.

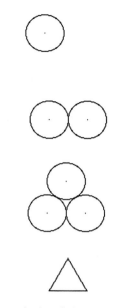

You can construct an equilateral triangle in MacPaint by connecting the centers of three equal circles, each of which just touches the other two.

If the triangle you construct is too large, just draw a horizontal line above the existing base and erase whatever you don't need. If the triangle is too small, extend the sides, add another base below the existing one, and then erase the existing base. You could use the selection rectangle and, holding down the Command and Shift keys, drag the triangle to another size, but doing that distorts the lines that make up the sides of the triangle.

Concentric shapes

You can construct a series of equally spaced concentric circles, squares, ovals, or rectangles without measuring. Here are the instructions for drawing equally spaced concentric circles in MacPaint:

1. Draw a 45-degree line across the window (hold down the Shift key as you start to draw).
2. At the top of the diagonal line, draw two short horizontal lines to mark off the distance you want between two circles.

3.   Lasso the segment of the diagonal line that contains the two marks, including the marks in the selection.

4.   Hold down the Option key, drag away a copy of the selected segment, and place the copy on the diagonal line so that the upper mark on the copy coincides with the lowest mark on the original.

5.   Repeat step 4 until the entire diagonal line has been marked off.

6.   Lasso the diagonal line with its marks, and choose Copy from the Edit menu to put a copy of the diagonal line on the Clipboard. You will use the copy to erase the original after drawing the circles.

7.   Draw the circles, starting and ending them only where a mark crosses the diagonal line. The circles themselves do not cross at the marks, but the invisible squares that bound them do.

8.   Erase the diagonal line and the horizontal marks. To erase with the copy of the diagonal line from the Clipboard, choose Paste from the Edit menu and drag the copy that appears exactly over the original diagonal line. While the copy is still selected, choose Invert from the Edit menu. Then click the mouse button anywhere, and the line is gone.

You can draw squares in step 7 instead of circles. If you want ovals or rectangles, draw the diagonal line in step 1 on some angle other than 45 degrees.

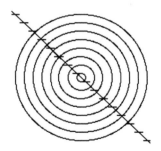

Using a diagonal line as a guide, you can draw equally spaced concentric circles, squares, ovals, and rectangles. The same basic method works in MacPaint and MacDraw.

A similar method works in MacDraw. The only variation is in the way the diagonal line and the horizontal marks are constructed and erased:

1. Draw a 45-degree line across the window (hold down the Shift key as you start to draw).

2. Draw a horizontal line across the top of the diagonal line.

3. Duplicate the horizontal line and drag the copy down the diagonal line to mark the distance you want between circles.

4. Duplicate again and again, until the entire diagonal line is marked off. MacDraw makes duplicates on a 45-degree line best with the grid on (use the Layout menu) at two times the grid interval. Otherwise you may have to drag the duplicates left or right until they cross the diagonal line.

5. Select all the lines, including the diagonal, by holding down the Shift key as you click on each in turn. Then choose Group from the Arrange menu so that all the lines will be treated as a single object.

6. Choose the None pattern from the Fill menu and draw the circles. Start and end them only where a mark crosses the diagonal line. The circles themselves do not cross at the marks, but the invisible squares that bound them do.

7. Select the group of lines and press the Backspace key to erase them.

Symmetry

You can draw a symmetrical object with MacPaint's paintbrush by turning on the brush-mirrors feature. MacDraw has no brush mirrors, but you can construct a symmetrical object in MacDraw as follows:

1. Draw half of the object—left or right for horizontal symmetry, or top or bottom for vertical symmetry.

2. Duplicate the half.

3. Flip the duplicate horizontally or vertically, as appropriate, to get the opposite half.

4. Put the two halves together and group them.

When you need symmetry on both horizontal and vertical axes, apply the method above to one quarter of the object to create a symmetrical half. Then apply the method to the symmetrical half to create a completely symmetrical whole.

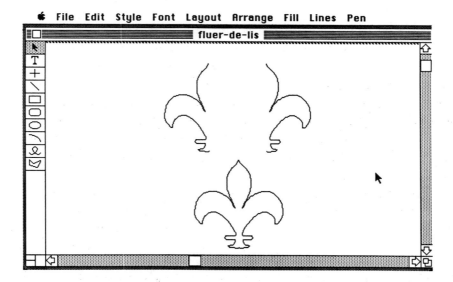

With MacDraw's Duplicate and Flip commands (from the Edit and Arrange menus), you can easily create symmetrical objects.

Blocking closure of a MacDraw polygon

When you are using MacDraw's polygon tool, clicking on an existing corner or the starting point of the polygon normally means you've finished and want MacDraw to complete the polygon. If instead you want to keep drawing, hold down the Option key as you click on the corner or starting point.

Creating curves from smoothed MacDraw lines

You can take advantage of MacDraw's Smooth and Reshape commands (from the Edit menu) to draw curved objects. Here's how:

1. Start by drawing an approximation of the curved object using either the freehand tool or the polygon tool. If you use the polygon tool, you'll find that

lots of short sides and wide-angled corners produce the best approximations (remember the connect-the-dots drawings from childhood?).

2. Choose Smooth from the Edit menu to smooth your rough picture. (Smoothing a freehand shape converts it to a smoothed polygon.)

3. Choose Reshape Polygon from the Edit menu. MacDraw displays a handle (black square) at each "corner" of the smoothed shape.

4. Drag the handles to change the object's shape. If you miss the handles and drag the edge of the shape, the object moves. Watch for this, since you may want to undo the move and try again.

As you begin reshaping, the object is redrawn with no fill pattern so you can see through it (even if it had no fill pattern to begin with). This takes a few seconds, so be patient with your first adjustment. When you finish reshaping and click elsewhere, the original fill pattern (if any) is restored.

Designating unsmoothable MacDraw cusps

Using MacDraw's polygon tool and Smooth command, you can create an object that has some smooth curves and some angular corners. You must designate the unsmoothable corners, called cusps, as you draw the object; you cannot conveniently go back and designate them once you've finished drawing.

You designate a cusp by holding down the Option key and double clicking. Corners so designated will not be smoothed when you later choose Smooth from the Edit menu. Any corner at which you click only once, with or without the Option key, is not a cusp and will be smoothed. Double clicking without holding down the Option key ends the polygon.

When you select a smoothed object with cusps and choose Reshape Polygon from the Edit menu, the cusps do not seem to have handles. Actually, each cusp has two handles stacked one on top of the other, making them both invisible. You can drag the cusp handles apart in order to turn the cusp into two smoothed corners. You can also drag two handles together to form a cusp, but you lose one corner in the process.

Retaining detail in smoothed MacDraw objects

The Smooth command in MacDraw's Edit window can help get rid of unwanted roughness in a freehand picture. Sometimes, though, it smooths out the detail along with the roughness. You can retain more of the detail by smoothing after enlarging, as follows:

1. Draw a small square near the object to be enlarged and select both the object and the square.
2. Choose Show Size from the Layout menu so you can keep track of the square's size as you change it.
3. Enlarge the square to several times its original size.
4. Choose Smooth from the Edit menu.
5. Reduce the square to its original size.

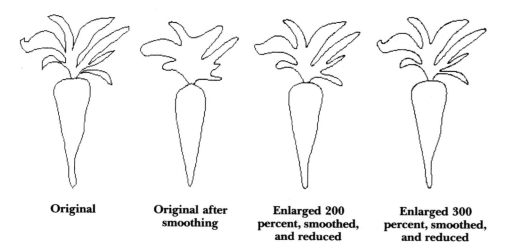

| Original | Original after smoothing | Enlarged 200 percent, smoothed, and reduced | Enlarged 300 percent, smoothed, and reduced |

To retain detail in a smoothed MacDraw object, enlarge it two or three times before smoothing, then reduce it to its original size.

The price you pay for smoothing

Use MacDraw's Smooth command sparingly. Because smoothed objects take longer to display, they slow down scrolling of the window and are slow to move. Smoothed objects also use more memory than unsmoothed ones.

ANIMATION AND SPECIAL EFFECTS

Using Undo for cheap animation

You can get really cheap animation in MacPaint by exploiting the Undo feature. Using a piece of clip art, one of the pictorial fonts such as Cairo, or something you have drawn yourself, you create two slightly different versions of a picture. Then you paste one version over the other and press the Tilde key, MacPaint's "undo" key. *Voila!* The picture appears to move. Here are step-by-step instructions:

1. Draw a picture and, to facilitate aligning it later with a second picture, draw a border around it at the edge of the window.

2. Double click the selection-rectangle tool to select the entire picture, then copy the picture to the Clipboard.

3. Use the Show Page view or the grabber to move to a vacant spot on the page, where you can draw the second picture.

4. Create the second picture by pasting the first picture from the Clipboard and making minor changes to it. Save the document at this point.

5. Paste the first picture exactly over the second and click on any tool to cancel the flashing selection rectangle.

6. Hold down the Tilde key and watch your picture move.

Change the Key Repeat Rate in the Control Panel desk accessory to slow down or speed up the animation. A slow rate yields the most convincing results.

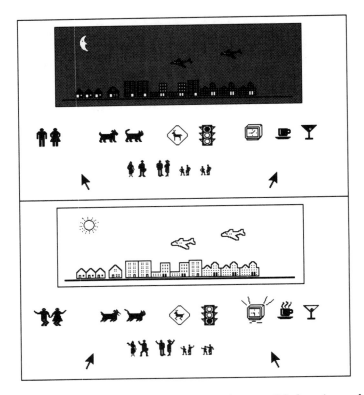

Paste a slightly modified version of a picture over the unmodified version and then hold down the Tilde key to make the picture "move."

Paste-anywhere animation

You may have noticed that it takes several seconds to display complicated MacDraw documents. This feature of MacDraw versions 1.7 and 1.9 makes it possible for you to assemble animated drawings in MacDraw for use in the Scrapbook and elsewhere. Be forewarned: This is tedious work! When you finish, you'll have gained a new appreciation for Walt Disney's animators.

You start by breaking down an action into a sequence of discrete events and drawing a separate picture for each event. The pictures are called frames. The frames might be a sample sequence of overlapping MacDraw objects, each one larger than the one before. Or they might be a sequence of small objects that fit together to make a larger object. To animate detailed drawings, you can draw each frame as a MacPaint picture and then import the pictures into MacDraw. Or you can compose a frame with MacDraw's polygon tool; round corners as needed with the Edit menu's Smooth command. Then create a new frame with the Duplicate command, and advance the motion of arms, legs, and so on by changing the objects with the Edit menu's Reshape command.

Generally, you must put a blank frame between every action frame; otherwise, each successive frame is overlaid on top of the one before it. However, you don't need a blank frame between action frames if the only action is growth of a nontransparent object, such as a rising thermometer, because in that case the growth in the second frame masks or adds to the condition shown in the first frame.

The shape of the blank frames affects timing. For fastest action, use borderless white rectangles for the blank frames. Slow the action down by using complex borderless shapes, such as polygons, instead of simple rectangles. Be careful not to make the blank shape too complex, or the animation will flicker. Smoothing the polygons yields a slow-motion effect.

The easiest way to handle a blank frame is to group it with the action frame that comes before it. Before grouping them, align the blank and action frames at their left/right centers and along their bottoms.

When you have paired a blank frame with every action frame that needs one, you are ready to stage the frames. If any of the action frames are obscured by blanks, you'll want to temporarily make the blanks transparent. To do that, select everything with the Select All command, choose None from the Fill menu, and choose the second line width from the Line menu. Move the frames into position one by one, starting with the frame you want displayed first. As you place each frame, use the Bring to Front command to make sure the desired frame is in front of all earlier frames.

Alignment of the frames is vital for realistic animation. If all the action occurs on a straight line, "ground" all the frames by selecting them all and then aligning their bottoms. If the sequence travels across the screen, do not align their side edges or left/right centers. If the sequence is stationary, however, the frames must be aligned at their left/right centers in addition to their bottoms.

After aligning the frames, select them all, and choose the white pattern from the Fill menu and the top line width from the Lines menu. Rerun your completed sequence by clicking either of the scroll boxes. If you're satisfied with the performance, group all the frames in the sequence. If not, pull the sequence apart and correct the faulty frames.

You can lengthen a performance by combining and repeating sequences. For example, if you have a sequence of six frames that show a dog walking ¾ inch across the screen, you can lengthen the dog's trip to 6 inches by duplicating the sequence seven times. To repeat a sequence, duplicate all the frames in it. Arrange the duplicates for continuous motion by placing each duplicate sequence a distance from the start of the foregoing sequence that is equal to the distance between the first and last frames of the original sequence. Thus, if the sequence moved ¾ inch across the screen, you would position a duplicate sequence ¾ inch from the start of the first frame in the sequence that precedes it.

The animation you assemble in MacDraw can be cut and pasted anywhere MacDraw objects are allowed, including into the Scrapbook, MacWrite, and Microsoft Word.

These nine figures, drawn in MacPaint, can be assembled into an animation sequence in MacDraw, which can then be pasted anywhere MacDraw objects are allowed. (Figures by Mark Stephen Pierce. Reproduced by permission of VideoWorks [Cambridge MA: SPINNAKER Software Corp., 1986], Sports file on Art disk.)

Pattern-variation animation

The patterns you use for shading or texture in a MacPaint picture can produce special effects, including animation and hidden messages. The special effects are achieved by drawing several objects, or several parts of one object, each in a different variation of a pattern. The pattern variations all look the same against a white background, but when dragged across a certain background pattern, they alternately stand out or disappear. The pattern variations are created by shifting the dots in the eight-by-eight pattern definition slightly in various directions. The necessary background pattern is the inverse, or negative image, of any one of the variations.

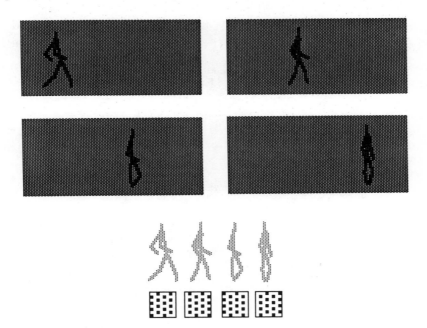

In MacPaint, objects drawn with different variations of a pattern alternately stand out and disappear as they are dragged across certain background patterns. Here, figures are drawn in four variations of a standard light gray pattern (left to right): the standard pattern, standard shifted one dot up and right, standard shifted one dot up, and standard shifted one dot down and right. The figures are shown against a background of the standard pattern inverted.

Not all patterns have the same number of variations. An all-black pattern has one variation; any way you shift it, it stays all black. At the other extreme, a pattern with one black dot has 64 variations, because there are 64 places to put the dot in an eight-dot-by-eight-dot pattern block. Regular patterns between those extremes have 2, 4, 8, 16, or 32 variations.

Hidden messages

You can use pattern variation-shifting to send a hidden message. All you do is write the message using one variation of a pattern and camouflage it with random lines drawn in a different variation. Be careful not to write over the message as you camouflage it. The hidden message is revealed by lassoing the camouflaged version and dragging it over a background pattern made of any variation of the pattern.

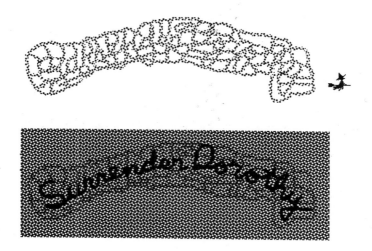

A message can be camouflaged by drawing random lines in a different variation of the pattern used to write the message. Lassoing and dragging the message over a background made of any variation of the same pattern reveals the message.

Spreadsheets

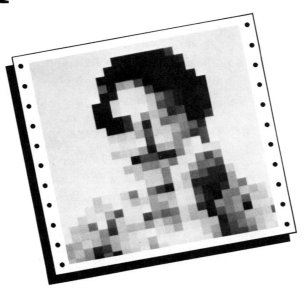

Some people call them spreadsheets, some call them worksheets—and still others call them names! Whatever you call them, try the hints in this chapter the next time you work with a collection of formulas, numbers, and bits of text all arranged in orderly rows and columns of cells.

SELECTING

Extending selection past window borders

All spreadsheet programs let you select a block of cells by dragging the pointer from the cell in one corner of the block to the cell in the diagonally opposite corner. With most programs, you can extend the selection into an area out of view by dragging the pointer into the column headings, the row headings, or one of the scroll bars. The spreadsheet scrolls automatically as long as you hold down the mouse button and keep the pointer just outside the cell area.

Selecting large areas

To select a large block of cells, click the cell in one corner, scroll to the cell in the diagonally opposite corner, press the Shift key, and click the cell. This method is faster than dragging from one corner of the block to the opposite corner.

Selecting nonadjacent cells

To select a group of nonadjacent cells in a Microsoft Excel or Multiplan worksheet, press the Command key as you click each cell or drag across each block of cells in the selection. You can use the Shift key in conjunction with the Command key to concurrently select more than one block of cells. The Command key does not work with all spreadsheet programs.

Selecting cells by name

There's no need to manually select a large or complex group of cells more than once in a Microsoft Excel or Multiplan worksheet. While the group of cells is still selected, you can name it and subsequently select it again by that name. To name a selected group of cells, use the Define Name command in Microsoft Excel's Formula menu or Multiplan's Select menu. To reselect the same group of cells, use the Goto command in Microsoft Excel's Formula menu or Multiplan's Select menu.

PERFORMANCE

Creating your own Microsoft Excel Command-key shortcuts

Have you ever wished Microsoft Excel had more keyboard shortcuts for its menu choices? Commands in the Format, Data, and Options menus in particular have very few Command-key equivalents. It's easy to create macros that not only choose commands from a menu, but that also select specific options in the dialog boxes that accompany the menu choices. And you can execute each command macro with a keyboard shortcut that you designate. For example, you could create a macro to assign the bold style to text in a cell, as follows:

1. Use Microsoft Excel's New command to create a new macro sheet, or open an existing macro sheet to which you wish to add this macro.

2. Choose Set Recorder from the Macro menu.

3. On the macro sheet, click any blank cell that has several blank cells below it and type a macro name such as *SetBold*. Press the Return key.

4. Go through the motions of selecting a cell—any cell, on the macro sheet or on a worksheet—to be made bold. Microsoft Excel is not recording now, so this action won't be part of the macro. You want to keep cell selection a manual operation so that you can select different cells each time you use the macro. If Microsoft Excel were recording cell selection, the macro would always make the same cells bold.

5. Choose Start Recorder from the Macro menu.

6. Choose Style from the Format menu and, in the dialog box that appears, select the Bold style. Press Return or click the OK button. Microsoft Excel watches what you do and places the necessary macro formulas on the macro sheet.

7. Choose Stop Recorder from the Macro menu.

8. Repeat steps 3 through 7 for each additional macro you wish to create. Of course, in step 3 you'll want to type a different name for each macro, in step 4 you'll go through the motions of setting up for the macro action, and in step 6 you'll do whatever it is you want the macro to do.

9. Save the macro sheet using the File menu's Save command.

```
┌─────────────────────────────────────┐
│ ▤□▤  Commands Macro  ▤▤▤            │
├─────────────────────────────────────┤
│        │            A           │   │
├────────┼────────────────────────┤ ⬆ │
│   1    │ SetBold                │   │
│   2    │ =STYLE(TRUE,FALSE)     │ ▢ │
│   3    │ =RETURN()              │   │
│   4    │                        │   │
│   5    │                        │   │
│   6    │                        │ ⬇ │
└─────────────────────────────────────┘
```

*Microsoft Excel macros can execute almost any command you can think of, not just
this simple one that sets the style to bold for everything in the cells you have selected.
By using the recorder commands in the Macro menu, you can have Microsoft Excel
create the macro for you as you show it what you want done. With the Formula menu's
Define Name command, you can also designate a keyboard shortcut
for the command macro.*

To designate a keyboard shortcut for a macro you've created, you must name it.
Open and activate the macro sheet if necessary, and proceed as follows:

1. Select the first cell of the macro on the macro sheet and choose Define Name
   from the Formula menu. A dialog box appears.

2. Microsoft Excel usually suggests a name for the macro based on the contents
   of the cell above the one you selected in step 1. If it doesn't, or if the suggested name is not to your liking, type the name of your choosing in the
   space provided.

3. At the bottom of the dialog box, click the Command option. This activates
   the adjacent Option-Command Key option.

4. Click in the space provided for the Option-Command Key, type a single letter, and click OK. Microsoft Excel differentiates between upper- and
   lowercase letters (*B* is not the same as *b*). You may not use digits, symbols, or
   the lowercase letters *e, u, i,* or *n*.

To run a macro for which you've designated a keyboard shortcut, make sure the
macro sheet that contains the macro is open (it need not be active), select cells or do
whatever other preparatory actions are required, and then press Command-Option
along with the letter you designated for the macro.

Clearing the Clipboard

After cutting or copying and then pasting a particularly large group of spreadsheet cells, it's a good idea to clear the cells from the Clipboard. The contents of the Clipboard occupy valuable space in the Macintosh's memory and therefore reduce the amount of space available for your spreadsheet.

To clear the Clipboard completely, select a single cell and choose Copy from the Edit menu twice. The first Copy command clears the Clipboard, but holds onto its contents in another area of memory so that you can, if necessary, undo the copy operation. The second Copy command clears the large cell selection from the undo area of memory.

Increasing accuracy by rounding

Calculations based on formatted cell values may often appear to come out wrong because the calculations are made with the cells' precise values, which may not have the same number of decimal places as their displayed values. For example, if a list of numbers were calculated to 14 decimal places but displayed to the nearest cent, the sum of the calculated values, when displayed to the nearest cent, would probably not equal the sum of the displayed values. To avoid such discrepancies, most spreadsheet programs have a ROUND function that you can use to limit the number of decimal places in a calculated value.

Microsoft Excel's Options menu has a Precision As Displayed command, which forces the stored value of every cell on the worksheet to match its displayed precision. The penalty for using this command is slower worksheet calculation, because Microsoft Excel rounds every cell value whether it needs it or not. Also, any constant values you may have entered with extra decimal places are permanently rounded; you can't get the extra precision back later by choosing Full Precision from the Options menu.

Copying quickly to many cells

Here's a quick way to copy the contents of one cell to any group of cells in a Microsoft Excel worksheet:

1. Select the group of cells to which you want to copy. Use the Shift key for large selections and the Command key for nonadjacent selections.
2. Press the Command key and then click the cell whose contents you want to copy.

3. Click the formula-editing area, and edit the cell contents or enter the new contents.

4. Press Option-Enter or press Option and click the enter box in the formula-editing area.

Using the Option key to propagate cell contents adjusts relative cell references in a formula the same way as using the Copy and Paste commands. Relative cell references in each copy of a formula refer to different cells than they refer to in the original formula.

Resetting Microsoft Excel dialog boxes

To quickly reset a section of a Microsoft Excel dialog box to its previous settings, click the section title.

This technique works only with a section whose title overlaps the border surrounding the section. For example, in the Find dialog box (Formula menu), the technique works with the Look in, Look at, and Look by subtitles, but not with the Find What subtitle.

Designating the order of cell entry

It's possible to preselect a group of cells in a Microsoft Excel or Multiplan worksheet for which you will later enter values, and to designate in advance the order in which the values must be entered later. To do this, open the worksheet and proceed as follows:

1. Select the group of cells for which values must be entered, using the Command key and possibly the Shift key, as described in "Selecting non-adjacent cells." Select the cells in the order in which you want their values entered.

2. After selecting the last cell in the group, press the Enter key once. This makes the first cell of the group the active cell.

3. Give the group of select cells a name, something like *Entry,* using the Define Name command, as described in "Selecting cells by name."

4. Save the worksheet to disk.

When it's time to enter values, open the worksheet and use the Goto command to select the named group of cells. Enter the value for the active cell, which has a heavy white border. Then press the Enter key, not the Return key, to end the entry and advance to the next selected cell. If you need to back up to a previous cell, press Shift-Enter.

Hiding columns

Spreadsheets often contain tables, auxiliary and intermediate calculations, proprietary formulas, or other information that you'd rather keep out of the public eye. In Microsoft Excel and Multiplan, you can hide private cells, by putting them in columns outside the public part of your worksheet and then setting the widths of those columns to zero. To change a column width to zero:

1. Move the pointer over the label of the column you want to change, at the very top of the column.

2. Move the pointer right, over the column boundary line, and drag the right boundary to the left until it overlaps the left boundary. If you want to hide several adjacent columns, drag the right boundary of the rightmost column you want hidden to the left until it overlaps the left boundary of the leftmost column you want hidden.

You can also set column widths to zero by selecting the columns and using the Column Width command from the Format menu.

If you change your mind about hiding a column or you need to make changes, you can expose it as follows:

1. Move the pointer above the column to the right of the hidden column, near but not over its left boundary.

2. Drag to the right until the information in the newly exposed column is visible.

In Microsoft Excel, you can also hide cells with numeric values by changing their formats to single semicolons.

FORMULAS

Copying formulas to a new worksheet

Microsoft Excel's Cut, Copy, and Paste commands transfer both formulas and values from one worksheet to another, provided the source worksheet is open when you choose the Paste command.

In Multiplan, the Cut, Copy, and Paste commands normally transfer only cell values—not the formulas in the cells—from one worksheet to another. You can retain the formulas by disguising them as text before cutting or copying and removing the disguise after pasting. Here's how:

1. Open the worksheet you want to copy from, and choose Save As from the File menu to make a copy of the worksheet. Experiment with the copy, not the original.

2. Choose Show Formulas from the Options menu.

3. One at a time, select each cell that contains a formula you want to transfer and, in the formula-editing area below the menu bar, use standard text-editing methods to remove the equal sign. Then press the Enter key to disguise the formula as text. Don't bother disguising any formulas that can be replicated by filling down or filling right.

4. Select the group of cells you want to transfer, and choose Cut or Copy from the Edit menu.

5. Open another worksheet or create a new one.

6. Select the location at which you want pasting to begin, and choose Paste from the Edit menu.

7. One at a time, select a disguised formula and, in the formula-editing area below the menu bar, insert an equal sign. Then press the Enter key to convert the text back to a true formula.

8. If necessary, use the Copy Down and Copy Right commands from the Edit menu to recreate similar formulas that you didn't disguise in step 2.

Bypassing formula errors

When nothing you do seems to rid a formula of an elusive error and you'd like to move on without erasing the formula completely, just remove the equal sign at the beginning of the formula. Microsoft Excel, Multiplan, Jazz, and most other spreadsheet programs won't let you put an erroneous formula in your spreadsheet. But without the equal sign, the spreadsheet program considers the formula to be text and lets you enter it. Later, you can return for another try at resolving the error.

Converting formulas to fixed values

Want to convert the calculated values in a group of cells that now contain formulas to constants? Use the Cut, Copy, and Paste commands with the Scrapbook, as follows:

1. Select the cells and choose Copy from the Edit menu. This puts a copy of the cell contents, including any formulas, on the Clipboard.
2. Choose Scrapbook from the Apple menu and then choose Paste from the Edit menu. The Paste command evaluates any formulas on the Clipboard and puts the resulting values in the Scrapbook.
3. Choose Cut from the Edit menu to put the calculated values on the Clipboard in place of the formulas, and close the Scrapbook.
4. The cells you selected in step 1 should still be selected. Choose Paste to return the calculated values to their respective cells.

If you want to convert the calculated value of just one cell of a Microsoft Excel or Multiplan worksheet to a constant, select the cell, click anywhere in the formula-editing area, and choose Calculate Now from Microsoft Excel's Option menu or Multiplan's Calculate menu.

Saving time with manual calculation

Save time when working on a large spreadsheet by using the manual calculation option. In Microsoft Excel, for example, choose Calculation from the Options menu and, in the dialog box that appears, select the Manual option. In Multiplan, choose Manual Calculation from the Calculate menu. You can force Microsoft Excel or Multiplan to calculate at any time by pressing Command-=, which is the shortcut for the Calculate Now command. In Jazz, use the recalculate command in the Range menu to set manual calculation, and recalculate as needed by pressing Command = R.

Calculating the difference between two dates

Multiplan, unlike Microsoft Excel, has no built-in date-calculating ability. Thus, you can't simply subtract two dates to determine the number of days between them. Instead, you must set up a series of formulas and a table to make the calculation. These are the required formulas:

Date1	=	a date such as 02/28/87
Date2	=	a date such as 03/01/88
Year1	=	VALUE(MID(Date1,7,4))
Month1	=	VALUE(MID(Date1,1,2))
Day1	=	VALUE(MID(Date1,4,2))
Leap1	=	IF(AND(Month1>2,OR(Year1/400=INT(Year1/400), AND(Year1/4=INT(Year1/4),Year1/100<> INT(Year1/100)))),1,0)
Year2	=	VALUE(MID(Date2,7,4))
Month2	=	VALUE(MID(Date2,1,2))
Day2	=	VALUE(MID(Date2,4,2))
Leap2	=	IF(AND(Month2>2,OR(Year2/400=INT(Year2/400), AND(Year2/4=INT(Year2/4),Year2/100<> INT(Year2/100)))),1,0)
DaysBetween	=	ABS((Year1*365+Leap1+LOOKUP(Month1, MonthAsDays)+Day1) −(Year2*365+Leap2+LOOKUP(Month2,MonthAsDays)+Day2))

Each of the two dates is entered as text in a separate cell. You can use any punctuation to separate the month, day, and year, but you must enter both the month and the day as two digits (use a leading zero if necessary) and the year as four digits. For example, enter *03/01/1988* or *03-01-1988*, but not *3/1/88*.

Auxiliary formulas use the text dates to calculate the month, day, and year as numbers, and to calculate whether or not each year is a leap year. A table supplies the number of days from the first of the year to the first of each of the twelve months. Using values from the table and auxiliary formulas, the main formula converts each date into a number of days since the imaginary date 00/00/0000, and subtracts the difference to get the number of days between the dates.

 ** File   Edit   Select   Format   Options   Calculate**

| R4C2 | =ABS((Year1*365+Leap1+LOOKUP(Month1,MonthAsDays)+
Day1)-(Year2*365+Leap2+LOOKUP(Month2,MonthAsDays)+
Day2)) |

DaysBetweenDates

	1	2	3	4	5
1					
2	Date1	02-28-1987		Year1	1987
3	Date2	03/01/1988		Month1	2
4	Days Between	367		Day1	28
5				Leap1	0
6					
7				Year2	1988
8				Month2	3
9				Day2	1
10				Leap2	1
11					

DaysBetweenDates:2

	4	5
12	---MonthAsDays Table---	
13	Month	Days
14	1	0
15	2	31
16	3	59
17	4	90
18	5	120
19	6	151
20	7	181
21	8	212
22	9	243
23	10	273
24	11	304
25	12	334

Accurately calculating the number of days between two dates in a Multiplan work-sheet is no simple matter. In addition to the main formula (shown here in cell R4C2), you need several auxiliary formulas (shown in R4C5 through R10C5) and a table (shown in R14C4 through R25C5).

HEADERS AND FOOTERS

Viewing long headers and footers

Microsoft Excel and Multiplan can print a one-line page header at the top and a one-line page footer at the bottom of every page. You enter the header and footer text in the Page Setup dialog box. If all the text of a long header or footer is not visible at once in the Page Setup dialog box, you can use the I-beam pointer to scroll the text right or left. To do that, place the pointer anywhere over the text, press the mouse button, and drag the pointer to either end of the text. When the pointer reaches the end, the text starts to scroll slowly in the opposite direction. The farther away you drag the pointer from the edge of the text, the faster the text scrolls.

Microsoft Excel and Multiplan header and footer commands

In addition to regular text, you can include special commands in a header or footer to have Microsoft Excel or Multiplan print the current date, time, page number, and document name. Other commands affect the text style and alignment. Here is a list of the available commands:

Command	Effect
&L	Aligns text that follows at left margin
&C	Centers text that follows
&R	Aligns text that follows at right margin
&P	Prints page number
&D	Prints current date
&T	Prints current time
&F	Prints document name
&B	Prints immediately following text (left, right, or center part) in bold
&I	Prints immediately following text (left, right, or center part) in italic
&&	Prints one ampersand

WORKSHEET GRAPHING

Creating bar graphs in Multiplan

Multiplan doesn't have the built-in graphing capabilities of other spreadsheet programs. But where it's meaningful to show the relative magnitude of several values, you can use the Bar Graph format to have numbers displayed graphically.

The Bar Graph format is designed to work best in standard-width columns with values between 0 and 10. If values are mostly out of that range, they must be multiplied by a scaling factor or the bar graph will not look good. For example, percentages commonly have values between 0 and 1 (the Percent format automatically multiplies them by 100 for display purposes only), and they should be multiplied by 10 for best bar-graph results. If the range of values is very wide, you may also want to widen the column that contains the bar graph.

When there are positive and negative values to be graphed, use IF functions to separate them into two columns, with negative values in the left column and positive values in the right. Align the negative values on the right and the positive values on the left. This makes the boundary between the columns a zero line, with negative values extending to the left and positive values to the right of the line. Multiplan automatically graphs negative values in light gray and positive values in dark gray.

 File   Edit   Select   Format   Options   Calculate

| R4C14 | =IF(RC[-1]<0,RC[-1]*10,0) |

Stock Performance

	1	10	13	14	15
		CURRENT	PERCENT	--- RELATIVE	PERFORMANCE ---
1					
2	COMPANY NAME	VALUE	GAIN(LOSS)	LOSING ISSUES	GAINING ISSUES
3					
4	American Quasar Petroleum	1200.00	-45.79%	████████▨▨	
5	Apple Computer	5825.00	56.23%		▨▨▨
6	Apple Computer	5825.00	-1.13%		
7	Church's Fried Chicken	12750.00	44.83%		▨▨▨
8	Coca Cola Company	5600.00	12.63%		▨
9	Eastman Kodak	19575.00	-17.73%	▨	
10	Mary Kay Cosmetics	2400.00	7.11%		▮
11	Ozark Airlines	787.50	-37.49%	▨▨▨	
12	Pan American World Airways	1100.00	11.64%		▨
13	Pay 'n Save Corp.	1725.00	75.99%		▨▨▨▨
14	Rolm Corp	3462.50	-0.37%		
15	Sunshine Mining	2375.00	-8.46%	▯	
16	Texas Oil and Gas	7537.50	119.41%		▨▨▨▨▨▨
17	Yellow Freight Systems	4950.00	56.15%		▨▨▨
18		=========			
19	Totals	75112.50	11.21%		▨
20	Averages		19.50%		▨

Multiplan's Bar Graph format lets you easily compare the magnitude of several values. Values to be graphed must be scaled to be between 0 and 10. An IF function in each cell separates positive and negative values. Aligning the two columns against their common boundary makes that boundary a zero line. The dark and light shading variations are automatic.

Creating Microsoft Excel scatter graphs

A scatter graph is normally used to analyze the relationship between two variables, usually called the X variable and the Y variable. If you can establish a high degree of correlation in observed values of the two variables, you can predict with some certainty the value of one variable that will correspond to a hypothetical value of the other. However, creating a scatter graph with Microsoft Excel is not as straightforward as with other types of graphs. Collect your observed data and proceed as follows:

1. Arrange the known values of the X and Y variables into a two-column table in a worksheet. The first column of the table lists the X values, which are the values for the category (horizontal) axis, and the second column lists the Y values, which are the values for the value (vertical) axis.

2. After setting up the table, select all of the values in both columns and choose Copy from the Edit menu.

3. Use the New command in Excel's File menu to create a new chart window.

4. Choose Paste Special from the Edit menu. Do not choose the Paste command. Because both columns of the table contain values, if you use Paste, Microsoft Excel will assume that you do not want category-axis labels on your chart and will plot both the X and Y values along the value axis as two data series, instead of plotting one point for each pair of X and Y values.

5. In the Paste Special dialog box, select the Categories in First Column option to tell Microsoft Excel to use the values in the first column for the category (horizontal) axis. Click OK, and Microsoft Excel plots the chart using its standard chart type, which is normally a column chart. In a column chart, each tick mark on the category axis corresponds to one X value from the worksheet.

6. Change the chart to a scatter graph by choosing Scatter from the Gallery menu and selecting a scatter-graph style in the dialog box that appears. As Microsoft Excel draws the scatter graph, it adjusts the category axis so the tick marks measure equal X-value increments, from the lowest value on the worksheet's list of X values to the highest.

7. Label the axes and the data points with the Attach Text command from the Chart menu. Unfortunately, you cannot link labels from the worksheet to the axes or data points in the chart; you have to retype them.

In step 1, you may arrange the X and Y values in rows instead of columns, in which case the X values go in the first row. You can also use a short macro to do most of the work of steps 2 through 7. After setting up the two-column table of X and Y values, run this macro:

	A	B
1		ScatterGram
2		=COPY()
3		=NEW(2)
4		=PASTE.SPECIAL(2,FALSE,TRUE)
5		=GALLERY.SCATTER(1)
6		=RETURN()

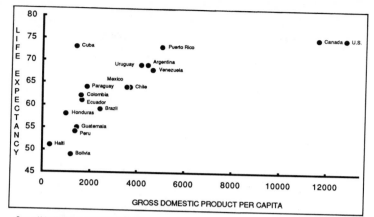

Source: United Nations 1982 Statistical Yearbook

	GDP per Capita	Life Expectancy
U.S.	$12829	75
Canada	$11677	75
Venezuela	$4670	68
Argentina	$4430	69
Chile	$3699	64
Mexico	$3555	64
Brazil	$2428	59
Ecuador	$1663	61
Colombia	$1632	62
Guatemala	$1433	55
Cuba	$1393	73
Peru	$1368	54
Bolivia	$1194	49
Haiti	$307	51
Puerto Rico	$5055	73
Paraguay	$1859	64
Uruguay	$4172	69
Honduras	$996	58

Scatter graphs are useful for spotting relationships between two variables. Here, actual data suggest that people live longer in richer countries, but that the relationship is not linear. To set up a scatter graph in Microsoft Excel, you create a table of known values for each variable, use the Copy and Paste Special commands to transfer the values to a new chart, and add labels to the data points and axes.

Communications

Getting two computers to communicate,
whether they're connected over phone lines with modems or
directly cabled, is not a task for the faint-hearted.
Don't let the technical complexity daunt you.
Look through this chapter for some ideas that will
help you get online successfully.

GETTING READY TO COMMUNICATE

Connecting directly to another computer

You can bypass modems and telephone calls by directly connecting the Mac and a nearby computer with a cable. What you need is a null-modem cable, which swaps the incoming and outgoing data lines. In most cases, an ImageWriter cable works. One end of the cable plugs into the Mac's modem port, and the other end plugs into the other computer's serial port.

If the serial port on the other computer is wired for a non-null-modem cable, then a null-modem cable such as the ImageWriter cable won't work. In that case, you should use the ImageWriter cable with a null-modem adapter or a non-null-modem cable, which you can purchase in most computer stores.

First-time settings

If you don't know what options to select in the Compatibility Settings dialog box the first time you call an information service or a remote computer, try 300 or 1200 baud, 8 bits per character, no parity, 1 stop bit (not an option with MacTerminal), and XOn/XOff handshake.

Best time to call

For best performance when communicating with an information service or other remote computer, contact it late at night or very early in the morning. More people call during daytime and evening hours. The busier the remote computer becomes, the longer it takes to handle your requests and, as a result, the more expensive your communications session will be.

Reducing the risk of full disks

When the terminal program records or captures a telecommunications session in a disk file, there is always the risk of running out of disk space while that particular session is in progress, especially with a single-sided (400K) disk. You can minimize the chance of the disk becoming full by saving the information recorded during the last session on a different disk and then recording the new session in a file on an otherwise blank disk.

Using MacTerminal, you can save the last session and clear the disk as follows:

1.   Choose Save As from the File menu and, in the Save As dialog box, use the Drive and Eject buttons to store the previous session's document on a blank disk.

2.   After saving, choose Clear Lines Off Top from the Commands menu.

Automatic answering

Many terminal programs do not answer incoming calls. In MacTerminal versions 1.0 and 1.1, for example, the Wait for Call command on the Phone menu does not work, and neither does the Number of Rings Before Answer setting in the Phone Settings dialog box. However, most modems, including the AppleModem 1200, the Apple Personal Modem, and other modems compatible with the Hayes SmartModem, will answer an incoming call even if your terminal program will not.

To institute automatic answering, you must type a command to the modem, as follows:

1.   Make sure the terminal program is on line. (In MacTerminal, check the On Line setting in the Terminal Settings dialog box.)

2.   Turn on the modem.

3.   Type the following command in capital letters:

     `ATS0 = 1`

This command tells the modem to answer the phone after one ring. The number after the equal sign determines how many rings the modem waits before answering.

4.   Stop automatic answering by typing the following command:

     `ATS0 = 0`

     or turn the modem off and back on again.

MAKING THE CALL

Typing modem commands directly

Although you will probably want to use your terminal program to have your modem dial often-used numbers automatically, you can also send commands directly to your modem by typing them on the Mac's keyboard. With any modem compatible with the Hayes SmartModem, for example, typing *ATD14155559196* and pressing Return dials the number 1/415/555-9196 directly; in MacTerminal, this bypasses the Phone menu altogether. When typing modem commands, use all capital letters or the commands will not take effect.

After you establish connection with another computer, the modem stops watching for commands. To get its attention, wait at least a second, type three plus signs (+ + +), and wait another full second. You should see *OK* appear on the screen, after which you can type commands to the modem. For example, you might need to bring a communication session to a hasty conclusion by typing *ATH* (the command to hang up).

Inserting commas for pauses

You can instruct any modem compatible with the Hayes SmartModem to pause during dialing. For each two-second pause required in a dialing sequence, insert one comma.

Escaping from PBX

To dial out of a private branch exchange (PBX), prefix the number you're calling with a 9. If you normally have to wait for a second dial tone before dialing the outside number, insert one or two commas between the 9 and the outside number.

```
┌─────────────────────────────────────────────────────────┐
│ Phone Settings                                          │
│                                                         │
│ Phone Number                                            │
│ ┌─────────────────────────────────────────────────────┐ │
│ │9,555-1212                                           │ │
│ └─────────────────────────────────────────────────────┘ │
│ Dial    ▸   ◉ Tone      ○ Pulse       ○ Mixed          │
│                                                         │
│ Number of Rings Before Answer        │1│               │
│                                                         │
│ Modem     ○ Apple 300   ◉ Apple 1200  ○ Other          │
│                                                         │
│                            ┌──────┐  ┌────────┐          │
│                            │  OK  │  │ Cancel │          │
│                            └──────┘  └────────┘          │
└─────────────────────────────────────────────────────────┘
```

*This phone number dials a 9 to get an outside line from a PBX, waits two seconds,
and then dials the remote computer at 555-1212.*

Special modem commands

Some modems have special dialing commands. For example, the Prometheus
ProModem 1200 recognizes the letter *W* in a dialing sequence as an instruction to
wait up to 20 seconds for a second dial tone or an access tone. Using this command
means that you don't have to estimate how long the wait will be, as you do with commas. The following example is equivalent to the previous one:

```
┌─────────────────────────────────────────────────────────┐
│ Phone Settings                                          │
│                                                         │
│ Phone Number                                            │
│ ┌─────────────────────────────────────────────────────┐ │
│ │9W555-1212                                           │ │
│ └─────────────────────────────────────────────────────┘ │
│ Dial    ▸   ◉ Tone      ○ Pulse       ○ Mixed          │
│                                                         │
│ Number of Rings Before Answer        │1│               │
│                                                         │
│ Modem     ○ Apple 300   ◉ Apple 1200  ○ Other          │
│                                                         │
│                            ┌──────┐  ┌────────┐          │
│                            │  OK  │  │ Cancel │          │
│                            └──────┘  └────────┘          │
└─────────────────────────────────────────────────────────┘
```

*This phone number dials a 9 to get an outside line from a PBX, waits for a second
dial tone, and then dials the remote computer at 555-1212.*

Alternate long-distance companies

Your modem will dial a long-distance number using an alternate company if you enter the dial command as follows:

1. Prefix the remote computer's number with the local-access phone number and your account number.

2. Insert commas between the local-access number and the account number to allow time for the long-distance company to answer and sound its tone.

```
┌─────────────────────────────────────────────────────┐
│  Phone Settings                                      │
│                                                       │
│  Phone Number                                         │
│  ┌─────────────────────────────────────────────┐     │
│  │832-5016,,,1234567 214-555-1212               │     │
│  └─────────────────────────────────────────────┘     │
│  Dial    ▶  ● Tone      ○ Pulse       ○ Mixed         │
│  Number of Rings Before Answer        ┌───┐           │
│                                       │ 1 │           │
│                                       └───┘           │
│  Modem     ○ Apple 300   ● Apple 1200  ○ Other        │
│                              ┌────────┐ ┌────────┐    │
│                              │   OK   │ │ Cancel │    │
│                              └────────┘ └────────┘    │
└─────────────────────────────────────────────────────┘
```

This phone number dials 832-5016 (a long-distance company's local-access number), waits six seconds, dials account number 1234567, and then dials the remote computer at 214-555-1212.

Credit-card calls

From most touch-tone phone lines, your modem will provide all the billing information for an AT&T credit-card call if you enter the dial command as follows:

1. Prefix the area code with a 0 (instead of a 1).

2. Add three commas, the credit-card number, and another comma to the end of the remote computer's phone number.

```
┌─────────────────────────────────────────────────────────────┐
│  Phone Settings                                               │
│                                                               │
│  Phone Number                                                 │
│  ┌──────────────────────────────────────────────────────┐   │
│  │ 0-214-555-1212,,,415 555 1212 9876,                  │   │
│  └──────────────────────────────────────────────────────┘   │
│  Dial    ▶  ⦿ Tone      ○ Pulse        ○ Mixed               │
│  Number of Rings Before Answer      ┌───┐                    │
│                                     │ 1 │                    │
│                                     └───┘                    │
│  Modem     ○ Apple 300   ⦿ Apple 1200   ○ Other             │
│                                  ┌──────┐  ┌────────┐        │
│                                  │  OK  │  │ Cancel │        │
│                                  └──────┘  └────────┘        │
└─────────────────────────────────────────────────────────────┘
```

This phone number dials the remote computer at 214-555-1212, waits six seconds, dials credit-card number 415 555 1212 9876, and then waits two more seconds before connecting.

Suspending Call Waiting

The click or beep that announces that a call is waiting on a phone line equipped with the Call Waiting feature wreaks havoc with telecommunications. But in many areas, you can suspend the Call Waiting feature for the duration of the ensuing call by dialing a three- or four-digit code, waiting for a second dial tone, and then dialing a regular phone number. This feature is available in so-called easy-access areas, in which you are automatically connected to the long-distance company of your choice and need not dial special access numbers to use a company other than AT&T.

```
┌─────────────────────────────────────────────────────────────┐
│  Phone Settings                                               │
│                                                               │
│  Phone Number                                                 │
│  ┌──────────────────────────────────────────────────────┐   │
│  │ *70,555-1212                                          │   │
│  └──────────────────────────────────────────────────────┘   │
│  Dial    ▶  ⦿ Tone      ○ Pulse        ○ Mixed               │
│  Number of Rings Before Answer      ┌───┐                    │
│                                     │ 1 │                    │
│                                     └───┘                    │
│  Modem     ○ Apple 300   ⦿ Apple 1200   ○ Other             │
│                                  ┌──────┐  ┌────────┐        │
│                                  │  OK  │  │ Cancel │        │
│                                  └──────┘  └────────┘        │
└─────────────────────────────────────────────────────────────┘
```

This phone number dials the code *70 to suspend Call Waiting on a touch-tone line, waits two seconds for a second dial tone, and then dials the remote computer at 555-1212.

To suspend Call Waiting on a touch-tone phone line, type the four characters *70, in front of the phone number. To suspend Call Waiting on a rotary or pulse-dial phone line, type the five characters 1170, in front of the phone number.

If you are not in an easy-access area, it is best to avoid using a phone line that has Call Waiting for telecommunications.

Staying connected

If your terminal program always seems to disconnect shortly after the number you dial is answered, try suffixing the number with two or three commas.

Busy...busy...busy

MacTerminal has no special command to redial a busy number. A few seconds after detecting a busy signal, it displays the message *The call was answered, but no computer responded* and waits for you to do something. You could redial by choosing Dial from the Phone menu, but here's a faster method: Assuming the last command you chose was Dial from the Phone menu, type A/ to redial a busy number. Do not press the Return key or you will cancel this repeat command. Typing A/ tells any modem compatible with the Hayes SmartModem to repeat the last command it received.

Redialing continuously

Anyone who uses electronic bulletin boards knows a remote computer can be busy for 20 minutes straight. In a situation like that, manual redialing quickly gets tedious. Few terminal programs or modems have an automatic redial-on-busy command; certainly MacTerminal and the Apple modems do not. But you can give MacTerminal an unintelligent continuous-redial capability with some preliminary word processing and these temporary changes to its file-transfer settings:

1. Use MacWrite or another word processor to create a text document containing about 60 lines that each have a capital A followed by a slash (A/, the modem's repeat command).

2. Save the document—on the MacTerminal disk if possible—using the Text Only option. MacWrite asks whether to put a return character at the end of each paragraph or the end of each line; choose Paragraphs.

3. Start MacTerminal and dial the number. If the number is busy, MacTerminal will hang up within 10 seconds.

4. In the File Transfer Settings dialog box, note the setting for Delay Between Lines and temporarily change it to 1800 (30 seconds). Also, note the setting for Transfer Method and then select Text. Click OK.

5. Choose Send File from the File menu and double click on the name of the redial-command document. MacTerminal will start sending one line of the document, which contains one redial command, every 30 seconds.

6. Listen to the modem speaker. When you hear the remote phone ring, immediately type Command-Period to stop MacTerminal from sending any more redial commands. Another A/ command will cause the modem to hang up!

7. After logging onto the remote computer, restore the Delay Between Lines and Transfer Method settings in the File Transfer Setting dialog box to their states prior to step 4.

If your modem won't respond to the repeated A/ commands, try turning it off and back on again. Then redial the number. If the number is still busy, continue with step 5.

AVOIDING GIBBERISH

Normal gibberish

It is normal to see gibberish on the screen when you first connect with some information services or bulletin boards. To stop it, try pressing the Return key once or twice, or press Command-C.

Extraneous characters

The most likely cause of extraneous characters, such as], {, or }, in the information you receive is a bad phone connection creating static on the line. Long-distance calls are particularly susceptible to noisy lines. Some long-distance companies have noisier connections than others, but bad connections are possible with any company. Here are some possible solutions:

- [ ] Hang up and try again. If you were using an alternate long-distance company (via a local-access number), place the call directly, through your normal long-distance company.
- [ ] Try another number for the information service. In major metropolitan areas, you often have a choice of several local numbers for one service.
- [ ] Use a slower baud rate. Modems are less sensitive to static at 300 baud than at 1200 baud.
- [ ] Activate XOn/XOff "handshake" protocol (in MacTerminal's Phone Settings dialog box).
- [ ] Try a different modem. Some models filter noise better than others.

Invisible typing

If what you type doesn't appear on the screen, choose your terminal program's local echo or half-duplex option. In MacTerminal, for example, you select the Local Echo setting in the Terminal Settings menu.

DDoouubbllee ttyyppee

If every letter you type appears doubled, disable your terminal program's local echo or full-duplex option. In MacTerminal, for example, make sure the Local Echo setting in the Terminal Settings menu is not selected.

Missing characters

Intermittent missing characters may mean the remote computer is sending information faster than your terminal program can receive it. To correct this problem:

- [ ] Make sure both computers are using the same baud rate; try a slower rate at both ends, such as 300 baud.
- [ ] See if activating the XOn/XOff "handshake" protocol helps. (Check Mac-Terminal's Compatibility Settings dialog box.)
- [ ] Stop capturing or recording incoming information on disk. (In Mac-Terminal, choose Don't Record Lines Off Top from the Commands menu.)

THE MACTERMINAL KEYBOARD

The Control key

When using MacTerminal and most other terminal programs, the Mac's Command key is equivalent to the Control key on other computer keyboards. For example, most information services recognize Command-S (Control-S) as a command to stop sending information until you press Command-Q (Control-Q).

Most Control-key combinations have direct Command-key equivalents. However, MacTerminal handles two Control-key combinations peculiarly: If you need to send a Control- ^ , press Command-6 (without the Shift key), and if you need to send a Control__, press Command-/.

The Delete key

The Mac keyboard has no Delete key (also called Del, Rubout, or Rub).

Many terminal programs let you make the Backspace key simulate a Delete key. MacTerminal version 2.0, for example, offers the option of treating the Backspace key as a Delete key or as a Backspace key; whichever you pick, you can still type the other by pressing Command-Backspace. Indicate your preference by choosing Keyboard from MacTerminal's Settings menu.

The Escape key

The Escape or Esc key found on most computers does not exist on the Mac. MacTerminal simulates the Escape key when you press the Tilde key.

Tildes and accents

Because MacTerminal uses the Tilde key as an Escape key, you must press Command-Tilde to type an accent grave (`). Pressing Command-Shift-Tilde types a tilde (~).

The Break key

When using MacTerminal in its VT100 mode, pressing the Enter key simulates the Break key found on VT100 keyboards.

Using MacTracks with terminal programs

The MacTracks desk accessory may interfere with MacTerminal's ability to use the Command key in simulating the Control, Delete, and Escape keys. For best results, record all MacTracks "tracks" to be used in a terminal program as combination keystrokes that include the Option and/or Shift keys in addition to the requisite Command key. For example, use Command-Option-C or Command-Option-Shift-C for a track, but not Command-C, which is the equivalent of the Control-C character used by many computers to stop processes.

TRANSFERRING INFORMATION

Don't use XOn/XOff with XModem

For accurate file transfer from a remote computer, use the XModem error-checking protocol, but make sure your terminal program's XOn/XOff feature is inactive. Otherwise, the XOn/XOff feature may introduce spurious errors during file transfer, causing blocks of information to be re-sent needlessly. When that happens, the receiving computer gets duplicate blocks of information. In Mac-Terminal, you set the Xon/Xoff option by choosing Compatibility from the Settings menu.

Unsuccessful XModem

When an attempt at transferring information to or from an information service is unsuccessful, it could just mean the service is too busy. When lots of people are using the service, XModem transfer does not work reliably.

Preventing screen clearing

Does CompuServe clear your screen while you have MacTerminal set to Record Lines Off Top? You don't want the screen cleared before the lines have a chance to move off the top, or they'll never be recorded.

To prevent unwanted screen clearing in MacTerminal versions 2.0 and above, choose File Transfer from the Settings menu and select the Save Screens Before

Clearing option. In MacTerminal versions 1.0 and 1.1, you must set MacTerminal to act like a TTY terminal, not a VT100 terminal, like this:

1. Select the TTY option in MacTerminal's Terminal Settings dialog box.

2. You must also tell CompuServe which terminal type you are using, so once you are connected to CompuServe, type *GO TERMINAL* at any exclamation-point prompt. This transfers you to CompuServe's TERMINAL/OPTIONS menu.

3. Choose option 2, Setting Your Terminal Type, to proceed to the TERMINAL TYPE menu.

4. Choose type 6, which is "Other (General Purpose)."

You are now ready to type any standard CompuServe navigational command, such as *GO MACUS* to go to CompuServe's Mac user group, and can proceed with your communications session with no further screen-clearing problems.

Direct Mac-IBM PC (MS-DOS) file transfer

An IBM PC or other computer that uses the MS-DOS operating system does not need a terminal program for simple file transfer when it is connected directly to the Mac. The DOS MODE and COPY commands suffice. The Mac does require a terminal program, however. To transfer files between the PC and the Mac:

1. Make sure the PC is waiting for a DOS command. The flashing cursor should be right next to a prompt, such as A>.

2. Type an appropriate MODE command on the PC to set up the serial port to match the settings in the terminal program on the Mac. For example, the following command sets serial port COM1: for 9600 baud, no parity, 8 data bits per character, and 1 stop bit:

    MODE COM1:9600,N,8,1

3. To send a file from the PC, prepare the Mac terminal program to capture or receive a file and then type an appropriate COPY command on the PC. The following example copies from the file named *PCSTUFF.TXT* on drive B to the COM1: serial port:

    COPY B:PCSTUFF.TXT COM1:

4. To receive a file on the PC, type an appropriate COPY command on the PC and then have the Mac's terminal program start sending the file.

When the Mac finishes, you usually have to press Command-Z on the Mac to tell the PC that the Mac is done sending. The following COPY command receives a file from serial port COM1: and saves it in a disk file named *MACSTUFF.TXT* on drive A:

```
COPY COM1: A:MACSTUFF.TXT
```

Direct Mac-CP/M file transfer

Any computer that uses the CP/M operating system does not need a terminal program for simple file transfer when it is connected directly to a Mac. CP/M's STAT and PIP commands do the job. The Mac does require a terminal program, however. To transfer files between the CP/M machine and the Mac:

1. Set the baud rate, parity, bits per character, and other compatibility settings in the terminal program on the Mac to match the standard port settings on the CP/M computer. If the CP/M computer's manual doesn't say what those settings are, try 1200 baud, no parity, and 8 data bits per character.

2. Make sure the CP/M computer is waiting for a command. The cursor should be right next to a prompt, such as A>.

3. Type the following STAT commands on the CP/M computer to set up the serial port to send and receive files:

```
STAT PUN: = PTP:
STAT RDR: = PTR:
```

4. To send a file from the CP/M computer, prepare the Mac's terminal program to capture or receive a file and then type an appropriate PIP command on the CP/M computer. The following example copies from the file named *CPMSTUFF.TXT* on drive B to the serial port:

```
PIP PUN: = B:CPMSTUFF.TXT
```

5. To receive a file on the CP/M computer, type an appropriate PIP command on the CP/M computer and then have the Mac's terminal program start sending the file. When the Mac finishes, you usually have to press Command-Z on the Mac to tell the CP/M computer that the Mac is done sending. The following PIP command receives a file from the serial port and saves it in a disk file named *MACSTUFF.TXT* on drive A:

```
PIP A:MACSTUFF.TXT = RDR:
```

CP/M computers include KayPro, Morrow, Osborne, Digital Microsystems, Micromation, Dynabyte, Onyx, Altos, Industrial Micro Systems, Exidy, Vector Graphic, and the Apple II with a CP/M card.

Direct Mac-Radio Shack model 100 file transfer

The Radio Shack Model 100 computer is 100 percent compatible with most Mac terminal programs, and you can use the ImageWriter cable to connect the two computers. MacTerminal, however, cannot receive files from the Model 100 unless you first perform temporary software surgery on the Model 100, like this:

1. Start the Model 100's built-in BASIC by pressing the Enter key while the main menu is displayed.
2. Type the command *POKE 63066,255*. Double-check the accuracy of your typing and backspace to correct if necessary. Press Enter.
3. Quit BASIC.

After the command in step 2, the Model 100 computer sends an invisible linefeed character after the return character at the end of each line. Without these characters, MacTerminal displays all the text it receives on the same line. The Model 100 change stays in effect until you perform a "cold start" or start BASIC and type the command *POKE 63066,0*.

AFTER TRANSFERRING INFORMATION

Cleaning up captured information

After using Recording Lines Off Top with MacTerminal to capture an entire communications session in a single disk file, you'll probably want to split the single file into several files and get rid of the junk that inevitably accumulates. You can't clean up the file with MacTerminal, but you can with MacWrite or Microsoft Word. To do this:

1. Quit MacTerminal.
2. Start MacWrite or Microsoft Word.

3. Using the word processor's Open command, open the MacTerminal document that contains the information you recorded. Before MacWrite opens a MacTerminal document, it asks whether return characters should signify the ends of lines or the ends of paragraphs; click the Paragraphs button. (The Line Breaks button may be the right choice with documents saved by other terminal programs. Experiment and see which looks best.)

4. Edit the file as you would any other word-processing document.

Once you have saved the document with MacWrite or Microsoft Word, MacTerminal will no longer be able to open it.

Using MacWrite on a Mac 512K, you won't be able to open MacTerminal documents longer than 2047 lines; on a 128K Mac, the limit is 500 lines. Every line of a MacTerminal document ends with a return character, and MacWrite limits the number of return characters in a single document.

Quick text selection in a MacTerminal document

You may want to simply copy some text from a MacTerminal document and paste it into another type of document or the Scrapbook. To quickly select a large block of text before choosing Copy from the Edit menu, click once before the first word, use the scroll bar to bring the last word into view, and hold down the Shift key while you click after the last word.

Strange characters

Strange characters appear when one application program encounters formatting codes embedded in a document by another application program. Almost all word processors allow boldface text, variable margins, and page headers, for example, but WordStar accomplishes that formatting one way on an IBM PC, and MacWrite does it another way on a Macintosh. If you simply transfer a WordStar document to the Mac and open it with MacWrite, the document will be full of strange characters — the result of MacWrite's misinterpreting the WordStar formatting conventions.

You can use a special file-transfer program to convert document formats. For example, MacLink converts between WordStar, Multimate, or Displaywrite documents on the PC and MacWrite documents on the Mac.

** File   Edit   Search   Format   Font   Style**

▨▨▨▨▨▨▨▨▨▨▨▨▨▨▨▨ Untitled ▨▨▨▨▨▨▨▨▨▨▨▨

□Th□ Mac □ mode□ deskto□ retain□ it□ familiarit□ n□ matte□ ç□wha□
kin□ o□ informatio□ yo□ proces□ o□ it--words" pictures" ç□column□ o□
numbers" an□ s□ on Æ I□ i□ consistentl□ familia□ ç□i□ al□
applications Æ Everythin□ yo□ d□ o□ th□ Ma□ use□ th□ ç□sam□
familia□ methods Æ Lear□ ho□ t□ d□ somethin□ i□ on□ ç□applicatio□
an□ yo□ wil□ kno□ ho□ t□ d□ □ simila□ tas□ i□ ç□anothe□ application Æ
N□ nee□ t□ lear□ ne□ method□ wit□ eac□ ç□ne□ application Æ Fo□
example" i□ yo□ lear□ ho□ t□ inser□ ç□an□ edi□ tex□ usin□ MacWrite"
yo□ ca□ expec□ th□ sam□ basi□ ç□technique□ t□ wor□ whe□ yo□ typ□
i□ MacPain□ an□ Multiplan Æ ç□□□ course" MacWrite" bein□ □ wor□
processor" wil□ le□ yo□ d□ ç□mor□ thing□ wit□ tex□ tha□ wil□
MacPain□ o□ Multiplan" bu□ ç□al□ Ma□ application□ approac□ simila□
tas□ lik□ tex□ ç□editin□ i□ □ unifor□ way Æ
□
□Th□ atmosphere□ an□ method□ ar□ s□ familia□ an□ consisten□ ç□fro□
on□ Ma□ applicatio□ t□ th□ nex□ tha□ yo□ wil□ fin□ ç□yoursel□
accomplishin□ task□ yo□ neve□ dreame□ yo□ woul□ ç□eve□ try" o□ o□
of□ □ computer Æ Explorin□ □ ne□ applicatio□ ç□wil□ no□ b□
intimidatin□ o□ frustrating" becaus□ yo□ wil□ b□ ç□abl□ t□ appl□ th□

Strange characters appear when MacWrite tries to interpret formatting codes embedded in a document by WordStar.

Converting to plain text

Often, the only way to use a Mac document on another computer, or vice versa, is to first convert the document to plain text, eliminating all formatting codes. On the Macintosh you do this by selecting the Text Only option in the Save As dialog box, the form of which may vary depending on the program. Many application programs on other computers have similar options.

Formatting detritus can also be removed from a word-processing document by a "filter" program such as the public-domain File Filter program, either before or after transfer. Naturally, you lose all formatting, such as margin settings, pagination, and text styles, in the process. After conversion, you can open each plain-text document with MacWrite or Word and add character, paragraph, and document formatting.

APPENDIX

Products Mentioned in This Book

*Accessory Pak I,*Silicon Beach Software, P.O. Box 261430, San Diego, CA 92126, (619) 695-6956

BitFixer, All Star Computer Services, 3822 19th Street, #5, San Francisco, CA 94114, (415) 282-0540

ClickArt Effects, T/Maker Graphics Company, 2115 Landings Drive, Mountain View, CA 94043, (415) 962-0195

CompuServe, CompuServe Information Service, P.O. Box 20212, 5000 Arlington Centre Blvd., Columbus, OH 43260, (800) 848-8199, (614) 457-0802 in OH

Coordinates, see *Accessory Pak I*

Dayton Fonts, Plugh Incorporated, P.O. Box 358, Dayton, OH 45459

Dvorak, from users groups such as BMUG, 1442A Walnut Street, Suite 162, Berkeley, CA 94709, (415) 849-9114

Fade to Black, Brian L. Matthews, 10513 S.E. 219th Street, Kent, WA 98031; or from users groups

Fanny Mac, Beck-Tech, 41 Tunnel Road, Berkeley, CA 94705, (415) 548-4054

Fedit, MacMaster Software, 939 East El Camino Real, Suite 122, Sunnyvale, CA 94087

FONTastic, Altsys Corp., P.O. Box 865410, Plano, TX 75086, (214) 596-4970

Helix, Odesta Corporation, 4084 Commercial Avenue, Northbrook, IL 60062, (800) 323-5423, (312) 498-5615 in IL

Jazz, Lotus Development Corp., 55 Cambridge Parkway, Cambridge, MA 02142, (617) 253-9150

Lisa Vision, LisaVision, 2541 Ninth Avenue, Sacramento, CA 95818, (800) 538-8157, Ext. 816, (800) 672-3470 in CA

MacBreeze, Levco, 6160 Lusk Boulevard, Suite C-203, San Diego, CA 92121, (619) 457-2011

MacDraw, Apple Computer, Incorporated, 20525 Mariani Avenue, Cupertino, CA 95014, (800) 538-9696, (800) 662-9238 in CA

MacLink, DataViz, 16 Winfield Street, Norwalk, CT 06855, (203) 866-4944

Mac Memory Disk, Assimilation, 485 Alberto Way, Los Gatos, CA 95030, (800) 662-5464, (800) 421-0243 in CA

MacBooster, Mainstay, 28611B Canwood St. Agonva Hills, CA 91301, (818) 991-6540.

MacPaint, Apple Computer, Incorporated, 20525 Mariani Avenue, Cupertino, CA 95014, (800) 538-9696, (800) 662-9238 in CA

MacProject, Apple Computer, Incorporated, 20525 Mariani Avenue, Cupertino, CA 95014, (800) 538-9696, (800) 662-9238 in CA

MacTerminal, Apple Computer, Incorporated, 20525 Mariani Avenue, Cupertino, CA 95014, (800) 538-9696, (800) 662-9238 in CA

MacWrite, Apple Computer, Incorporated, 20525 Mariani Avenue, Cupertino, CA 95014, (800) 538-9696, (800) 662-9238 in CA

MDC II, New Canaan MicroCode, 136 Beech Road, New Canaan, CT 06840, (203) 966-6969

Microsoft Chart, Microsoft Corporation, 16011 N.E. 36th Way, Box 97017, Redmond, WA 98073-9717, (800) 426-9400, (206) 882-8080 in WA and AK, (416) 673-7638 in Canada

Microsoft Excel, Microsoft Corporation, 16011 N.E. 36th Way, Box 97017, Redmond, WA 98073-9717, (800) 426-9400, (206) 882-8080 in WA and AK, (416) 673-7638 in Canada

Microsoft Multiplan, Microsoft Corporation, 16011 N.E. 36th Way, Box 97017, Redmond, WA 98073-9717, (800) 426-9400, (206) 882-8080 in WA and AK, (416) 673-7638 in Canada

Microsoft Word, Microsoft Corporation, 16011 N.E. 36th Way, Box 97017, Redmond, WA 98073-9717, (800) 426-9400, (206) 882-8080 in WA and AK, (416) 673-7638 in Canada

Mock Write, CE Software, 801 73rd Street, Des Moines, IA 50312, (515) 224-1995

Mouse Mover, Magnum Software, 21115 Devonshire Street, Suite 337, Chatsworth, CA 91311, (818) 700-0510

Paint Cutter, see *Accessory Pak I*

Paint Mover, prerelease version from users groups such as BMUG, 1442A Walnut Street, Suite 162, Berkeley, CA 94709, (415) 849-9114

QuickPaint, Enterset, 410 Townsend Street, San Francisco, CA 94107, (415) 543-7644

RamStart from users groups such as BMUG, 1442A Walnut Street, Suite 162, Berkeley, CA 94709, (415) 849-9114

ResEdit, from users groups such as BMUG, 1442A Walnut Street, Suite 162, Berkeley, CA 94709, (415) 849-9114

Rulers, see *Accessory Pak I*

SciFonts, Paragon Courseware, 4954 Sun Valley Road, Del Mar, CA 92014, (619) 481-1477

SideKick, Borland International, Incorporated, 4585 Scotts Valley Drive, Scotts Valley, CA 95066, (800) 255-8008, (800) 742-1133 in CA

Switcher, Apple Computer, Incorporated, 20525 Mariani Avenue, Cupertino, CA 95014, (800) 538-9696, (800) 662-9238 in CA

ThinkTank, Living Videotext, Incorporated, 2432 Charleston Road, Mountain View, CA 94043, (415) 964-6300

TurboCharger, Nevins Microsystems, Incorporated, P.O. Box 1249, Capitola, CA 95010, (408) 479-0860

INDEX

Q

R

S

Lon Poole writes the popular "Get Info" column for *Macworld* magazine, and is the author of the classic *Apple II User's Guide*. His first book for Microsoft Press was the best-selling *MacWork, MacPlay*. Lon Poole lives in Oakland, California.

The manuscript for this book was prepared and submitted to Microsoft Press in electronic form. Text files were processed and formatted using Microsoft Word.

Cover design by Ted Mader and Associates
Interior text design by Darcie S. Furlan
Illustrations by Chuck Solway
Principal typography by Lisa Iversen
The high-resolution screen displays were created on the Apple Macintosh and printed on the Apple LaserWriter

Text composition by Microsoft Press in Baskerville with display in Baskerville Bold, using the CCI composition system and the Mergenthaler Linotron 202 digital phototypesetter.

Lon Poole writes the popular "Get Info" column for *Macworld* magazine, and is the author of the classic *Apple II User's Guide*. His first book for Microsoft Press was the best-selling *MacWork, MacPlay*. Lon Poole lives in Oakland, California.

Trademarks

BitFixer™ is a trademark of All Star Computer Services.

FONTastic™ is a trademark of Altsys Corporation.

Apple® is a registered trademark and ImageWriter™, LaserWriter™, Lisa™, MacDraw™, MacPaint™, MacProject™, MacTerminal™, MacWrite™, and Switcher™ are trademarks of Apple Computer, Incorporated.

Mac Memory Disk™ is a trademark of Assimilation, Incorporated.

Touch Tone® is a registered trademark of AT&T.

Fanny Mac™ is a trademark of Beck-Tech.

SideKick™ is a trademark of Borland International, Incorporated.

CompuServe™ is a trademark of CompuServe Incorporated.

EnterSet™ and QuickPaint™ are trademarks of EnterSet.

Hayes® is a registered trademark of Hayes Microcomputer Products Incorporated.

IBM® is a registered trademark of International Business Machines.

ThinkTank™ is a trademark of Living Videotext, Incorporated.

Jazz™ is a trademark of Lotus Development Corporation.

MacBooster™ is a trademark of Mainstay.

Macintosh™ is a trademark of McIntosh Laboratories, Incorporated.

Microsoft® and Multiplan® are registered trademarks of Microsoft Corporation.

TurboCharger™ is a trademark of Nevins Microsystems, Incorporated.

MDC II™ is a trademark of New Canaan MicroCode.

Odesta Helix® is a registered trademark of Odesta Corporation.

Macworld™ is a trademark of PC Word Communications, Incorporated.

Accessory Pak I™ and Paint Cutter™ are trademarks of Silicon Beach Software, Incorporated.

ClickArt® is a registered trademark of T/Maker Graphics Company.